Terje Tvedt is Professor of Geography at the University of Bergen and Professor of Political Science and of Global History at the University of Oslo. A Past President of the International Water History Association, he has published extensively on water-related topics and is the author of a number of influential books, including *The River Nile in the Age of the British* (I.B.Tauris, 2004). He is editor of the series *History of Water* (I.B.Tauris) and has written and presented two successful television documentaries on water, shown in 150 countries.

TERJE TVEDT

A Journey in the Future of Water

Translated by Richard Daly

I.B.TAURIS
LONDON · NEW YORK

This translation has been published with the financial support of Norwegian Literature Abroad, NORLA.

The publisher and author acknowledge the kind assistance of the University of Bergen toward the cost of translation, and of Norwegian Literature Abroad.

Published in 2014 by I.B.Tauris & Co Ltd
6 Salem Road, London W2 4BU
175 Fifth Avenue, New York NY 10010
www.ibtauris.com

Distributed in the United States and Canada Exclusively by Palgrave Macmillan
175 Fifth Avenue, New York NY 10010

ISBN: 978 1 84885 744 5 (hb)
ISBN: 978 1 84885 745 2 (pb)

A full CIP record for this book is available from the British Library
A full CIP record is available from the Library of Congress

Library of Congress Catalog Card Number: available

Typeset in Garamond Premier Pro by Ellipsis Digital Limited, Glasgow
Printed and bound by TJ International Ltd, Padstow, Cornwall

FSC www.fsc.org MIX Paper from responsible sources FSC® C013056

CONTENTS

ACKNOWLEDGEMENTS

There are many to be thanked: All the researchers and colleagues who have inspired me and from whom I have learned, and all the individuals I have met in the course of my travels and who have willingly given me their time. But since there are so very many who fall within these categories, I have adhered to the following guideline: nobody mentioned, nobody forgotten. Many of the journeys were undertaken in relation to the making of two comprehensive documentary films about water, *A Journey in the History of Water* and *The Future of Water*. This book would not have come into being without the close collaboration of the photographers, producers and production leaders over a period of several years. In addition, I want to thank my family who, for year after year, have devoted their holiday time and spare time to joining me on my water travels, although I do not believe they have regretted one day of it.

To my children Nikolai, Tale, Ida and Geirr

PREFACE

The first picture of Earth from outer space was a defining moment in the history of ideas. At last it was possible to see our planet from the outside, freed from the conceptual grip imposed by the singularity of place. On Christmas Eve 1968 an astronaut on board *Apollo 8* – the first spaceship to circle the moon – took the photograph. Almost immediately new metaphors burst into being. It became normal to talk about 'Spaceship Earth', 'One World' and 'Gaia'. But more than anything else, what this picture shows us – and indeed what all subsequent pictures taken of our planet from space show us and what they accentuate – is that this planet, distinct from all the others whirling through space, is unique in being composed overwhelmingly of water.

What we see from this first photograph from space are blue oceans covering three-quarters of the surface of the earth, the white polar ice caps of the Arctic and Antarctica, and large cloud systems. All this water gives the planet its special identity. Over the course of billions of years it furnished the basis from which life has come into being. The way that water has moved on Earth – in plants and in and between all organisms – has given rise to the origin of species and the characteristics of all landscapes. In the last 100,000 years, the way that water has flowed in the valleys and across the plains it helped to form has also decisively affected not only the history of society but also how people have managed to live and work, as well as their religious ceremonies, cultural rituals and political relations. Yet despite its prominent role, the social significance of water has impressed itself surprisingly little in terms of our contemporary understanding of history and the processes of evolution and development.

In contrast to such 'water blindness', water is central to my understanding of the history of humanity and I ask the following questions: from a global and historical perspective, firstly, how do we understand the relationship between water and society? and, secondly, how have human beings changed nature and themselves through their efforts to gain mastery over water?[1]

1. For several decades I have researched and written about the significance of water to the development of society. As a historian with a particular interest in development studies, and as a professor of political science and geography, I have attempted to approach the problem from a variety of angles. In the photograph, I am giving a lecture in my role as President of the International Water History Association at its meeting in 2003 in the Library of Alexandria.

I have read everything I can lay my hands on – from 3,000-year-old Chinese treatises on the character of water to Herodotus' epic accounts of history from Egypt and Ancient Greece; from descriptions taken from the world's religions about how the gods created the world with the help of water to dry engineering reports on water control in one waterway or another. I have read the latest climate research scenarios on future floods and droughts, and I have hunted down dust-laden sources all the way from Khartoum to Kansas. In addition, I have travelled to more than 70 countries to witness the constantly new forms assumed by water in its eternal motion and variation, and to see how different societies culturally construct meaning in relation to water. This book is a narrative of some of these journeys into the world of water. It tells what happens when the spotlight is focused on riverbanks, at dam sites and fountains, instead of rather simply letting such places form the backdrop to the travel routes that so many have chosen to follow previously. Thus I am concerned not just with travelling to often distant and exciting places around the world, but also with seeing through new eyes that which is customary and everyday.

Until the end of the 1990s there were very few scientists studying the role of water in shaping society and looking at how it might affect the future. Then, in the course of a single decade, water moved to centre stage with the present doomsday scenarios regarding the future. Nourished by worldwide fears of global warming and climate change, by events such as Hurricane Katrina, floods across Europe and drought in the USA, water has suddenly come to public attention. Indeed, the inception of discussions about climate change above all has to do with potential changes in the waterscape and in the quantity and form of water. It has become common to argue that the ice is melting at the Poles, across Greenland and in the Himalayas, in the Alps and the Andes, and that these constantly increasing amounts of water will run into the oceans, causing sea levels to rise. Is flooding in Europe, New Orleans and India a warning of more extreme weather conditions in times to come? Or could there be less rain, so that three-quarters of the earth becomes desert by 2100, as some researchers predict? And will there be war over access to water, because people cannot exist without the water of which their bodies are mainly composed? Fundamental questions about the future of humanity are being posed around the world, and for the first time in history they have to do with the role of water and our ability to control it.

In today's world the formative value of travel is perhaps exaggerated, when 'the exotic' is to be found in the back streets of every large city. But when it comes to understanding the role of water in society, how water has been used, and how it shapes the development of society, 'going on a journey' remains a necessity. Goethe said that if one wanted to understand China, one had to be able to identify the smell of China. Or, to put it more precisely, it is better to see things with one's own eyes, with all one's senses open and receptive. And so it was for me essential to see and feel and hear how the rivers run, how the precipitation falls, to experience how human beings everywhere try to adapt to and control water, and the different ways in which they do so. Travel is one way to engage with water's distinctive characteristics: the fact that it is both universal and particular at the same time, that it is at one and the same time both part of nature and part of culture.

The grand classical river journeys are still enveloped in an aura of adventure. Think, for example, of the river expedition in Joseph Conrad's *Heart of Darkness*, where the journey up the Congo itself becomes a symbol of a journey into the bowels of evil. Or we may think of Mark Twain and his Tom Sawyer and Huck Finn on their Mississippi, where the river propels the raft, and thereby the story, onwards, lightly and effortlessly. There are many metres of bookshelves devoted to descriptions of journeys on the great rivers such as the Amazon, the Yangtze, the Ganges or the Rhine. The fascination of river travel has not abated. And since half of humanity lives along waterways that are divided between more than one country, then if one allows oneself to 'flow with the current' of a great river one discovers important truths about the whole world.

Nevertheless, water travel has a different architecture in this book. It is built on the basis of contrasts, both with regard to the geography of water and the characteristics of the different societies I encounter – from the Colorado waterway and Las Vegas, to the sources of the Brahmaputra in Tibet and the Three Gorges Dam in China; from poor nomadic societies in Africa and Asia, to great cities with enormous water problems; from water in abundance in America and Europe to the Sahara and the desert in Oman; from ancient fountains where water cascades freely, to the world's largest dams where water is tamed and brought to heel. I have looked into water in all its forms, travelled down the great river

2. The author standing at a place that future history books will describe as being of world significance historically. In the background is the station that pumps water from the Yangtze almost 2,000 kilometres northwards in China, and which has the official aim of erasing the regional imbalance in China's economy.

valleys, and spoken with water experts and politicians from around the world. I have travelled, absorbed by the diversity and beauty of water, fascinated by its properties: eternally pulsating, always with a direction or a bearing that no one can stop completely, yet which yields before obstructions with apparent humility.

My travels began in a manner as trivial as it is possible to imagine – on a bench in Hyde Park, London. The park is world famous for its Speakers' Corner but now, above all else, what draws people here are the lawns, the trees and the Serpentine – a lake first excavated about 1730 and formed by damming up Westbourne brook, a tributary of the Thames, but today one of London's lost rivers running through underground pipes that discharge into the main river at Chelsea about 300 metres beyond Chelsea Bridge. Even though heavy rain clouds hang low above the treetops, I am far from being the only one sitting here quietly in a state of rather soulless tranquillity. For there is something about water – I do not know whether it is the singular way that the surface appears calm, or how it mirrors the sky and the sun or the trees, or whether it is the repetitive but never identical movement of water as it gushes from fountains – but whatever it is it draws people in all countries and throughout the ages to itself. Water has been celebrated and used as a metaphor in music and literature down the ages and played a central role in both religious cosmology and cultural rituals. What puzzles me is that, as I sit here, there are probably millions of people across the globe visiting a fountain, a spring, a river or a waterfall that has a particular meaning or purpose for them.

The very nature of water seems to demonstrate again and again, day after day, the fact that even when it is at its most suppressed, no other resource can bring all the elements together in the way that water does, binding land, sea, air and people in an endless living cycle. For in the hydrological cycle, water changes, transforms and becomes itself again and again. The water that I drink in my cafe latté could have been running in a clear mountain stream last year or it could be emerging from a spring again next year. It may well have been part of the water in Socrates' goblet of poison or the bathwater of a Chinese emperor or it could have poured forth from the fountain that stands in the middle of the Serpentine. Thus water binds together all people in all ages in a unique way.[2] Eternally in motion, forever changing, the property of all and the property of none, essential to all societies and to all ecosystems: it is these unique and far-reaching qualities of water that has made my journey into water so necessary.

I am on the escalator in the London Underground at Victoria Station. The station is full of people. A busker plays a Neil Young classic and a London bobby gives a friendly wave. In other words, it is a very normal day and I am quite sure that I am the only one with his head full of thoughts about water as we are borne downward into the depths, past the advertising posters for the West End theatres. The atmosphere would become rather more unsettling, and indeed more claustrophobic, were I to sing out, 'The station is in the process of filling with water!' People would undoubtedly look up from their newspapers and perhaps feel a certain alarm. But I would immediately be able to reassure them: 'But the pumps are in place and they are pumping water; you don't see them but they will save you.' People would perhaps cast a suspicious glance in my direction, turn back to their newspapers, shrug their shoulders – and dismiss me as just another of the many eccentrics who populate London's Underground.

But in fact there *are* actual pumps in place in Victoria Station: they pump hour after hour, day after day, about 35 litres of water per second. They do an absolutely essential job of preventing water from seeping through the walls and inundating the London Underground system. As people rush on to the platforms and train doors open, the water is being pumped away; as their train pulls away and enters the nearest tunnel, the water is being pumped away. The reason is not that it rains excessively in London or that the sea seeps in from the east, but rather that the groundwater is rising under London. In the 1960s the breweries and the paper industry which established themselves here during and after the Industrial Revolution, moved away from the core of the city. As a result, the amount of groundwater in regular use was reduced. When its level of use falls, so the water table rises – and it rises inexorably. Thus today the reality is that were it not for the pumps, Victoria Station would be underwater. Were the pumps to stop functioning, large sections of the London Tube system would be below water level.[3]

And so, grey and dull though it may be, Victoria Station, in the triviality of its daily activities, conceals an important truth: although human beings can control water, force it into pipes, imprison it behind dams and consume it, such control is never complete. We can never manage to control it fully, completely and for ever – water will always in the end find a way to escape from any human embrace. Yet every society must attempt to control water because no society can exist without it – though each chooses, and will always choose, to do so by a variety of means and in different ways. And all societies discover that if at a certain point in time there is a balance between water and society, this will, inevitably, lead to an imbalance at another point in time; the struggle to control water is thus a never-ending activity.

So groundwater is rising under London because of changes in society. Yet at the same time, London and the Thames constitute a prime example of how changes in *nature* can also create changes in the 'landscape of water.' Every time

3. The Thames Barrier was built between 1974 and 1984 to protect London from floods and flood tides: nine cupolas, 30 metres high, and a platform of reinforced concrete, in the middle of the Thames. London can be glimpsed stretching 10 kilometres upstream. In a matter of minutes the installation can be closed to prevent London from being flooded by the sea. Between 1993 and 2003 the river had to be sealed off 79 times.

I am in London I take either a boat tour on the Thames or along one of the canals in the city. This is my way of paying homage to this unassuming water course which nevertheless provided the basis on which London became the centre of world trade for many centuries, when wooden sailing ships were able to sail up the river and far into the country, thanks to the tides. In this way, the river itself contributed definitively to world history. Its future significance, however, will be of a completely different character.

I have paid several visits to a fantastic hydraulic construction situated at a right angle to the flow of the river and somewhat downstream from London – the Thames Barrier, built in the 1970s to defend the city against flooding. An enormous defensive wall of steel, between the city and the sea. It is composed of nine snail-shaped cupolas, each of them 30 metres high, and a platform of concrete that in a couple of minutes can close off the whole Thames to prevent seawater from forcing its way up over the barrier. Due to the rising sea levels and the fact that Britain is tilting – the southerly portions of England are sinking into the sea at the rate of 1–2 millimetres annually as a consequence of the last Ice Age – the danger from flooding is increasing. During the first decade that the Thames Barrier was in operation it closed 11 times due to danger of flooding. In the following ten-year period, from 1993 to 2003, it had to be closed 79 times. The great day of reckoning will be whether or not the barrier is adequate if the seas happen to rise more than calculated. There are some who believe that even in 20 – 25 years' time the Thames Barrier will not be able to protect the city. In that event it would be transformed from a regional symbol of the human ability to control the water to a universal monument to how human beings fall short whenever they try to exert eternal control over this volatile, ever-changing resource.

As I depart from Britain the autumn rains are pouring down as they often do in this 'Sceptred Isle'. They splatter across the fuselage of the aircraft as I gaze out at the Atlantic Ocean and the English Channel below us. And as I do so I am struck by a paradox about the name of our planet. In English it is called 'the Earth'; in Afrikaans, 'aarde'; in Arabic أض ['land or earth', with a definite article] pronounced as 'arD'; in Hebrew it is called 'ertz', in German 'Erde' and in the Scandinavian languages 'jord'. The English word *Earth* developed from the Old English word *eorðe*, which means 'ground, soil, dry land'. Thus the earth got its name from the diametrical opposite of the wet elements. This is perhaps natural because the planet was 'baptised' around 1400, a time when everything was focused on getting more out of the earth, and human understanding of the planet was extremely limited: human beings had not yet seen the planet from outer space and they knew nothing of the other planets to be able to compare; they did not understand photosynthesis, nor the hydrological cycle. We now know that the one-sidedness of the name blinds us to our planet's great distinctive characteristic – its water – and to the eternal, changeable relationship between earth and water, society and water, and people and water.

Our journey is divided into three parts. The first deals with the fact that we are living in an age of uncertainty – an uncertainty about climate change – and with the consequences that follow from that. The second part deals with the power struggles going on to become the water barons and water lords of the future. The fact that we are living in an age of water uncertainty combined with the existence of new water technology and threatening water crises, will lead to a situation where the struggle for power over water will become a central axis around which future history will turn. And since everyone must have water, this will be a power struggle that will involve all of us and from which no one will be completely exempt. The third part deals with how large regions of the world will be radically changed in the coming years by water projects that are more extensive, and which will have far greater consequences, than any previous projects in human history.

And so our journey begins.

Arctic Ocean
GREENLAND
ICELAND
CANADA
UNITED STATES
Pacific
Atlantic
MEXICO
MAURITANIA
Ocean
BRAZIL
BOLIVIA
ARGENTINA
Ocean

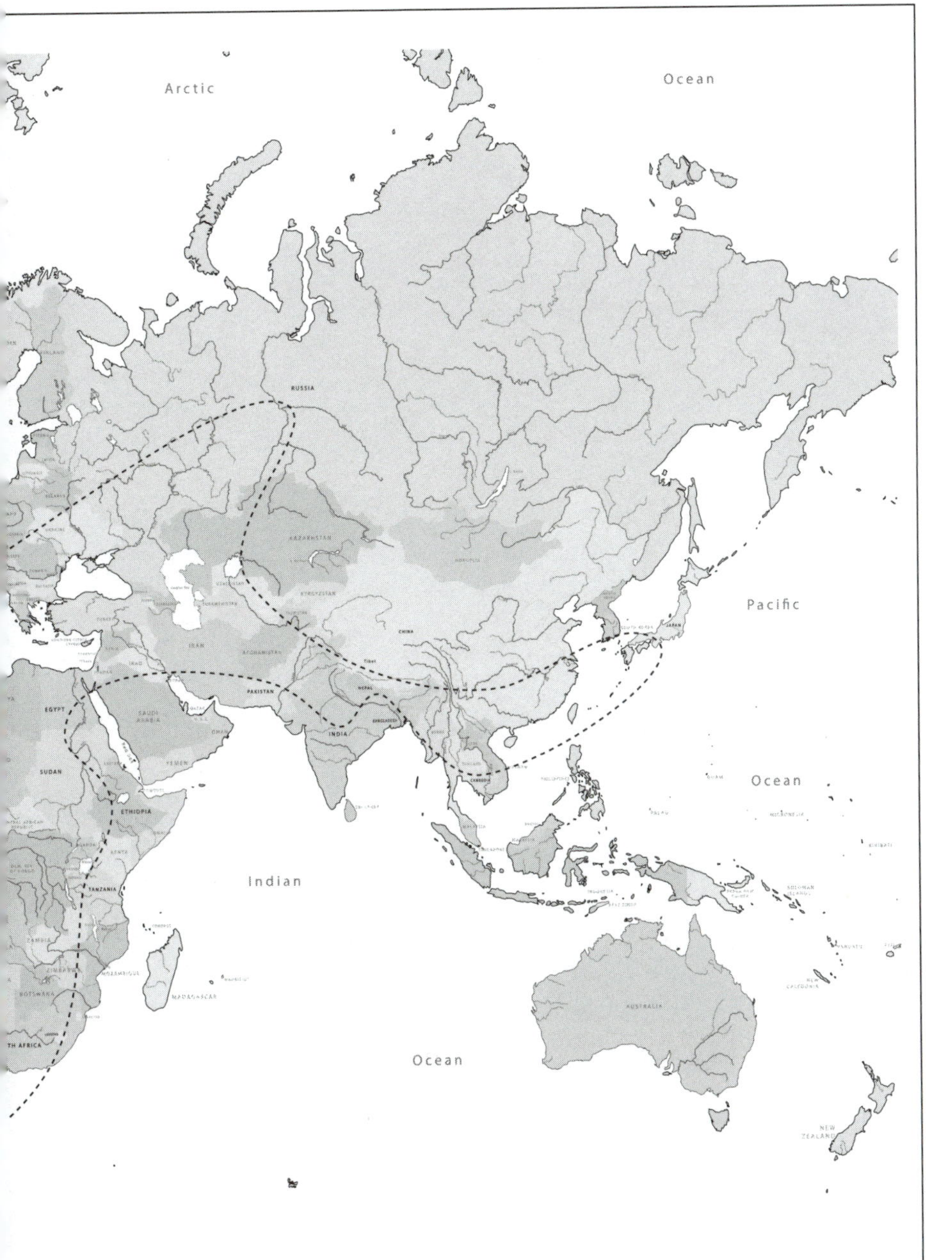
Arctic
Ocean
RUSSIA
KAZAKHSTAN
CHINA
JAPAN
Pacific
Ocean
PAKISTAN
INDIA
EGYPT
SUDAN
ETHIOPIA
TANZANIA
Indian
Ocean
MADAGASCAR
AUSTRALIA
NEW ZEALAND

PART 1
THE NEW UNCERTAINTY ABOUT WATER

4. We are now living in the new Age of Uncertainty. Everywhere people are wondering how they can secure themselves a future that no one can know with certainty: will there be more precipitation or less, more floods and more droughts, greater melting of ice and higher sea levels?

INTRODUCTION TO PART I

In the mid-1990s, when I went travelling to almost 30 countries in connection with research and a television series I was making on the role of water in history, virtually nobody talked of global warming and changing water landscapes. Now, people everywhere are interpreting unusual weather as profound expressions of threatening climatic change. Nearly 3,000 metres above sea level among mud huts in Lesotho I encounter an old woman who wants to talk about the recent bad weather and who explains it as 'global warming.' At a reception in a beach hotel in Cancun, Yucatán, a Mexican Elvis impersonator complains that the weather is different now from what it was, due too so much CO_2 in the atmosphere. And along the battered riverbank of the Bagmati in Nepal, an old engineer with large sad eyes and the firm conviction that the extremely modest volume of water in the river this year is due to global warming, has decided to devote the last years of his life to saving the country's most sacred river from death by local pollution. Everywhere I go, I meet people sharing the same view; a new insecurity about precipitation, drought, glaciers and sea level is woven into the world's collective consciousness.

In the course of a few short years the language of climate science has come to predominate in the grand narratives about the future of the planet and human responsibility for it. Hardly at any time in history have so many, so quickly, changed their ideas about such fundamental questions and to such a great extent. Since climate change in societies will first and foremost manifest itself in terms of the way that water flows in the landscape, the grand and mighty narratives about the future of humanity have suddenly become stories that rest on definitions and conceptualisations about how water will flow in that future.[4]

Given this background one can say that humanity has entered the age of uncertainty.

The new era will be shaped fundamentally by the permanent and growing insecurity regarding the water landscapes of the future. The media speculate and politicians and scientists discuss: are we standing at the beginning of centuries

5. Homo sapiens has developed into the world's dominant species over the course of the last 10,000 years. Viewed from the perspective of long geological time spans this has been a period wherein the climate and the hydrological cycles have been unusually stable, providing our species with a relative paradise compared with earlier climatic periods.

of drought and will a third of the planet become desert in 100 years time? Or are we living in the century of floods – of the melting of the ice? Will the world's oceans rise by several metres and, if so, when will it actually happen? Predictions of such disasters involving water strike a deep chord in the human psyche.

In the course of my travels I have been re-reading the famous ancient flood myths: the 5,000-year-old epic of Gilgamesh from the lands between the Tigris and the Euphrates; the story of Noah's Ark in the Bible; the final destruction of the world by flood in Buddhism; and some of the innumerable stories of disastrous floods that are to be found in different shades and variations in almost all religions and many grand cultural narratives. I have tried to hunt down depictions of the Great Flood by painters, and not only the well-known drawings and paintings by Michelangelo and Leonardo da Vinci. My favourite is Gustave Doré's painting from 1865 having the very mundane yet precise title: *World Destroyed by Water*. It is full of contradictions: characterised by existential darkness

6. The more developed and complex a society is, the greater the costs society will have to bear and, indeed, the greater the challenges that have to be tackled in order to adapt to a changed waterscape. This is Lake Tana, Ethiopia, a lake that has lain undisturbed for thousands of years, but no longer.

yet at the same time it shows how the catastrophe releases the best side of human nature. People are portrayed desperately trying to flee from the rising seas. A father is attempting to keep his wife and children above the water. Above him, two parents are trying to push their children up on to dry land. In the middle of the picture we see the arm of a drowning parent trying to give their child a few more moments of life. And the sinners sacrifice themselves to save the innocent.[5] These Doomsday portrayals are both appealing and appalling, yet they appear anachronistic because they lack what modern Doomsday prophets rely upon – the status of modern science. Thus, water now fights back, not as a boomerang, but as the familiar, returning in completely unfamiliar ways.

In the very long term what is certain is that there will be great changes in local and regional water cycles. In the land of the Dogon people in Mali, on the edge of the Sahara, people have survived for generations with both little water and huge variations in precipitation. Here, what is constant in the water cycle is its inconstancy; what is normal is the certainty of the abnormal – that catastrophes will occur and that they will batter society. Lakes appear and disappear annually in this region, and as such they are natural barometers of the absolutely unique and eternal fickleness of the climate and the waterscape.

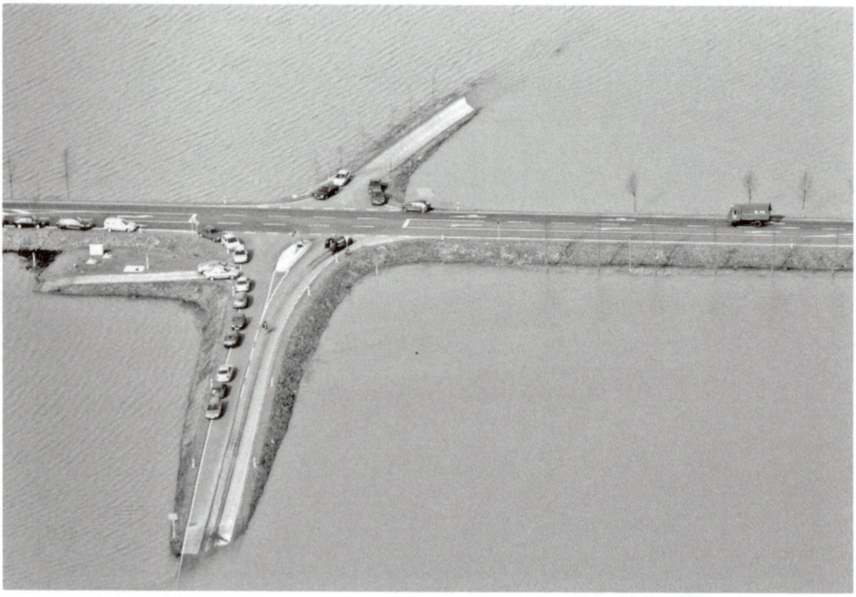

7. Ideas of flood and catastrophic flood damage are central to most religions. Thus we find that Doomsday prophecies have deep cultural traditions to draw upon and they are constantly reactivated, influenced by great floods like this one in Germany.

Once a year, the small Antogo lake is the scene of an extraordinary event: people come from far and wide to go fishing. The traditional belief is that the fish come from the neighbouring mountains. When the annual rains come, the water rises. The fish wash out of hidden lakes in the mountains, down the mountainsides and into the lake. On the great day, thousands of people gather around the little body of water. They sit in silence on the banks encircling the lake, waiting for the signal that is given when the water level is optimal for catching fish with their hands. At that point, they storm out into the water in their thousands. In the course of a few minutes the lake is emptied of fish. The people wade back, climb the banks, and in a little while the lake is no more.

From the perspective of climatic history this ritual fishery symbolises human impotence in the face of the power of the changing cycle of water. If the conditions of the last millennium have constituted a blissful climatic paradise, then, fundamentally, humanity finds itself in the same situation as the fishers at Lake Antogo when the water conditions are ideal. We have, of course, no reason to believe that the water conditions of the present will last. The extraordinary event at Lake Antogo is a fertility ritual that also underlines another paradox of history: the relative autonomy of poor village people in the face of the power of nature and water. Even though the lake disappears, the existence of the society is not threatened. People simply do something else, or migrate with their scant belongings to some other place. Modern society, with its huge cities of millions of people cramped together in very small areas, does not have the same options.

8. In China, 37,000 people are employed to influence the climate to a small extent. They shoot chemicals into the clouds in the hope of controlling local precipitation. This is done both to increase rainfall and, on occasion, to drive the clouds away whenever the government deems this appropriate. But what will be the long-term societal consequences if, demanding better weather, people go to the ballot box to choose a new government?

9. Tibetans rowing across the Brahmaputra in a yak-skin boat, surrounded by dry river banks and sandy deserts that remind one of the Sahara.

CHAPTER 1
TO THE RIVERS OF HEAVEN AND THE CENTRE OF THE WORLD

'There is no doubt,' he says, with an unflinching, rather sombre glance, 'Many of the glaciers in Tibet will certainly melt.'

I am sitting with Yao Tang Dong, one of China's leading glaciologists, in his office, a little outside the centre of Beijing. His friendly appearance adds to the drama of his research findings. He is certainly aware, I think to myself as I look through some of the reports he shows me, that his analyses will indirectly affect the future of 3 billion people and contribute to making remote Tibet into one of the most centrally strategic regions on earth.

When, six months later, I travel to Tibet I do so in the way that seems most appropriate for one who is interested in the country's strategic significance for the future of the planet. I do not go by air, which distorts topographical proportions and earth-bound perceptions, such as *descending* to the alpine plateau; rather, I will climb up to it. I have therefore chosen to take the train to Tibet from Beijing.

On the first day, we pass through the landscape of the Yellow River, which is both the mother of joy and the mother of sorrow to the people of China. Unlike most rivers, the Yellow River is in fact completely brown and in some stretches contains seven parts muddy ooze to three parts water. I gaze upon what, over thousands of years, has been not only the begetter of a civilisation, but also a violent, terrifying river, the cause of more mass deaths than any other force in the history of the world. In 1887 alone it killed between 900,000 and 2 million people, and in 1931, between 1 million and 3.7 million. China's history has revolved around this river and its control. It is the river that laid the basis for where the imperial kingdom of China was born: Xian; and where some years ago the mass grave of thousands of terracotta warriors, each formed with individual features was discovered. Here the river curls its way between an infinity of hilltops that more than anything else resemble earthenware pots with striated surfaces – but which are in fact laboriously constructed terraces that bear witness

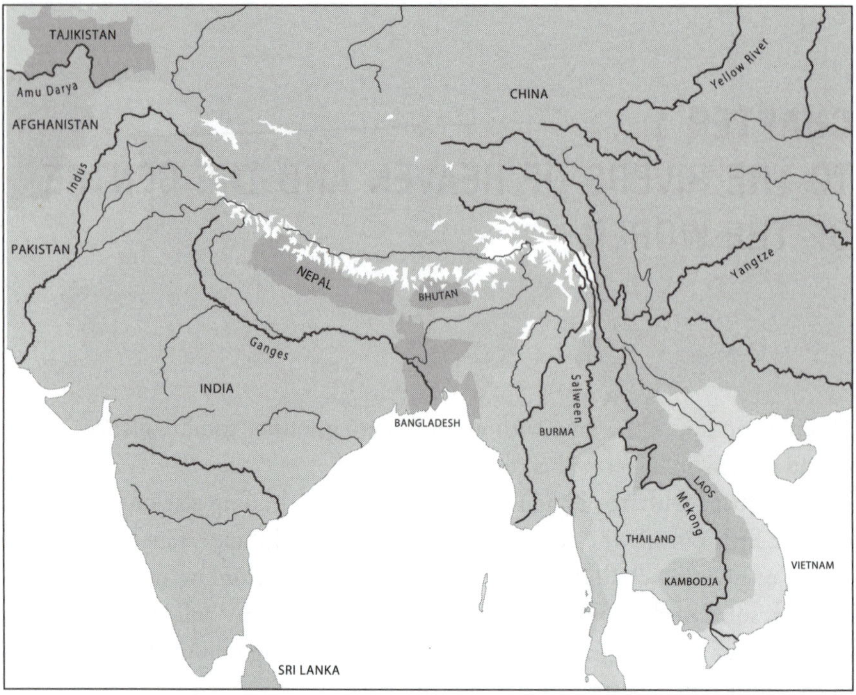

Map 1. If the ice of the Himalayas and other high-altitude plains melts, this will have a radical effect on the flow of water to the major rivers of Asia – the Yangtze, Yellow, Indus, Ganges, Brahmaputra, Salween, Amu Darya and Mekong rivers – which have shaped Asia's history for thousands of years, and which will have increasing importance in the future.

to the indomitable, millennia-old struggle of the Chinese against the very nature of water. Their aim has been to hold on to the fertile soil, such that even more of it will not wash into the river and increase the danger of flooding on the plains downstream toward the China Sea.

The train reaches the alpine plateau on the second day and it becomes immediately evident that I have come to the water tower of Asia. I sit for hour after hour in the restaurant car of the train, dumbfounded, indeed bewitched, by a landscape that I have never seen anywhere else – barren rolling hills with flowing water almost covering the whole horizon, as though the rivers flow directly down from heaven. In the distance can be seen parts of the great Kunlun mountain chain that forms the physical and historical division between the Yellow and Yangtze River basins, or between southern and northern China. In China's mythology this was the Taoist paradise, for it was here that King Mu, according to the legend, discovered the Jade Palace of Huang Di, the mythic Golden Emperor, creator of Chinese culture. We pass Tanggula Station – at 5,072 metres

10. This is the Yangtze, more than 4,000 metres above sea level, one of the many rivers that run through the rather sparsely populated Quinghai–Tibet plateau, before heading downstream.

above sea level it is the world's highest railway station – which has a building that seems to stretch up toward heaven as though in competition with the mountains in the distance.

The dining car steward interrupts me:

'You sit here all day?'

Naturally enough, he wants to free up my table for subsequent business.

'Yes,' I say, 'Absolutely, the whole day.'

I make the arrangements for a new order of noodles in order to keep my place at the panoramic viewing window. I try to identify the rivers from the map that I have spread out on the dining table between the chopsticks and the rice bowl, and follow their course, as lines of blue, down the Asian continent. The names are bewildering: like most other large rivers, the Yangtze has different names; here it is called Tuotuo and Tongtian ('the river that passes into heaven'), while the Tibetan name is Drichu, or 'the river of the female yak'.

'How much cultural hubris and theoretical narrow-mindedness is there in intellectual traditions which maintain that the development of society and modernity have made the power of geography irrelevant?' I wonder. I have a strong desire to shout this out for the whole dining car to hear, but there are only a few non-English-speaking Chinese sitting here, enveloped in clouds of cigarette smoke.[6]

The Tibetan Plateau is the source of the great river systems that gave birth to civilisations: not only the Yangtze and the Yellow rivers, but also the Indus, the Ganges, the Brahmaputra, the Salween, the Mekong rivers that over thousands of years have helped shape the history of Asia, and which in the future will have an increased significance economically, politically and culturally in China, India, Pakistan, Vietnam, Cambodia, Laos, Thailand, Nepal, Bangladesh, Burma and Bhutan. This region holds the key to the future of large parts of Asia. To an ever-increasing degree, Tibet will become one of the most strategically important areas on the globe. And this will be so whatever happens with the climate.

The landscape makes a profound impression – the crystal clear air, the blue ice-crested mountains in the distance, the cold light-green colour of the lakes, and the rivers with their innumerable tributaries, both large and small, flowing down the distant barren hills. Forty or 50 million years ago the Indian subcontinent collided with the rest of the landmass of Asia and the mountaintops then rose toward the heavens. In the twentieth century the area was popularised in exotic travel accounts as the land of 'eternal ice and snow.' This ice constitutes Asia's water bank – 15,000 glaciers that collectively cover an area of more than 30 million square kilometres in the Himalayas. Questions about the future of these glaciers will to an ever-increasing degree concern all humanity, not only this year and next year, but thousand years from now.

As the sun makes its way across the sky, I leaf through the notes I made of my discussion with Yao the previous year, as well as interviews he has given and articles he has written.[7] These reinforce his message: the glaciers recede every year, producing an amount of meltwater approximately equal to the annual water flow of the Yellow River. Many of the glaciers will soon be gone, as soon as 2035 it is argued, and they will all completely disappear by 2100! The temperature has increased, it is claimed, by one degree since 1950.

It has been said that only historians are mightier than God because they are in a position to change the past. The predictions of Yao and his colleagues – and they are only predictions, even should they happen to come true – imply that the researchers possess a defining power with regard to future development and will have a vital influence over how societies of billions of people will tackle the new future. What they find out and, not least, how they interpret their data and which scenarios they suggest, will have dramatic but completely unforeseeable consequences – and this will be so, irrespective of whether they prove to be right or wrong. When Yao says that 54 per cent of China's glaciers will be history by 2050 if current trends continue, he is thus warning of an environmental catastrophe of almost inconceivable dimensions and which it is too late to avoid as long as global warming is seen as the cause of the increased release of carbon dioxide (CO_2) into the atmosphere. For if this is the cause, then these glaciers of the Himalayas will disappear before the current trend of rising temperatures can be turned around or stopped.

Whether Yao and his colleagues happen to be right, and indeed all those who are even more strident and who unconditionally maintain that the glaciers of the Himalayas are in the process of disappearing, Asia's future will be a chaotic one. Under such a scenario, there would first be a period of flooding. Bangladesh would be underwater even more frequently. Pakistan would face disaster, even should they build the enormous planned dam on the Indus not far from Skardu, since most of the water in the Indus comes from glaciers. The Mekong also flows out of the Himalayas and Tibet and waters parts of China and Vietnam, Cambodia, Laos and Thailand. What will happen, for instance, at Tonle Sap, the beautiful lake not far from the temples of Ankor Wat in Cambodia, which I crossed one beautiful silent dawn some years ago, and where fishers dwell in stilt houses above the highly productive waters that rise and fall in concert with the flow of the Mekong? Large portions of India will be hit by floods, and thereafter by drought, since 37 of the country's great rivers arise in the Himalayas and 45 per cent of the water of the Ganges comes from glaciers there.[8] It has been estimated that between the months of July and September the Ganges will contain two-thirds less water once the glaciers have disappeared. This will mean a shortage of water for half a billion people and affect one-third of the area under irrigation across India.

The consequences for China will also be great. If the flow of water in the Yangtze, Brahmaputra and Mekong becomes significantly reduced, this will threaten the country's economic growth and political stability. And if the glaciers melt as suggested, there will be a greatly increased flow of water and it is uncertain whether the mega-dams being built on the Yangtze and the Yellow rivers will be capable of withstanding the millennial floods – the prognoses are that the normal flow of water will increase radically during the melting period. Following the predicted floods, the rivers would be mere shadows of their former selves. China's gigantic water diversion projects might well be left standing as tragic testament to naive climatic optimism. For the 23 per cent of the country's population who live in oases in western China, such a scenario is alarming in the extreme. Many of the Central Asian states on the northern side of the Himalayas, which were part of the former Soviet Union, and which already find that the lack of water is one of their most important development obstacles, also face completely new challenges because many of their great rivers find their source in the Himalayas.

Even if all these predictions that the glaciers will melt are not borne out in practice, a dark cloud nonetheless hangs over, and will continue to threaten, the hopes of hundreds of millions of people for the future. But the conditions that determine the state of the glaciers – what is known as the mass balance – are enormously complicated, not least in the Himalayas due to the dry air and the altitude, and the data series do not span long enough periods from which to draw definite conclusions about how things will look in 50, 100 or 200 years. Here, as elsewhere, the role of researchers as interpreters of the uncertain future of the waterscape will grow in potency and power. In contrast to fortune-tellers and the four-line prophetic verse composed by the sixteenth-century French astrologist and doctor, Nostradamus, the analyses of today's researchers rest on the legitimacy of modern science. No matter how many measurements they make, and how they interpret them, they will, due to the new political and ideological atmosphere of climate insecurity, have both acquired and been awarded a degree of power over the future, a power that is of a completely new type, since no one can with certainty say what will happen, and no one will live long enough to witness whether a particular scenario proves right or wrong.

New discoveries about the past climate constantly nourish the uncertainty surrounding the future of the water landscape here, too. Some years ago scientists discovered that enormous ice dams formed across the Brahmaputra in the Himalayas 1,000 years from now. Between AD 600 and 900 the water broke through the walls of ice that had formed the lakes. For India, this led to one of the greatest flood catastrophes following the last Ice Age. Predictions about the future will increasingly be anchored in interpretations of new discoveries about our past, and this is one main reason why the age of uncertainty has come to stay.

Late in the evening we reached Lhasa. Having wandered through the old city – a must for all visitors to Lhasa – and having sat on a street corner and watched devout Buddhists spinning their prayer wheels while they went about their traditional rounds across the city on what, in the course of a decade, has transformed into dusty car-choked streets, I leave the following morning by car for a tour along the Brahmaputra to the mountain pass of Kamba-la, almost 5,000 metres above sea level. One of the largest glaciers in this part of Tibet stretched its dirty self almost down to the road. Some faded prayer flags had been hung where it ended. I scrambled up on to it – I had to touch the ice, because what I was touching was an insurance policy for civilisation that would, however, soon be history if the predictions about the future of this and other glaciers in Tibet and the Himalayas are true.

But what gives my journey through the Tibetan landscape its greatest meaning, the pivotal moment amongst all my other impressions, is walking alone, encircled by mountains 6,000 metres high, in a blazing hot alpine desert on the banks of Asia's main artery, the Brahmaputra. Like many others, I have been fascinated by Tibetan religious and philosophical traditions[9] and have leafed through *The Tibetan Book of the Dead*, which in the original language has the more powerful title *Emancipation through Knowledge of Life after Death*.

I have been told about the symbolism of the Buddhist Tsa Tsa statuary made from sacred clay and still being offered on the streets of Lhasa. And as with every historian concerned with global historical issues, I am aware that as early as AD 600 the Tibetans developed their own phonetic alphabet and in the eleventh century they developed a kind of theocratic feudal state, with priests – or lamas – ruling over the serfs, who cultivated the land for them. But the crumbling Buddhist monasteries clinging to the Tibetan mountainsides, the shivering, thinly-dressed monks with their characteristic dark-red robes wrapped tightly around themselves, the introspective gaze of the faithful who throw themselves down on all fours, innumerable times, then rise up and slide down onto their stomachs with their faces to the ground, right in amongst the cars and the Chinese tourists, and the heavenly burials, where the dead, whose souls have already departed, are carried to the tops of the mountains and hacked into bits so that the vultures can clean the bones of all flesh – all of this only peripherally interested me now. I was on the trail of something much more important.

Wandering through the sand dunes, the beauty of which reminds me of the finest in the Sahara, I catch glimpses of the Brahmaputra – or Yarlung Tsangpo as it is called in Chinese – which seems rather close due to the thin air, and spy deep-blue mountainsides with ice that appears to cling to the jagged peaks. This gets one just about as close as it is possible to get regarding the truth about Tibet's fate. The geographical configuration – or contradiction – that encapsulates Tibet's situation is the following. The region has thousands of square kilometres of sand desert and enormous areas threatened by desertification while at the same time being the water tower for almost half the population of the planet.[10] The Himalayas, and the mountains whose summits Sir Edmund Hillary and others risked their lives to reach, act as a barrier to precipitation here. They protect Tibet from the monsoon rains and at the same time turn large tracts of the region into desert. In central Tibet the annual rainfall is only 25–50 millimetres (a global definition of a desert climate is a region with less than

200 millimetres of precipitation per year). Other places on the plateau get even less rain.

According to classic Buddhist philosophy, Manasarovar – the highest altitude lake in the world and reachable after several days' journey by car inland over the alpine plateau from Lhasa – is mother to all the rivers. It is sacred to Hindus as well as to Buddhists. Pilgrims believe that, by circling around the edge of the lake on foot and by bathing at the four holy bathing places, one may be absolved of one's sins and attain good fortune. The nearby Mount Kailas is known by the Tibetans as Khang Rimpoche, which literally translated means 'precious jewel in the snow.' According to Hindus this is the home of Lord Shiva. Just as the mountain is central to the mythic narrative of both classic Tibetan Buddhism and to Hinduism, so, in the context of water policy, it is one of the geopolitical centres of the future. From this region four rivers flow down to the dry plains

11. Buddhists in Lhasa prostrate themselves as they pray in front of the country's most holy building, the Potala Palace. They have done so for hundreds of years. The Chinese flag was raised above the palace in 1959. Until that point it had been an administrative and religious centre for Tibetan attempts to secure independence. For a long time the rest of the world has been preoccupied with the question of religion in Tibet's relationship with China but, above all, it is Tibet's role as a water tower that will decide its long-term relations with Beijing.

where 1 billion people live: the Karnali southwards toward the Ganges; the Indus toward the north; the Sutlej to the west until it joins the Indus; and the Brahmaputra toward the east. For me, Manasarovar and Mount Kailas, which in travel literature have become thoroughly immersed in mysticism, symbolise Tibet's ever more central role as the water tower for the wider region and a climatic thermometer for the whole globe. A whole continent will be casting anxious glances toward this mountain that Tibetans for centuries have called this 'precious jewel in the snow'.

Back in Lhasa, I go to the park below the Potala Palace. The Potala was built by King Songtsen Gampo in the seventh century, destroyed by war and lightning, rebuilt by the fifth Dalai Lama in 1645 and since then has been Tibet's political centre. Here I sit immersed in an atmosphere of devout spirituality and piety created by the profound, concentrated prayer of the Tibetans outside the front of the palace. It feels out of place – indeed even heretical – to conclude that the future of this region will be decided by something as prosaic as the advance or retreat of the ice at the Roof of the World.

12. In the Netherlands plans to build a new airport in the sea are being discussed, and several architectural firms are designing floating cities.

CHAPTER 2
A PUMP TOUR IN THE NETHERLANDS

Every time I fly over the Netherlands and we prepare for landing at Schiphol Airport outside Amsterdam, I gather up my reading material, place it in the pocket of the seat in front of me, stow the table, fold my napkin, lean toward the window and try my best to get a glimpse of one of those construction projects that make the Netherlands unique: a 63-kilometre long drainage canal that encircles the airport, dug by hand more than 100 years ago. All honour must be given to a pump and to an idea. Around 1850, the Netherlands placed an order in Great Britain for the largest steam engine ever built. It was put to work doing what pumps have always done in the Netherlands – pumping away surplus water. Many hundreds of millions of cubic metres of water were removed from the Haarlemmermeer sea, and eventually the land appeared upon which the airport would later be built.

The canal had to be constructed not – as is the case in many other areas of the world – in order to carry its water to dry and thirsty fields, but rather to get rid of the surplus, taking it out to sea. That pump and drainage canal became the founding conditions for Schiphol, and as I scurry along the lengthy passageways between Hugo Boss and Jack Jones shops in continental Europe's busiest airport, I always remind myself that I am walking on laboriously reclaimed land, 6 metres below sea level.

On this occasion I am visiting the Netherlands to see what the country and its leaders plan to do if the glaciers in the Alps are indeed melting. The struggle against the sea is familiar and well-known, but what will happen to Europe's river deltas if the meltwater runoff increases? Researchers have elicited that the total area covered by Switzerland's 940 glaciers decreased by 18 per cent between 1973 and 1999. The speed of their decrease is six times as rapid as the annual reduction between 1850 and 1973; moreover, all glaciers below an altitude of 2,000 metres will have disappeared by 2070. Some researchers, like Roland Psenner, argue that if the glaciers continue to melt at today's rate, there will be none remaining by 2037, with the exception of a handful that lie above the 4,000-metre level.[11] Maybe these catastrophic predictions about the Alps are completely wrong – and there are researchers who argue that they are – but the fear that the ice will melt and precipitation increase has already attained great political significance across Central Europe. The authorities in the Netherlands calculated at the beginning of the twenty-first century that the water level in the rivers would increase several decimetres in the course of a few decades – something that will demand extraordinary initiatives in a country where 60 per cent of the land lies 3.5 metres *below* sea level.

Almost anywhere one looks in Holland one sees the evidence of what is an artificially established but vulnerable balance between water and land. I like Amsterdam especially, and the unique intimacy created by the houses, cafes and people reflected in the city's network of canals that runs between and beneath the narrow streets. Approximately 1,300 bridges and viaducts are necessary to join the approximately 90 'islands' together. From the deck of one of the many canal boats carrying tourists slowly through the city, and near the large merchant houses from Amsterdam's heyday in the 1600s, what stands out clearly is the relationship between Amsterdam's geography and economic history. The city was founded 800 years ago when farmers and fishermen simply built a dam across the Amstel River to hold back the waters of the Isselmeer, thereby giving the city its name. Later, other cities were established in the same manner, as reflected in the names of cities as such as Rotterdam, Monnikendam, Edam and Zaandam.

But this relationship, marked by constant imbalance and conflict, yet held in check by water engineers, will determine the future of both the country and the city. Many consider the cafes and hashish bars to be typically Dutch, but if one were to look for what it is that distinguishes the Netherlands from all other European countries, then one must visit other parts of this most heavily-populated country on the continent. Four hundred years ago, the philosopher René Descartes was reputed to have said, 'God created the world. Man created the Netherlands'. This was an accurate observation since this country, to a degree greater than any other, is a centuries-long engineering project, created by organisation, cooperation and determination.[12] The unique historical tradition of the Dutch has been to wrestle the land free from the embrace of water. For me, there are precisely three places that symbolise the uniqueness of Holland, and which at the same time can recapitulate the long and crucial connecting line between the past with its future.

Kinderdijk, or 'the child's dyke' as it denotes in Dutch, is located right by Alblasserwaard, or 'the land by the water's edge'. On the journey to Kinderdijk it is impossible not to be reminded of the unique quality of the Netherlands: there are 27 signs around and about that indicate one is now driving below the surface of the sea. The Kinderdijk area has always been threatened by water, and the most famous flood catastrophe occurred there on 18–19 November 1421. On that occasion, 60 villages were inundated. According to legend, a cat managed to save a child in a cradle while the water welled up around them and the dyke on which the cradle came to rest became known as 'the child's dyke', which became the name of the place as well. There are still 1,000 windmills in Holland but their concentration here is unmatched elsewhere. Nineteen majestic windmills line the horizon, painted brown and organised as though intended to be part of a painting by Rembrandt. They continue to cast their reflections into canals that were constructed in the 1740s.

The windmills have functioned mainly to remove the water from the earth – not to grind the grain, as in other countries. The great sails – which reach toward the sky and to the clouds that race rapidly by here on the flat plains along the North Sea – stand as symbols of the Netherlands' history. The pop and crackle of the sails as they turn and the torrents of water being scooped up by the mill

13. The most important task of the windmills in the Netherlands has been to pump water out of the reclaimed polder lands and into canals and rivers, so that it can be sent out to sea. The windmills have made the country livable, but they would be woefully inadequate as a weapon in a struggle against greater precipitation and rivers with greater quantities of water in them.

blades and dumped into the canals that carry the water away and out to sea, are the sounds that have accompanied human activity in the Netherlands polders for hundreds of years. The mills' form is at once archaic and futuristic, a type of timeless machinery that rests upon the elements, but which ever more importantly belongs to the past – for they will not afford Holland the necessary protection from the insecurity and threat of the waterscape of the future.

But it is Alkmaar, a little northwest of Amsterdam, and not the windmills of Kinderdijk, that summarises for me the situation and unique features of Holland. Alkmaar resembles the rest of the country but at the same time its poignant history points inexorably toward the future. Alkmaar encompasses both the country's history and its future. It was not far from here that the first polder was reclaimed from the water in 1533; and it was here, in 1573, at the beginning of the 80-year war with Spain, that the Dutch used water as a weapon to break the Spanish siege. What makes this place particularly interesting now is that here, for the first time, the Dutch actually sacrificed the precious land they had reclaimed at great effort from the water's embrace. They decided that it was necessary to give up hard-won land so that the nation as a whole would endure. The Dutch are now facing, according to the government, a comparable situation, but this time it is not the Spanish who are the enemy: it is the water itself.

The Netherlanders have the unique but enormous problem of a structural nature because the balance they have managed to strike between land and water is now fundamentally threatened. As a consequence, they have launched what is described as a completely new method of controlling the rivers. Land must now be sacrificed to water, but on a much greater scale than in Alkmaar in 1573.

'The Dutch no longer realise that they are completely dependent upon water control. The polder mentality – or rather, the cooperative spirit that created the country – has disappeared: We feel as though we are speaking not to deaf ears but simply to people who have forgotten where they live.' The water engineer who is taking me along to one of the pumping stations outside Delft stretches out an arm and points to the canals beside which we are driving.[13]

'They don't realise that we are the ones who are controlling how much water runs through the canals at any point in time and who are always the determining factor as to whether they can drive their cars into their garages or, in dry shoes, take their girlfriends to an outdoor restaurant for the evening.'

I am out for a pump tour together with my Dutch engineer friend, who is also a historian. It gives one an additional, rather odd, joy to travel around avant-garde Holland on a hunt for something as traditional and as unspectacular as water pumps and pumping stations. The water experts we encounter express the same irritation: today's Netherlanders take water security for granted, they say

– as though the balance between water and society was created by nature or as though nature had been tamed and domesticated. There can be no doubt that the key guardians of the Netherlands are the water engineers who now also manage the thousands of pumps that stand pumping day and night, year after year, over large areas of the country. These pumps are the nerve centre of the country's life because they determine where people can live, where people can drive and what people can do. And they must pump ever more and more due to changes in the national water cycle.

The lowest polders are 7 metres below sea level, while spring floods can increase sea level as much as 5 metres above normal. Rainwater must therefore be constantly pumped away. Having visited pumping station after pumping station, and with the sounds of their repetitive rhythm still clear in my ears, it was easy to conclude that the land I was travelling in was, first and foremost, the land of pumps and moreover, pumps that would need to perform their task for all eternity.

But, according to the authorities, it has now become evident that even this will not suffice.

They are afraid that the water stored in the Alps will flow down the major rivers in greater quantities than previously thought and that this could occur at unusual or unexpected times. At the same time, precipitation will increase. The rivers will naturally collect more water, but they are already full to overflowing with all the water being pumped up from the polders and off the land. The authorities are afraid that the vulnerable and delicate balance that has been established cannot be maintained much longer. As Deputy Minister for Water and Transport Melanie Schultz van Haegen told me: 'We cannot cope with all this water in the old-fashioned way.'[14]

The authorities in the Netherlands believe that 1,430 kilometres of dykes and the most effective river management system in the world are no longer sufficient to meet future scenarios. In the country where the dyke-builder has been a national hero, and which has sent water engineers to tame water around the world (they built the first canals that bound together the Hanseatic towns with the Elbe and Hamburg in the 1400s; they were the leading engineers in the water control works that were one of the conditions for the Japanese economic revolution at the end of the nineteenth century; and they are now being asked for advice from New Orleans to Shanghai), they have decided to do something drastic. The Netherlands – whose mythic hero-figure, Hans Brinker, the eight-year-old boy who put his finger in the dyke that was about to burst – has now decided to knock down its dykes! Earlier it was said, 'He who will not work with the dykes must leave his land'. Now, however, dykes have to be done away with and the rivers given more room – and this in a country where space is at a premium.

I pay a visit to the Dordrecht region, here the future has already arrived. It borders the rivers Oude Maas, Beneden Merwede, Nieuwe Merwede, Hollands Diep and Dordtsche Kil. From the name Dordrecht – 'river crossing' – it is understandable that this is an area that will have problems if the water levels rise in the rivers. Here, farmers were in the process of moving, because some farms would soon be inundated under 3 metres of water.

'It is all for the people in the cities,' says a farmer's wife bitterly, but at the same time appreciative that the government had to take action. Indeed, some people's interests have to be sacrificed to more important national interests. But what is most moving is not the fate of individuals but the nation's U-turn in water policy, a fresh example of how the Netherlanders' eternal conflict with water has been, and will continue to be, a struggle against processes they themselves first set in motion.

There is hardly any other country that has done more than the Netherlands in dealing with the practical consequences of potential future climate change and a potentially changed waterscape. But a Dutch colleague, and an expert in the country's hydrology, made a point of stressing to me that these initiatives are far from sufficient.

'They will learn only when catastrophe strikes, and it always does so with despotic power,' he says, and draws parallels with the epoch-making floods in the history of the country.

This time, as the aircraft takes off from Schiphol, I gaze with an extra eagerness at the canal below. 'Who is right about what is needed to cope with the future of water?' I ask myself and wonder if I can see yet another pumping station on the horizon. Are the initiatives being taken completely insufficient, or are they too drastic, and whose interests are to be sacrificed in this the most densely populated country in Europe so that the remainder of the Netherlands' population can live in security, safe from the threat of river water in the coming decades?

What the Netherlands unambiguously shows is that the New Age of Water Uncertainty has definitively reached the European continent, and that even in Europe, the bastion of modernity, a struggle of enormous dimensions and unanticipated consequences is underway to establish definitive power over how the water landscape of the future will look.

14. The east coast of Greenland is closed to marine traffic almost year-round due to the ice in the arms of the fjords. In a very short period of time, the region has come under the world political spotlight due to the fear that 10 per cent of the world's water mass, now in the form of ice, will melt into the sea, causing waves to lick at the first-floor windows of the Empire State Building in New York, along the Bund in Shanghai, the jazz cafes of New Orleans, and inundate large portions of Bangladesh and the Netherlands.

CHAPTER 3
THE ICY BARRENS THAT ARE BECOMING THE WORLD'S 'HOT SPOT'

Along the 2,600-kilometre coastline of eastern Greenland there are two towns and seven small settlements with a total population of 3,500 people. It is possible to visit this coast by boat, but only for five months each year. The rest of the time the ice is impenetrable. And so it is that I make my journey to Tasiilaq by helicopter. The spring sun is shining and, as we fly toward our goal encircled by an infinitely cloud-free sky, in crystal-clear air, the colour of the fjord gives new meaning to the phrase 'deep blue'. With each kilometre the feeling that we are leaving civilisation and entering a barren land of ice is reinforced.

The pilot, clearly just as fascinated as I am by this unusually fine spring day, flies the helicopter low, despite regulations, and brushes the tops of enormous icebergs that lie like huge rafts all over the surface of the fjord. As we go in for landing, we can see the houses, which cling to their foundation walls several metres high to help them withstand the fierce wind squalls. They are painted in strong primary colours: dark red, yellow, blue and bright red. I check into Hotel Red House, which is run by a German and enjoys a panoramic view over King Oscar's Fjord, the ice, the mountains and the glaciers. I quickly find out that on Greenland there are quite a few who look forward to the day when some of the ice *has* melted away!

'We are not quite following your famous countryman's footsteps. While Nansen went across Greenland on skis, we plan to kite-board the length of Greenland.' A tall Frenchman, who in no way resembles an athlete, and with his arm in a sling after having broken it the previous day, wants to set a speed record together with a friend traversing Greenland's inland ice from south to north tearing along behind a snow kite. Astounding, of course, but his prowess is of peripheral interest to me. Thus, while his mother, who was here as support staff, mixes and stirs a cup of powdered coffee in the sparsely equipped kitchen, and while his co-kiter gives free reign to his imagination about someone at some time in the future managing to cross Greenland on roller-skates, I find some classic Greenland books from the hotel shelves. I sit down in a chair on the veranda facing the fjord. I took a deep breath, not only in response to the harsh beauty of the landscape but also to get a clean, deep lungful of fresh air.

The first Inuits settled on the east coast about 2,000 years ago, probably arriving in skin boats rowed along the shore, several thousand years after the first people came over from North America and landed on Greenland's west coast. During periods when the climate was colder than it is today, their society died out and some areas were abandoned for warmer places, until higher temperatures and easier ice conditions led to them being settled again.

Recent research speculates about whether changes in the climate were a determining reason why, for example, the Viking colonies started by Eirik Raude (Erik the Red) were abandoned. They were established in AD 984 and were in existence for 450 years. But then they disappeared suddenly, leaving almost nothing behind except for some bone fragments found by archaeologists.[15] Analyses of this bone material indicates that they suffered from constant hunger brought about by climate change. It is likely that during the Middle Ages most of eastern Greenland was uninhabited. Therefore, in the history books of the future, Erik the Red will not only be remembered as the discoverer of Greenland but also as the founder of a colony that failed to adapt to climatic variation.

The reason I have come to eastern Greenland is because the new uncertainty and insecurity about our water future has suddenly – in the course of a very few years – brought these icy barrens to the centre of world attention. As a matter of fact, it was when scientists hauled up ice-core samples from deep within Greenland's ice-fields that we learned for certain that the climate has undergone changes in the last millennium, and that sometimes there have been radical changes occurring in a short period of time. These new discoveries have been the primary source of our uncertainty about the future. The most venerable ice – that at the greatest depth – is almost 2 million years old and therefore provides source material from an era that hitherto we have been unable either to reconstruct or understand. Above all this new knowledge, deposited like tracks in the history of the ice, has rendered the hydrological cycle of the future, and thereby the development of human society, irrevocably more uncertain. It is because of the Greenland ice that we can now say with certainty that the climate has always been changing, and always will; and further, that human activity itself is a factor that affects these changes.

Greenland will remain at the centre of world policy for reasons that only a few decades ago would have seemed absurd: namely, that the island holds approximately 10 per cent of the world's fresh water bound up in the form of ice. The inland ice in places is up to three kilometres thick and encompasses a surface

15. Taking regular measurements of the hydrology of glacial rivers can inform researchers about changes in the quantity of water given off by glaciers. This is a river that runs out from Mittivakkat Glacier in eastern Greenland. There the runoff has increased definitively, but scientific findings about inland ice are still limited and predictions abound.

area as large as Britain. The Greenland ice has been remarkably stable for the past ten thousand years (although with great regional variations) but before that period it melted so much that sea levels rose dramatically. By the end of the Ice Age the oceans had risen by 20 metres in a period as short (in geological terms) as 400 years.[16] How much – or how little – the world's oceans will rise is dependent, ultimately, on what happens in Greenland and upon the fact that once the melted water is in the oceans it will warm up and, as a consequence, expand. Thus it is that this outpost of civilisation – Greenland, and not New York or Brussels or Beijing – holds the key not only to our understanding of the distant past but also provides the basis for making predictions that will affect a large proportion of humanity in the future.

The United Nations climate panel believes that it will take between 500 and 2,000 years for the Greenland ice cap to melt, and that the sea level will rise by 50–80 centimetres by the year 2100. Others believe that this is an alarmist prediction based upon thin empirical evidence and unreliable models. On the other hand, researchers at NASA maintain that Greenland's glaciers are slipping toward the sea much more quickly than the United Nations assumes and expects:

they predict that the ice cap will melt in the course of a mere 200 years and they show what happened at the end of the last Ice Age. Some researchers in California maintain that satellite photos show an increase in the loss of ice mass of 250 per cent between May 2004 and April 2006,[17] and that consequently the ice is melting much more rapidly; yet others argue that the thickness of the ice cap inland is increasing in many places. Those adopting the most extreme position argue that it will soon be time to jump into boats! It is obvious that a global struggle is underway in the interpretation of what is happening in Greenland and how it will affect landscapes around the world, with enormous, far-reaching political – economic consequences.

Some of the real veteran Greenland researchers are located at the Sermilik Research Station at the head of an arm of the fjord 20 kilometres north of Tasiilaq. It was built in 1970 and is owned by the University of Copenhagen. Once our helicopter had risen over the last mountain peak I could see the simple cabin, hemmed in between the glaciers and the icebergs. Standing on a dry patch outside it, surrounded on all sides by snow, are Bent and Niels. For several decades they have, unnoticed by the outside world, studied and measured developments in one of the many lesser glaciers. One of them confided that for a long time his wife has referred to him simply as a 'mud geographer' because he had devoted years of his life to measuring the quantity of silt and stone and water in the glacial rivers of Greenland! But such is the nature of research at its most useful: suddenly, data assembled silently and laboriously over many years, awaken global interest. While they investigate Mittivakkat Glacier they live in this spartan, simply equipped station: six beds, a stove in the living room where a sofa has been pushed into a corner, and where water must be fetched from the glacial stream one can hear through the cabin's thin walls. They are experienced foot soldiers in what has become a veritable army of researchers who have streamed into Greenland from all around the globe. In the spring sunshine, which causes the dry sandbanks down by the edge of the sea to steam in the warmth, we find the path up along the meltwater river, while icebergs as large as ships move slowly and majestically across the fjord in profound silence. Equipped with a rifle to protect us from polar bears, the researchers show us their measuring stations on the river and how they calculate the snow depth up on the ice. 'There is no doubt about it, Mittvakkat Glacier is receding about ten metres a year,' Bent says, pointing toward the arm of the glacier, indicating the point to which it used to extend. 'On the other hand it's difficult to say anything with certainty about the changes to the Greenland ice cap. It is reducing in many places and growing in others,' says Nils.

As icebergs the size of tall buildings glide past and out to sea right to the

16. Here we see the sandbars found near some lonely icebergs in Sermlikfjord. I am coming down the mountain with the Danish glacier researchers as they finish yet another day on the job.

horizon, the two Danish researchers report that they neither can, nor will, make unequivocal predictions about what will happen to the inland ice cap in the future. They stress the need for caution, since to date the research has shed surprisingly little light on how glaciers behave and why they act the way they do. They maintain that nobody yet understands the complicated mechanisms behind glacier mass balance, air temperature, wind, and ocean temperature in the Arctic Region.

At other locations in Greenland, scientists lower themselves into tunnels and wells created by water within the ice. Some of them believe that this meltwater, if its quantity increases, will cause the ice to slide out into the sea much more quickly than portrayed by the normal climate models. Therefore, hearing the sound of running water under the glaciers, the question one might pose is: is this the alarming sound of the future of humanity, the modest forerunner to 'the tipping point' when the world's oceans will rise much more precipitously than expected? For others, however, it is sweet music. For them the question might be: is this the sound of Greenland's future economic fairytale?

'Water power will be Greenland's new growth resource. The first hydro-station has already been built outside Tasiilaq.' The Danish hydro-electric engineer who drives me out of the little settlement in a battered pickup has no doubts about this as he will show me the local hydropower station, and after some kilometres on a twisty gravel road I am able to see it right down by the fjord. There is nothing to indicate that this modest architecture heralds a possible revolution in Greenland's economy and history. But with ever more meltwater in the rivers, and with 10 per cent of the world's water stored as ice in the mountains, it is clear that the potential is enormous. There are many in Greenland who view water power as an area of priority with which they can modernise and develop the whole island. They not only want to start aluminium smelting with the help of cheap power, but there are also those who talk about selling enormous amounts of electricity by sending it through underwater cables to Canada and the USA, and to Europe via Iceland and the Faroe Islands. The possibility of producing hydrogen from the water has also been discussed. Some estimate that Greenland's potential production of water power could be 8,000 terawatt hours per year – about four times the USA's annual energy consumption and about ten times that of Europe.

The gigantic masses of ice that many believe are melting due to global warming, and which will begin to flow down from the high mountains, will transform Greenland into a gigantic producer of power. And while the engineer is showing me on the screen how much energy is being produced, my mind slips back to the epoch before 'the new uncertainty' – that is, to the 1970s, when global warming was a completely unknown concept. Back then there were proposals put forward as to how to melt the ice of Greenland artificially in order to produce water power there. It was suggested, for example, that the ash from coal-driven factories in the USA and Great Britain could be spread out over the ice in Greenland in order to increase the melting of the glaciers by artificial means.

The changing ice conditions on Greenland have always had significance for climate patterns all over the world, but due to current awareness of climate change processes the political importance of the Greenland ice is much more crucial than before. If the ice melts, this will have great regional repercussions for the geopolitics of the region. Denmark's control of the island will certainly quickly become history. During the Cold War, Greenland was a frontline military strategic chip played by the superpowers; as such, it was a protective barren land for American bases. If the ice melts, Greenland will not only become a 'hot spot' as the planet's barometer over climate change, but also for the major powers in their manoeuvrings over new resources and control, since nobody yet knows what the ice is hiding.

American, Russian, Japanese, Indian, Chinese and Canadian political and economic interests are all preparing for a new world to open up if indeed there will be less ice on Greenland and less ice in the Arctic Ocean. Ships from the west coast of the USA going to north-east Asia will save approximately 40 per cent of their sailing time if they set course for the north coast of the continent and through the Northwest Passage instead of through Suez and the Panama

Canals. The savings for the shipping companies could be in the neighbourhood of $250,000 per sailing, and business people and politicians have already dug themselves into the starting line as they wait for more conspicuous signs of climate change. And what hides beneath the ice – not only in Greenland but also in Canada, Alaska and not least in Siberia? Will climate change make people in the northern hemisphere still more privileged? Will they not only retain their position of power in the world but also strengthen it?

One charmless grey afternoon, when the gusts of cold wind blew relentlessly, I went out in a small boat between the pack ice and the icebergs in the fjord beyond Tasiilaq. And while I shivered as I noted the intense concentration of the boat's operator – he had to ensure that the vessel did not become locked in by the mass of moving ice – and spied a few colourful painted houses that seemed to stand in stark contrast to the inhospitable nature surrounding them, it became very clear to me: changes in the climate are not changes that will unite human beings in a common struggle for the future of the planet. The social and political consequences of the new uncertainty can first be understood by grasping the fact that many will ask 'What's in it for me?'

'Good?' The pilot, who is about to take the helicopter back to Kullusuk, asks if the trip has been worthwhile. While the sun continues to shine with the same brilliance, we remove our bags from the cockpit. The fog, stubborn and unchanging, glides silently in, erasing the charm of the mountains, rendering them hostile and forbidding. I take a final glance across these barrens that now occupy a central place position in humanity's uncertain future. 'Yes,' I reply. 'And very instructive.'

17. The Four Rivers Fountain on Piazza Navona was created by Bernini and built in the 1600s. The powerful figures represent the rivers Nile, Danube, La Plata and Ganges.

CHAPTER 4
FROM ACQUA VERGINE TO THE CITY THAT REFUSES TO DROWN

Inscribed on the tombstone of English poet, John Keats (1795–1821), in Rome, one finds the words 'A Life Writ in Water'. Keats wanted to capture the fleeting, unsettled and always changing nature of existence and used water as a metaphor for what in his time was the romantic approach to existential questions. The image is poignant because water erases all traces, since water – and this is something that Keats would scarcely have been aware of – has chemical properties that make it unrivalled as a solvent. But from another point of view, one could say that both history and the future are 'writ in water', and this is well-illustrated in the country where Keats' life came to its end – Italy. The history of Rome and Venice, of Florence and Pisa of the Renaissance, the rise of the Mafia on the dry earth of Sicily, and the developments in the Po Valley, could all be written from such a water perspective – a history, as it happens, still waiting to be written.

Slightly above the Spanish Steps, and not far from streets filled with chic clothing boutiques, the caretaker of the Roman waterworks unlocks an unremarkable white door in a brick wall, and immediately I enter a completely different and silent world. I am descending a spiral staircase in a heavy darkness alleviated only by the caretaker's powerful light. We are on one of the companionways down into the Acqua Vergine aqueduct, which was commissioned 19 years before the birth of Christ, and at which time it was called Aqua Virgo. The name was taken from a legend. Thirsty Roman soldiers asked a young girl for water. She showed them to the spring that would later supply the aqueduct. In her honour the spring was called Aqua Virgo. It was 20 kilometres in length but it dropped in elevation only 4 metres over that distance, and most of the time it carried more than 100,000 cubic metres of water daily.

With every metre that I descend I hear the unmistakable susurrus of *aqua vitae*. I feel my way around in the cool darkness, along the Canal of the Virgin, far below the hot busy streets of Rome, and I know that I am walking beside what, perhaps more than anything else, provided the foundation upon which the magnificence of the imperial capital rests – for it was not the religious architecture, nor the bread and circuses, that made the city possible: it was the water that ran beneath its streets.

Imperial Rome is known above all else for the Pantheon and the Colosseum, while the Canal of the Virgin is just about as forgotten as it is hidden. Five hundred and seventy-eight kilometres of aqueduct brought the water in from the springs in the hills beyond Rome, above the Roman *campagna* and into the centre of the imperial capital. If one arrives in Rome by air or by train one can still see the remains of almost 20-metre high brick and mortar bridges with their open archways. In one's mind's eye one can still picture how they carried the closed, mortared water channels on their backs, so to speak. Some of them had two or three channels, one on top of the other. But what really counted were the underground aqueducts. Almost 90 per cent of the water was carried through installations like that of Acqua Vergine. Even though Rome was built on the banks of the Tiber and its water was considered both sacred and of especially good quality (for a long time the Popes would take bottles of water dipped from the Tiber when they travelled abroad), the City of the Seven Hills could not have developed or coped with the large increase in population during the centuries around the birth of Christ if it had not had large-scale supplies of additional water.

'Try to compare all these indispensable aqueducts with the completely pointless pyramids, or with the Greeks' useless but admirable constructions,' wrote Sextus Julius Frontinus, in charge of Rome's water supply between 104 and 83 BC, in his brilliant book *The Aqueducts of Rome*. Frontinus left behind living accounts of the aqueducts, the water distribution system and the relevant procedural law. It took 538 years to build the 11 aqueducts of the city. At its height, the system moved about a million cubic metres of water daily, or about 1,000 litres per inhabitant each day, many times more than in the world's large cities today. During the time of the emperors the city was the centre for the secular cult of water. It was said that for the Romans, the baths were their temples. The aqueducts also supplied 1,212 fountains. As early as around 150 BC the geographer Pausanias, who had travelled widely in the Mediterranean region, declared that no place had the right to call itself a city unless it possessed a decorated fountain dedicated to a god or a hero. Rome, more than any other urban conurbation, stood as an expression of this tradition.

Fountains are one of the most potent and frequently used symbols, not only of the cultural triumph of urbanisation but also of the sheer power of the sovereign. Fountains have so many different connotations that there is no one social or psychological explanation of their placement and design. And yet they have something in common: at one and the same time they express homage both to the free properties of water and to the power of nature as tamed by human beings. From a long-term historical perspective they can be interpreted as symbolising the idea that human beings are no longer enslaved by the whims of nature. Additionally, since they represent a special form of moving sculpture that utilises the visual and musical aspects of water, they enliven a city and bring a hint of nature into it.

The Four Rivers Fountain on Piazza Navona was created by Bernini and built in the 1600s. It is a must for anyone who wants to understand the history of Rome. It is at first glance an artistic portrayal of the Garden of Eden from the Bible; but at a little distance one also sees that it is an architectonic feat and an obligatory tribute to the ruler of Rome. The artist has set an obelisk (taken from Heliopolis in Egypt by Emperor Augustus 2,000 years earlier) on top of the fountain, and on top of that again, a dove – an emblem from the family crest of Pope Innocent X. Thus the fountain expresses not only the seventeenth-century conception of the Biblical story of the four rivers of Eden but it also reflects papal power and the symbolic role of fountains in confirming this power. The fountain's powerful manly figures stand for, and symbolise, the Nile, the Danube, La Plata and the Ganges.

The Popes restored and developed Rome as the foremost city of fountains. In the end, the aqueducts were destroyed by the Ostrogoths under King Witiges, who had them hacked to pieces in AD 537 in order finally to bring the Romans to their knees. When Rome picked itself up again during the Renaissance the old aqueducts were repaired and rebuilt. Now, in what gradually became the city of churches, water came to be regarded to a large degree as sacred. It became a symbol of the new life that the Catholic Church of the Popes brought to Rome; and it went even further, such that water became the 'Water of Life'. The fountains of living water now stood as expressions of power, immortality and purification. The Popes gave the people once again what the emperors had provided: grand, amazing fountains, like poems composed from stone and water.

Trevi Fountain marks the end of Acqua Vergine. It is one of the most famous fountains in the world, and is 'immortalised' in Fellini's film *La Dolce Vita*, with the Swedish actress Anita Ekberg. Both Romans and tourists have flocked to this monumental tribute to the circulation of water for more than 200 years, evening after evening. When Nicholas Salvi created the fountain in the eighteenth century, he wrote a small pamphlet about it, in which he reflected upon his work and the nature of water, 'that moving and eternally operative substance ... which can never really rest and relax, in contrast to the earth, which can do nothing other than accept impressions coming from external actors, and particularly from the water that created it.' The original fountains were to celebrate the arrival of water in the centre of the city. Thus the Trevi fountain is a celebration of both those who have power over water and of the power of water itself. It also symbolises water's dual and somewhat contradictory role as both serving humanity whilst simultaneously being an object of religious veneration.

From Rome, the imperial city where water was in abundance and controlled 2,000 years ago, I go north, following the mighty but now regulated Po until it enters into the sea and then move on to Venice – the city of canals. This Italian city tells a very different story about human relations to water. Venice sits on tree trunks pounded into the mud of a lagoon in the Adriatic Sea, and has always had a strange, faded beauty about it. Back in 1853, John Ruskin wrote that Venice was 'a ghost upon the sands of the sea, so weak – so quiet – so bereft of all but her loveliness'.[18] The decline and decadence of Venice has inspired other artists and intellectuals. In 1910, Filippo Tommaso Marinetti, the champion of Italian futurism, proposed to 'cure and heal' this 'decomposing city' while 'lifting its imposing geometry of metallic bridges and factories to the skies'. And in 1995, the French intellectual Jules Régis Debray, wrote in his pamphlet, *Against Venice*, that 'Venice is not a city but a representation of a city'.

But it is in late autumn, during the grey and misty months of November and December, that the city becomes most obviously imbued with the grandeur of its past and the melancholy of the present. The fate of the city is now, more and more, a compressed object lesson in the global consequences of uncertainty regarding the waterscape of the future. If the ice of Greenland melts as quickly as some maintain it will, and the sea level rises as dramatically as the Italian government believes, Venice will drown in the lagoon that created it.

It is early December and I am wandering slowly through the almost empty lanes and alleys. The sound of my footsteps is magnified by the deep silence of the early morning as I walk across the short arched bridges that cross more than 150 canals and link 117 small islands into a city. I cast a glance at the cafe tables wet from mist and dew before even the first chilly breakfast visitors are hunched over their morning coffees. The gondolas sit dark and abandoned in the morning mist and reinforce the morbid atmosphere. I am on my way to St Mark's Square, the very heart of the city, where the beautiful cathedral is standing, built over what are said to be the remains of St Mark (the myths tell that Mark's remains were stolen from Egypt and brought to Venice hidden under a load of pork so as to avoid a search of the ship by Muslims).

I round the corner from the cafe called *Harry's Bar*, once famously frequented by Ernest Hemingway, and I see an abrupt and shocking sight: the cathedral, standing with its base in water. Even before I manage to adapt to this sight, warning sirens ring out loud and strident between the palace walls. Civic employees are rapidly on the spot setting up a plank scaffolding on sawhorses so that pedestrians can cross the square and reach their jobs with dry feet. Sellers of yellow gumboots have appeared as well, adapting to a new market: tourists looking for protection against the water. To me, being here for the first time during high water, it is a very strange and rather alarming experience: I have to balance my way across some simple grey planks in order to traverse one of the most visited and exulted squares in the world.

The day before, in one of the city's museums, I had seen the famous painting of Gentile Bellini, *Processions of the Relic of the Cross*, a momentary scene from St Mark's Square from 1496. Now, a day later, I am surrounded by many of the same buildings that Bellini had painted back then; but from a distance they remind me more of large, ocean-going ships. Some restaurants have had to close, and instead of serving people at their tables are dangling green hoses out their windows to expel water from the cafe floor. It seems that Venetians are already used to what for me is a completely abnormal situation. The floods have already become the regular order of the day. They have become routine for Venetians because – and it is here that the uncertainty over the future climate kicks in literally – the city is more and more frequently under water.

18. More and more frequently, in order to cross St Mark's Square in Venice, inhabitants must use plank bridges that are set up by the authorities whenever water floods this famous square. It is under water ten times more frequently than it was a century ago. The authorities predict that the city will be inundated by 2050 if drastic steps are not taken.

Venetians have always struggled with water and the consequences of the way they have managed it. From a certain perspective, today's situation can be viewed as an extreme variation of a continuing and unique relationship between society and water. The city and the lagoon it rests upon were created by the Adriatic Sea and the three large rivers that run into the Adriatic. Over thousands of years the action of the waves and the sand from the rivers created hundreds of small islands. People gradually came to live here, first as fishers. Then, during the fifth century AD, many streamed in as refugees from Attila the Hun and his army. As early as the fourteenth century, the Venetians decided to divert the three rivers that ran into the lagoon, away from the city.[19] This reduced the danger of flooding. At the same time the lagoon was defended, both from a military point of view – attackers had problems manoeuvring their fleets in the shallow waters of the lagoon – and as a port. If, particularly during the Middle Ages, they had not intervened in the processes of nature and the sedimentation of the rivers, the lagoon would have filled in, and Venice, that city of canals, would have been part of the mainland.[20] Leonardo da Vinci was someone who understood the particular qualities of this waterscape. When the Ottoman Turks threatened the city in the 1500s, he proposed building a portable dam across the rivers so as to be able to drown the invaders. He also designed footwear to enable the soldiers to walk on water and over the shallow bottom of the lagoon, so they could attack the undersides of the Turkish ships.

Then, during the twentieth century the city sank by 23 centimetres, partly due to natural geographic causes but above all because the new industry on the mainland pumped the groundwater out from under Venice. After this was forbidden, in 1983, the city almost stopped sinking.[21] But now there is another challenge; that of the rising sea levels. According to the most dramatic predictions, rising sea levels will lead to a completely different relationship between the 'marble walls' and the 'water'. Lord Byron's famous poem from 1819 has proven prophetic:

> Oh Venice! Venice!
> When thy marble walls
> Are level with the waters, there shall be
> A cry of nations o'er thy sunken halls.
> A loud lament along the sweeping sea!

St Mark's Square is underwater ten times more frequently now than it was a century ago. At the beginning of the twentieth century the city was underwater four times a year. In 1996 water flooded across St Mark's Square 90 times. The most serious warning that something was going terribly wrong occurred on 4 November 1966, when water rose 194 centimetres above normal tidal levels and it was three days before it receded. In 2002 large portions of the city were inundated 15 times in the month of November alone. The authorities maintain that the city will be completely underwater by 2050 if drastic action is not taken to remedy the situation. The old Renaissance ground-floor salons have become warehouses, and some of these have already been vacated due to incoming water. The inhabitants are also fleeing from the ever-greater wave of tourists. Indeed, never before has Venice lived up to the image of it presented in Thomas Mann's *Death in Venice*, written two years before the outbreak of the Second World War, with its atmosphere of doom and destruction (the black gondolas reminded him of coffins), the conflict between passion and self-control, between life and death – an atmosphere that became immortalised in a film version of the same name, not least because it was accompanied by the music of Mahler's Fifth Symphony.

The city's unique colours contribute to this melancholy apocalyptic atmosphere. They are not like colours in other places, not least because of the way the light shines on the water, in the lagoon and the canals. In the Gallerie dell'Accademia, founded by Napoleon when he invaded the city, one is able to see how the Venetian painters, in contrast to their Italian colleagues of the sixteenth century, were possessed by their use of colour. Whereas others were concerned with composition, the Venetians were the masters of colour, clearly inspired by the way the light reflected and refracted up from the lagoon and seemed to obliterate contours and meld colours together in a kind of indeterminable blue atmosphere.

How to save Venice from destruction? Will the sea rise? And if so, by how much? There are few questions that have greater consequences for the city's future. Of course, in the final analysis the surface of the earth is always changing and, seen over a long historical perspective, the fate of cities, from Harappa to Venice, rise and, ultimately, disappear. But many would love to keep Venice alive, at least for some generations to come, and they are convinced that technology provides the solution. Down through the years the Venetians have dug up the mud from the bottom of the canals in order to stop the water from rising over the walls of the houses, as the bottom of the canals constantly silt up with mud. But this is not enough now, it is argued, and some experts suggest pumping sea water in under the city to lift it. But in 2003 the Italian government went for a project that would simply lock out the sea if necessary. They wanted to send a strong message: It was too early to organise a funeral for Venice.

Brim full with technological optimism, they called the plan Project Moses, or simply Moses. This modern Moses will also command the sea to part, but this

19. For several centuries the Venetians have tried to establish a balance between the lagoon and the city, through human intervention. Some believe that the technology of Project Moses will be the crowning glory in the Italians' historic struggle against the water; others believe it breaks fundamentally with the pragmatic way that Venetians formerly controlled it. Parts of the lagoon have become a hectic construction site.

time it will be engineers who decide how. This solution – the moveable gate solution, where gigantic doors will close and keep out the sea – is seen as the optimal solution compatible with local natural water conditions. Underwater gates at the bottom of the lagoon will rise upwards and prevent the Adriatic from rushing in over the streets of the city. The annual maintenance alone will cost about 9 million Euros. Former President Silvio Berlusconi pushed for this solution because, as he said, climate change has to be taken seriously. Berlusconi placed the first stone at the construction site at the bottom of the lagoon – with his name on it.

'The government is using the uncertainty about the climate to advance the interests of the technological – industrial complex,' said the environmental activist, pointing at the canal water washing its way up the walls of the palaces directly across from the restaurant where we were sitting.

'They say it is absolutely certain that the sea outside Venice will rise and that the city will be underwater by 2050 if something drastic isn't done.'

'But,' he continues, 'many environmental activists are less categoric in their predictions, because nobody knows how much or when the sea level will rise. Therefore we go in for less grand and a greater number of smaller initiatives.

Whatever is best for the lagoon, and is done properly, is what we consider appropriate.'

He looks at me and waits for my reaction because he knows that what he is saying poses a challenge to the conventional picture of the global environmental debates, where the traditional 'right' tend to pooh-pooh the question, while the traditional 'left' tend to speak of the need to take the warnings about global warming seriously. But in the case of Venice, this has been turned on its head. I answer politely that I am not actually surprised, that this merely confirms a common phenomenon of growing importance: how the assessment of future water landscapes and climate will be an intense political and politicised arena. At the core of this age of uncertainty one will find a power struggle of global dimensions – not only over interpretations of the weather of the future, but also between competing interests as to how one should deal with them. Some people want to utilise the threat to put forward projects in which they have economic and political interests, yet others seek political influence and power as self-styled champions of the environment.

When the decision was made about this project, one of the leaders of the World Wildlife Fund in Venice said, 'Today the fate of the city is balancing on a pretentious, costly and environmental technological gamble'.[22] At the same time, the president of the region, and member of the ruling party said, 'December 6th will be a historic day for Venice. The whole world will applaud, and only makers of galoshes will be sad'.[23] Prime Ministers Berlusconi and Prodi at the time were in favour but the mayor of Venice was opposed. The local authoritites felt that the project was based on what was already considered to be an out-dated model of the future rise in sea level (those building the swing gates were reckoning that the sea level will rise by 15–25 centimetres by 2100) and that it relies upon a simplified and too elementary understanding of the complex ecology of the lagoon. The opponents of the project would prefer to continue to do what Venice has always done, but to do so more intensively: that is, clean the bottom of the canals, dredge them out so they become deeper, and shore up the houses. They insisted that no one knew with any certainty what the climate will be in future and how the sea level will be affected. Many maintained that the project will destroy the local ecology under the guise of saving it. Ironically enough, and in keeping with the character of the uncertainty, in the year 2006, just after the decision had been taken, the sea level was lower than it had been for many years. Perhaps it was this that Berlusconi had in mind when the same year he said to Reuters: 'I am the Jesus Christ of politics, I am a patient victim. I put up with everyone, I sacrifice myself for everyone'.[24]

The disagreement over Project Moses in Italy is a telling one for the situation that is emerging around the world. For the first time we are all condemned to shape the future society by acting on the basis of predictions about what is going to happen to water in the future. In the Maldives, the government has built an artificial island – Hulhumale, 1.5 metres above sea level – out of fear of rising sea levels. About half the population of the country's roughly 250,000 people could seek refuge there – a modern Noah's Ark for water refugees. If the ocean rises higher they will have to build it up! If the Greenland icecap melts, then New York and London will be threatened. If Antarctica melts, the ocean will rise by 61 metres, and many more will be jumping into the lifeboats. Only very few believe firmly that this will happen, and then only over a very long time span. But almost all predictions calculate that greater proportions of the ice will melt into the seas and that many will face challenges; challenges that nobody knows how to tackle but which will affect and involve everyone.

One should not depart from this city of water and canals by train or car, but rather by boat. For here, the canals cannot be taken for the anachronisms they look like where the gondolas, laden with tourists, paddle carefully under the low bridges, but rather for what they are – the city's living arteries and the only route in for firemen and pasta deliveries. And as my ferry slips out of the lagoon in the December fog, and I hear the water slapping up against the walls of the houses, and as I know that record tides have occurred in recent years, it is easy to get a sense of foreboding, of fear for what might become the unknown tyranny of the future – rising sea level.

20. There are 3,000 *cenotes* on the Yucatán Peninsula in Mexico. These freshwater sink holes were the basis upon which the Mayan civilisation was able to survive after the urban centres in the southern portions of the Mayan Empire were abandoned due to catastrophic drought. The local population continues to use these wells.

CHAPTER 5
THE AZTEC 'LAND ON WATER' AND THE MAYAN HIDDEN WATER WORLD

Many associate Mexico City with pollution, slums and strident social injustice. Or with the place where in 1968 Bob Beamon set his fantastic world record in the long jump, landing 8.9 metres from the plank. Mexico City is all of this but, for me, one of the most interesting aspects of the city is revealed when flying in to the city. The plane came in late in the evening over the high mountains that ring Mexico City. As the pilot banked the aircraft into an exceptional sea of light, the word *megapolis* or mega-city, took on a new, concrete, observable significance. The pattern of light there below me reveals a unique aspect of this city: there are no dark strips to break the monotony, no rivers capable of reflecting light like the Hudson in New York, the Thames in London, the Edo in Tokyo, the Nile in Khartoum, the Seine in Paris or the Spree in Berlin. A basic structural fact of far-reaching importance is that Mexico City has no river it can utilise, and since it lies 2,200 metres above sea level, it has no large lakes either from which water could be drawn.

Almost every fifth Mexican, and one-half of the country's industry, is squeezed together within the boundaries of this one city. Seven thousand people are packed into each square kilometre. Mexico City covers 2,200 square kilometres, while the European cities of the nineteenth century were seldom greater in area than one could walk through on foot as one conducted one's business. In the time of the emperors, Rome covered approximately seven square kilometres, while London in the Middle Ages was only a little over 1.3 square kilometres. Sociologists and historians who work with urbanisation have had to re-evaluate many of their concepts and assumptions in relation to such mastodon cities.

Outside the world-famous anthropological museum in Mexico City there stands a statue several metres high of Tlaloc, the leader of a group of rain gods called *Tlaloques*. The statue was created during the era of the Aztecs, whose civilisation was an Indian high culture dominating Mexico's highland plateau from the beginning of the sixteenth century, and whose largest city, Tenochtitlán, was more populous than almost any in Europe with the possible exception of Naples. Where it stands, reflected in a small, almost square pool of water that is intended to remind the visitor of the importance of water to this civilisation, the statue appears more out of place than awe-inspiring. But Tlaloc provided rain. And he demanded, as all other Aztec gods did, human sacrifice. The Aztec gods were assuaged particularly by child sacrifice. The best way to satisfy the hunger of Tlaloc was to sacrifice children, especially those who cried loudly and shed many tears. The child would first be beaten so that it cried. Everyone in attendance hit each other with the same lugubrious aim of causing tears. Earthly tears would cause Tlaloc to release his heavenly tears from the sky. The ceremony concluded with the drowning of the child. Then piles of latex gum would be burned such that the gods would now permit the rains to come.

Despite their beliefs, rather than relying upon the rain or Tlaloc's tears, the population developed a unique system of agriculture: they built what some have called, in a rather misleading way, 'floating gardens', or *chinampas*. The core area of what would become the Aztec Empire was called the 'Land on Water' and their most famous city, the 'Stone in Rising Water'. In the middle of the lakes in the Valley of Mexico, which was located on the site of modern-day Mexico City, they built up a society economically founded on a great number of man-made small islands, each between six and ten metres wide and from 100 to 200 metres long. These agricultural islands were extremely fertile, made from mud accumulated from the bottom of the lakes. They were thus connected to the bottom of the lake; the plants received sufficient moisture and were fertilised by organic matter in the mud and from local aquatic life. Today, this can be found in only one small ecological park, Xochimilco, which is located some kilometres from the centre of Mexico City.

When the Spanish attacked the high plateau in 1519 they rather rapidly began to drain the lake. The motives of the Conquistadors were military. By running off the water they first reduced the military mobility of the Aztecs, and then weakened their means of subsistence. In 1607–8 they drained most of the water from the existing five lakes. By the nineteenth century, and particularly by the beginning of the twentieth, Texcoco Lake was emptied, partly to reduce the constant flooding and partly as a prescription for the gradual expansion of the city.

I have been invited to Xochimilco by the park leadership and I therefore manage to avoid the groups of musicians in colourful, too tight trousers and jackets who constantly, with 'languishing glance and voice' offer to play one or another serenade for the visitor. I am thus able to study the canals and 'floating gardens' in peace. Xochimilco is literally a lake of fertility; it is not only an actual example of the many ways water and soil have been linked together to create the basis for various types of society, it is also an impressive testament to a way of life that predominated for centuries, and remains above all an object lesson – its aquatic fertility stands in dramatic contrast to the lack of water and the stony desert that is today's Mexico City.

The visitor cannot help be impressed by the riches of the water in Xochimilco, which stand in stark contrast to the way that Mexico City obtains its water supply by pumping up groundwater. The city now has over 10,000 pumping stations and they pump up about 50,000 litres a second. But the water demand radically exceeds what the local groundwater reservoirs can furnish. Large and costly projects have therefore been set in motion to pump water from rivers and springs at distances as great as 200 kilometres, and from locations that are more than 1,000 metres lower than the city. The Cutzamala Project, which was completed in the 1990s, transfers 14.9 cubic metres of water per second from the Cutzamala River in the Balsas Basin in the southwest of the country, to Greater Mexico City to add to the city's supply of drinking water. It consists of seven reservoirs and a 127-kilometre long aqueduct with 21 kilometres of tunnels. It satisfies 20 per cent of the city's water needs. The costs are mounting as the quantity of water in underground reservoirs diminishes. This is happening even though water consumption by parts of the population is extremely low. Millions are dependent upon buying water from private water sellers, who are so common as to be part of the normal street scene in many places. Columns of tanker lorries drive around in the suburbs; the drivers stop their vehicles, unfurl the hose and run water from the tankers to drums outside where people live; in this way people obtain their drinking water, as well as water in which to wash themselves and their clothing, cook and clean their houses.

'Watch your head!' I am creeping behind the construction boss down in the passageways beneath the crypt of the central cathedral in Mexico City. As I walk, bent forward and careful not to trip over wheelbarrows or shovels leaning against the walls, a tragic and somewhat surreal scene appears: 200 construction workers are fiendishly struggling, not to renovate the old cathedral but rather to prevent it from cracking. They have been working there for years to save this sacred sanctuary from the city's thirst – and from the sins of the past. It has been said about the city that whenever the population drinks, the city sinks. On average the water level under the city has been sinking about one metre per annum – in some places only 0.1 metres and in others as much as 1.5 metres. But as the groundwater sinks, so do parts of the city. Certain areas have sunk as much as 9 metres in the past century. Parts of the centre are sinking at a rate of one centimetre every fortnight. It is thus somewhat misleading when some people call Mexico City Latin America's Venice. Mexico City is – literally – a lopsided, unsustainable development. The ground is sinking so easily because it was once the bottom of a lake, a lake that no longer exists. The buildings sink unevenly, and the cathedral stands and rests on the remains of the most important temple the Aztecs built in the centre of Tenochtitlán. The construction workers are unable to prevent the cathedral from continuing to sink, but what they can do is provide a permanent foundation for all the various parts of the church, so that it sinks evenly.

Deep in Xcaret Ecological Park, not far from a row of beach hotels at Playa des Maya at Cancun on the Yucatán Peninsula, and four days' drive by car south-east from Mexico City, I encounter a group of local Mayan actors who are trying to recreate the history of Mayan civilisation as a tourist attraction. The whirling drums and the awe-inspiring masks are intended to stress the exotic. The smoke from the campfire envelops the scene in a mystical veil. Usually I cannot stand such 'almost authentic' dramatisations of the past because they aim to lift history out of its contemporary context, making it easily recognised but also banal. But here my scepticism is won over by the music, the atmosphere, the rough-and-readiness of the theatrical expression and the running shoes beneath the costumes, and by the charm of what are today's marginalised Mayan Indians acting out the history of their own heyday without any indication of loss, sadness or sentimentality. They present the *gestalt* of their past as irrevocable, and seem happy to have got out of it – indifferent to the fact that the history and downfall of Mayan civilisation is being taken up by increasing numbers of historians, archaeologists – and climate researchers.

The water history of the Mayans is a warning about what can happen in the future. The civilisation lasted approximately 1,200 years, but enjoyed its heyday between AD 250 and AD 900. At its greatest extent, it covered a vast land area from Guatemala in the south to Mexico in the north, with more than 40 cities, each having a population of up to 50,000. Altogether the empire numbered around 2 million people. They pursued astronomy and mathematics and developed the forerunner to our calendar. Some of their myths are well-known, like Popul Vuh's creation stories, composed in the Quiché language of the high altitude plains of Guatemala;[25] and we are able to learn, particularly from Friar Diego de Landa's book written in 1556, many of their customs.[26] (Diego de Landa was a functionary of the Spanish Inquisition and a burner of Mayan manuscripts.)

Paradoxically a journey concerned with the future of water must also include journeys into the past, such as my visits to these overgrown centres of Mayan civilisation. Increasing numbers of researchers believe that it was changes to the climate and the waterscape that finally knocked out the core areas of this Central American civilisation (in combination with a series of other social and cultural circumstances). Agriculture here was based on precipitation and the Mayans created a complex system of dams and canals so as to conserve rainwater during dry periods. For example, a reservoir at Tikal – the largest of the cities lying in ruins, and dating from the heyday of the Mayan civilisation – which is in today's Guatemala, contained enough drinking water to sustain a population of about 10,000 people for a period of 18 months. (*Ti-akal* is a Mayan place name that means 'by the reservoirs'.) It has gradually become evident that the Mayans did not conduct a classic slash-and-burn horticulture but rather a more intensive form of agriculture, making use of both terracing and various forms of irrigation.

The Mayan civilisation expanded during a period when there was much regular precipitation.[27] When the climate worsened and no rain fell for several years in a row (between approximately AD 800 and AD 900), it sparked a chain reaction which ultimately led to the centres on the southern side of the Yucatán Peninsula being abandoned to the jungle. When these societies no longer received the water they needed, the cities and the agricultural societies could no longer be sustained. The position of the rulers of Mayan society depended on their ability to make sure the people got sufficient quantities of water, and demonstrations of their special relationship to the water gods was a central foundation for their legitimacy. When the water disappeared, the basis for their power eroded as well. Changes in the local hydrological cycle therefore also had great significance for relations of authority and, thereby, for the society's ability to deal with external stresses.

Water is a fluid, but at the same time a constant, structural factor capable of contributing to our understanding of the rise and fall of Mayan civilisation, also showing that it is too simple to talk about the collapse of this civilisation. These processes can be studied on the Yucatán Peninsula, especially in Chichén Itzá, the famous old Mayan city covering an area of 10 square kilometres. It reached its pinnacle after many of the central cities in the classical period of Mayan civilisation had been abandoned, and was able to survive here due to the existence of a different waterscape than in the Mayan heartland.

As the sun, through a faint band of mist, sent down its first, almost golden rays of light to illuminate the top of the 24-metre-high Quetzalcoátl Pyramid in the centre of Chichén Itzá, I mount its 91 steps. There is no sound other than my own footsteps, the barking of a dog and the tapping of a woodpecker in one of the trees behind the ruins of the Observatory. I recall Popul Vuh's creation myth and feel elated. In this classic Mayan text, which describes an otherwise incomprehensible world, the most important creation event is described as the dawn – and what a dawn it is here on the Quetzalcoátl Pyramid!

According to the myth, the world and human beings were engulfed in darkness until the gods created the sun, the moon and the dawn. The Mayans developed an observatory, a calendar and astronomy (although they never discovered the wheel, and they practised self-sacrifice). All the pyramids are built such that their sides are aligned with the four heavenly directions; each side a staircase of 365 steps, including the platform at the top. Indeed, as I reach the top of the pyramid it becomes easier to comprehend that Chichén Itzá lies in a seasonal desert and how the place name emphasises the importance of water. It derives from *chi* (mouths), *chen* (wells), and Itzá is the name of the tribe that lived here. From the top I catch a glimpse of the most famous of the three wells that made the place inhabitable – famous because researchers believe it was also used for offering sacrifices, particularly of young boys. In 1904 an American by the name of Edward Herbert Thompson purchased the whole area and started archaeological excavations. He also drained away the water and discovered skeletons and other sacrificial objects that served to confirm the hypothesis.

From the top of 'El Castillo', as the pyramid is also called, I get barely a glimpse of what I have come such a long distance to see: the *cenotes* or natural wells. Such permanent sources of water are located here and there around Chichén Itzá and the Yucatán Peninsula, and were there when the Mayans emigrated north. *Dzonot*, as the Mayans called them, had water in them even during periods of drought. There were no surface rivers that they could utilise – they did not exist – but they had at their disposal 3,000 such natural sink wells. They were created when the porous limestone collapsed due to chemical reactions caused by rain squalls, CO_2 and historical fluctuations in the sea level. The *cenotes* are unique to this region and they have been for Yucatán what the Nile has been for Egypt, although of course in a different way and on a much more modest scale.

The Zaci sink hole is located on an island in a landscape of innumerable blue-green hues, under an open sky on one side and a large limestone curtain of stalactites on the other. From the bottom, the modern world is inaudible – silence except for the sound of the swimming strokes of a young boy and a hoarse-voiced heron. Outside, the surroundings are barren, brown and sere from the sun, and to descend into the *cenote* one must clamber down stone steps hidden by a bright green, exuberant jungle landscape.

I moved restlessly from one *cenote* to the other, not only because of their beauty, which it should be said – and this is a warning to those who would go there at the wrong time – depends upon the position of the sun, but also to

21. The sink holes are like naturally created cathedrals. Thousands of years ago these grottos must have been dry. The stalactites which hang from the ceiling require dry air in order to form and grow. Therefore we know they were created in the course of the last ice age because at that time the sea off the coast of Mexico was much lower than it is today. When the ice melted, the sea level rose and the grottos were gradually filled with water. Since fresh water is lighter than salt water, it was fresh water that filled them and created many of the *cenotes*.

understand more their significance and variation. They were the centre of the Mayans' economic and ritual life. They were regarded as the abdomen of the earth, and as the wet portals to the underworld of the rain gods. They were thus the location of sacrifices – especially to appease their rain-god Chac.

The most spectacular of the *cenotes* is Dzitnup or Keken, 52 kilometres south of Merida, near the town of Abalá. It is completely hidden underground. As I descend into it and have to find my balance on the increasingly wet and slippery stones, I notice the marked contrast between the dry air I am leaving behind and the humid damp air beneath the roof of the *cenote*. Large trees are hanging suspended in the air in front of me; in their search for water, their roots have broken through the ceiling of the *cenote*. I bend down to pass below some of the low-hanging stalactites and I get a glimpse of the underground well itself. It is a blue-green oasis of completely pure water in which the local population bathes, protected from the burning sun; enormous stalactites of all shapes hang from the ceiling and down into the water, whilst stalagmites grow upwards from the bottom, almost right up to the ceiling. Not least, there is the light: it comes playfully through a small hole in the roof of earth that arches over the *cenote*. It is not difficult to understand that these places became the sites of religious cults: in architectural terms they remind one of cathedrals.

What makes the *cenotes* particularly fascinating is not the stalactites, impressive though they are, for such phenomena are found in many places, but rather the natural and social paradoxes contained within these sunken wells. Stalactites are not known to grow in damp, wet conditions, so why are they here? And where does the freshwater come from which has contributed to keeping Yucatán's civilisation alive? The *cenotes* are, in fact, the most visible part of an enormous underground river system.

It is midday, siesta time and the heat shimmers over the forest road. Bill, an American who turned his back on his homeland following the Vietnam War, is going to show me a subterranean river that he himself has investigated and illuminated. Behind us the air is filled with a massive white wave, created by enormous swarms of butterflies that our car has disturbed. Bill stops the vehicle in the middle of the forest and we walk along a trail that runs down into a cave entrance in the ground; the entrance is encircled by dry bushes. We descend by ladder several metres below the ground, when a fantastic natural phenomenon appears: the entrance to a huge river system that stretches mile upon mile under the Yucatán Peninsula, the longest known subterranean river in the world.

It is these underground rivers that provide water to the *cenotes* and that made it possible for Mayan agriculture to survive on the Yucatán Peninsula. They provided durable security against climatic variation and the uncertainty in precipitation. In an even longer climatic historical perspective it is interesting to note that the rivers run through what were once dry grottos (stalactites require dry air before they are able to form), and thus water covers still earlier cultures. When the ice melted, the sea level rose, and since fresh water is lighter than salt water, fresh-water rivers were formed. It has thus been changes in the water cycle that have provided the foundation for both the development of Mayan civilisation and its partial downfall. Even while under the earth in the pitch black, and with the sound of water licking against the walls of the grotto, I was able to see – for once rather clearly – how changes in the waterscape became catalysts for deep historical processes of change that turned some communities into winners and others into losers.

Later, I am seated watching the late afternoon waves rolling across the Gulf of Mexico whilst a gecko crawls across the ceiling of the outdoor balcony in an apparent defiance of the law of gravity. I try to imagine how the Mayans must have reacted in the ninth century when the rains they relied upon did not fall for several years. Could they have saved their centres if they had been better prepared? What were the consequences of these catastrophes for their view of the world and their ideas of development? And to what extent is today's more complex society in a better position to tackle radical changes in the waterscape? And as I sat there with my thoughts, I could hear in the background, providing an emotional backdrop, the sound of the whirling drums at Xcaret, those historically imitative but sharp rhythms from a world that has disappeared.

Once again I am struck by the idea that it is possible for a historian to write about water's future because water can be perceived as a kind of talisman for the continuity and deep structures of history and human evolution. Trying to understand the role of water in society, the relevance of yesterday therefore continues, more than is usual in other areas of society, into tomorrow. The sunken wells and subterranean rivers of Yucatán, surrounded by the fading radiance of the Mayan ruins, provide us with a reminder that when it comes to controlling water's fundamental capriciousness, human beings have made surprisingly little progress, and the Mayans, from such a long-term water perspective, are our contemporaries.

PART 2
THE AGE OF THE WATER LORDS

22. Following a lengthy drought, this well in Gujarat, India, provides highly uncertain life insurance for many people.

INTRODUCTION TO PART 2

What makes wars start? Fights over water, changes in patterns of rainfall, fights over food production. This is an issue that threatens the peace and security of the whole planet.

Margaret Beckett, Minister of Foreign Affairs, Great Britain

Under Heaven there is nothing more pliant and weak than water,
But for attacking the firm and the strong, nothing surpasses it,
nothing can replace it.

Dao De Jing verse[28]

On 28 February 2006, Britain's Defence Secretary John Reid made a remarkable speech at Chatham House. He delivered a stark assessment of the potential impact of climate change and signalled that Britain's armed forces would have to be prepared to tackle conflicts over dwindling resources, and that military planners had already started considering the potential impact of global warming for Britain's armed forces over the next 20 to 30 years. The Labour Defence Secretary warned of increasing uncertainty about the future of the countries least well-equipped to deal with flooding, water shortages and valuable agricultural land turning to desert, and that Britain must be prepared for humanitarian disaster relief, peacekeeping and warfare to deal with the dramatic social and political consequences of climate change. He said: 'Impacts such as flooding, melting permafrost and desertification could lead to loss of agricultural land, poisoning of water supplies and destruction of economic infrastructure'. He also made the erroneous, but at the time widely shared standpoint that 'the blunt truth is that the lack of water and agricultural land is a significant contributory factor to the tragic conflict we see unfolding in Darfur. We should see this as a warning sign'.

The year after, early in 2007, Britain used its presidency of the UN Security Council to lead its first debate on climate change and conflict. 'What makes wars start?' asked the Foreign Secretary, Margaret Beckett. 'Fights over water. Changing patterns of rainfall. Fights over food production, land use. There are few greater potential threats . . . to peace and security itself.'

A secret report prepared for the Pentagon in 2004 had stated that climate change in the coming 20 years could create natural disasters claiming the lives of tens of millions of people; there could be wars over food, energy, and not least, water; and the situation could lead to huge waves of migration, and to wars for the very survival of countries.[29] Typically for a growing mood among politicians, the Minister of Water for India, Dasmunshi, laconically declared, 'I am not the Minister of Water Resources but rather the Minister of Water Conflicts.'

It is well-known that water has been a source of power and conflict ever since the first society came into being. The novelty in such conflicts will therefore be the magnitude of the danger they pose. Uncertainty about whether we are living in the century of drought, the century of rising sea levels, or the century of great floods will ensure that the question of who has power over water resources is one of growing strategic importance in both an economic and a political sense.

The struggle over water will, indeed, come to threaten peace and security. But to maintain that the water crisis will lead to war reflects a simple mechanical view of relations between society and water, and undervalues human ingenuity, adaptability and willingness to make compromises. But at the same time, analyses of society that refuse to accept that there *could* be wars or conflicts in which fresh water is one of the many important factors, or that there is *no* conflict-engendering dynamic that links scarcity of resources with migration, are also simplistic.In the press and media one continually finds commentators maintaining that water will overtake oil as the most significant source of conflict. But the comparison is inadequate, because the struggle for power over water will, in a completely different way, be a question of life and death. And it will be eternal and concern absolutely everyone. Its results will turn out to be completely different as well, and they will be more subtle because the rights of ownership to a common resource like water, and a resource that is in constant flux, are much more obscure.

Water is extremely unevenly disbursed in different regions within a single country and this subjects the country's national unity – where it is often already weak – to additional pressures. And there are few things that can express more nakedly the enormous social disparities in the world than water, since both poor and rich require equal amounts in order to live. The planet's 900 million slum-dwellers have at their disposition between five and ten litres of water daily, and as a rule this costs more than the piped-in water of the well-off inhabitants of the same cities.[30] Such inequality will lead to social and economic conflict in the world's large cities. There will thus be struggle between individuals, between companies, between town and countryside and between states and regions. It will also be a struggle over vital religious symbols and cultural traditions, since rivers and lakes often have religious meaning as well. Half of our species live in watersheds shared by two or more countries, and since it has proven difficult to establish a binding international statutory framework, power over water resources could indeed have global and continental significance.

When, a couple of centuries ago, the German philosopher Immanuel Kant, in an essay entitled 'Eternal Peace', wrote that the world was condemned to eternal peace, either due to human foresight or through a series of catastrophes that give them no other choice, he overlooked a fundamental and well-known aspect of the human condition: our eternal but ever-changing need for water, and the indifference of water to political boundaries and differing consumptive needs. The highly uneven distribution of fresh water, changing in form and quantity as it crosses national, cultural and social boundaries, creates constant and ongoing frictions. None of the existing theories on the relationship between the state and the market, or the positioning of the state in the international arena, or the relationship between resource-utilisation and power – none of these manages to encompass the complex global, regional and local game played about water.

23. In the coming decades, obtaining enough water for the needs of all inhabitants will become an ever more demanding task in the world's large cities. In 1800 only 3 per cent of the world population lived in cities. Now, for the first time in history, the majority of the population is composed of urban dwellers. In 1950 there was only one city in the world with a population of more than 10 million; now there are 25. There are few places where the contrast between the rich and the slums is sharper than in Johannesburg, between modern Sandton and the suburb of Alexandra, as indicated by this picture.

CHAPTER 6
SOUTH AFRICA'S BRIEF 'WATER WAR'

'To travel is an illusory flight from the unbearable boredom of middle-class life', wrote J. G. Ballard. He had a point if by travelling he meant a search, simply for the sake of stimulation, to find the outlandish, the different or the degraded. It has become unnecessary to search for the exotic and the strange in 'far-away places' when, to an ever greater degree, in step with globalisation and patterns of human migration one can find them in the back alleys of one's own locale. But even allowing for this, Ballard is wrong, because middle class people themselves do not consider their life boring, and because travel to an ever greater degree – in league with increased knowledge about the world – can be an ever more specific and goal-oriented journey aimed at intellectual enrichment.

Sun City is located a little north of Johannesburg and Pretoria in South Africa, in the middle of a dry bush landscape, and is known as Africa's answer to Las Vegas. It is an artificial, kitsch metropolis with casinos, luxury restaurants and trendy music scenes. I have come here to see a concrete, much discussed and very eloquent example of the total conquest of nature, made more forceful through its contrast with all those women on this continent who devote a great proportion of their lives to fetching water from places that are a great distance from where they are living.

Sun City's architects have overcome the natural limits of the place with the help of water, and in so doing have made it clear that the question of the lack of water and of conflict over water is much more complex than is frequently described. They pump water up out of the ground and have created a new oasis. Cascade Hotel is located right beside an artificial waterfall in this oasis. The water that feeds this fall runs through a 250,000 square metre artificial jungle, past 3,500 trees of various types brought in from different countries in the world, and with a flock of tropical birds that sing here as beautifully and exotically as they might in a natural jungle. Here one finds emerald-green golf courses and groomed pathways between a linked system of artificial lakes, rivers, waterfalls and rapids, and a tropical beach where almost two-metre-high artificial surfing waves recreate the sound of the sea and where people surf as though they were on the ocean.

Even the local national park has been created with artificial water. Pilanesberg National Game Park is organised around artificial lakes and waterholes, and almost 6,000 animals – elephants, giraffes, lions, rhinos and buffalo – were transported here in what was called Operation Genesis, to date the largest animal transport in history. I spent the night in a nearby lodge, and then as the sun came up over what looked like a completely normal African savannah landscape, I stood in the back of a pickup lorry with other tourists and believed I was 'on safari'.

Sun City is interesting as a backdrop to the water situation in South Africa, as well as to the situation in the world's other large cities. This kitsch metropolis demonstrates the possibilities offered by money and technology: when they are made to work together it is possible to overcome the scarcity of water. One reason why the water question increases in seriousness until it becomes political dynamite is precisely due to the fact that it is indeed possible to solve the water crisis if one invests enough money and use available modern technology – even where the natural waterscape is blessed with surprisingly few positive attributes.

Johannesburg is barely a two-hour drive from Sun City. It is the financial hub of South Africa, where the skyscrapers stretch heavenward as if in defiance of the images of misery that dominate the view of Africa presented by the Western media. I walk down to Sandton City, boasting of 144,000 square metres of retail space and allegedly the largest shopping mall in the southern hemisphere. Johannesburg is one of those cities that undermine the theories that society must develop gradually over time and in keeping with its traditions. A little more than a hundred years ago there was nothing here. But then George Harrison, a name that should be easy for most people to remember, discovered gold here, and since then no city has grown more quickly. There is now a population of 8 million in Greater Johannesburg.

Chance events have thrust Johannesburg into the centre of the global water discourse and they have done so in three specific ways. First, Johannesburg is the financial centre of the first country in the world to declare the right of access to water to be a human right. It did so in 1996. Developments in Johannesburg will therefore be keenly observed, and what happens there will have significance for the global discussion on rights-based development and the pricing of water. Second, it was here that the world's top leaders gathered in 2002 and agreed to place water at the top of the political – economic agenda.

The city will therefore be associated with the struggle for millennium goals in the water sector.[31] Third, Johannesburg is the first capital city that survives on imported drinking-water obtained from a neighbouring country. It thereby foreshadows a future where drinking-water can become an item of trade, on a large scale, between nations. For the region is dry and is poor in terms of water resources, and almost all scenarios regarding the world's future climate predict that precipitation will sink dramatically and thus the water crisis will worsen.

The combination of these factors has made Johannesburg a global symbol in the struggle against what activists call 'the privatisation of water', a struggle that has flared up in cities around the world, from Cochabamba in Bolivia to Dar es Salaam in Tanzania, from Accra in Ghana to Dhaka in Bangladesh.[32] Whilst indoors the leaders of the world deliberated on the wording of a global declaration on the importance of water for development, outside, thousands from Johannesburg's shanty towns were marching and shouting, 'Water for the thirsty!' The demonstrators invited journalists and photographers to visit Alexandra, for there standing among the shacks clad in corrugated iron sheets, they could see the skyscrapers and fashionable establishments only a few thousand metres away. Geographical proximity coupled with extreme social differences lent the demonstration extra potency: their message to the world could easily be filmed, and therefore, in our modern times, it existed.

The demand was for free water. The demonstrators said that whatever constitutes a right according to the Constitution must be provided free. They demanded that the authorities not hand over the distribution of water to large private French corporations, which had been the plan. They also wanted the elimination of the water metres that measured consumption. The demonstrations got results. The authorities put their collaboration with the large international corporations on ice, and announced that all householders should get some free water. But, the government warned, if people used more than the quota, they would have to pay and they would have to pay in advance. The authorities said their goal was to get people to waste less water because the city does not have enough for its needs. In summing up their initiative, the authorities called it a success and a prototype that should be copied, because consumption is reduced whilst at the same time they argue that most households finally have access to clean water.

A dilemma is in the making: the threat of climate change and the increasing gap between water availability and increasing demand will force an investment of trillions in the coming decades – and someone has to pay. But who will this be if access to water is a basic human right? The state? But many states do not have sufficient resources to do this. The international community? Most likely people in the rich countries, who themselves often pay for consumption of water,

24. The Government of South Africa has decreed that the right to water is a basic human right and has provided millions of people with running water since taking power after Apartheid. Nonetheless, demonstrations still occur in the large cities across the country. People are refusing to pay for what they consider a basic human right. Here we see members of the ANC in Cape Town demonstrating against, among other things, the water policy of the authorities.

will not be willing to establish a system whereby people in poor countries get water for free. The idea of water as a human right has certainly mobilized political action for improved water services, but it is very difficult to reconcile the right to water as a basic human right with a practically-orientated graduated tariff system. In contradiction to what its advocates believe, the slogan of human rights to water might in some cases prevent both necessary reforms of the water sector in favour of the poor and the development of the water system itself.[33]

In Johannesburg, as in many other large cities, the struggle over water is part and parcel of a wider struggle against international big capital. Some of the world's largest corporations are involved in the supply of water. Some of them have international holdings and try to control the supply of water to large cities around the world. Their marketing stresses that they can provide better and cheaper water to more people than can the bureaucratic public institutions found in poor countries. Generally speaking, though, they have been met with opposition, and at the same time they are often among the major targets of the opponents of globalisation. Bolstered by ideas about the unique nature of water – for unlike other goods bought and sold, it is an absolute necessity for life; and because it is always in motion how can it really be owned by anyone – water will by its very nature always be subject to the objection that it cannot be treated as just another commodity. Adam Smith's theories about water, as expressed in his book, *The Wealth of Nations*, published in the eighteenth century, have risen once again, given new life and relevance by present-day experience. Smith wrote that water is a good that due to its unique qualities cannot fall within the framework of the basic laws of economics that determine the price that consumers are willing to pay to get their hands on goods. People around the office of the activists in Soweto have not been reading Smith, but they certainly do not want to pay a single penny for water because they do not regard it to be a commodity.

25. The boy in the picture is playing and singing a song about the price of water in Lesotho, which is the water tower for the country of South Africa. Lesotho is the only country in the world where the whole land mass is more than 1,100 metres above sea level, and so it is relatively easy to send water down to the South African plains below.

But the Johannesburg region has one great advantage: only a few hundred kilometres away from this economic centre of the country, and from Soweto and Alexandra, there is a small, poor, mountain country completely surrounded by South Africa. From this location the Johannesburg region is able to obtain its water, and it does so. The country, Lesotho, is poor in most things, except for this 'blue gold'.

I have never had the feeling of crossing the border between two worlds, in the same way and over such a short distance, as the day I crossed the border between South Africa and Lesotho, between two countries that lie, according to the obscurantist rhetoric of the development aid community, in the 'south'. On the one side, South Africa: modern, high-tech, spectacular buildings, well-manicured gardens, a cosy inn that served whisky and cornflakes; on the other side of the Caledon River, Lesotho: poverty, African mud huts, colourful riders on Basuto ponies, donkeys everywhere carrying much too heavy loads, and herdsmen – boys from six to about fifteen, with a cloth, of what traditionalists consider typical of Basuto culture, slung over their shoulders. (In fact, this garment did not come into being until manufactured cotton goods exported from Manchester and Liverpool reached the country a little more than a century ago.) The UN describes 40 per cent of the population as being 'extremely poor', and few countries in the world have a higher rate of AIDS. The Basutos moved here a few centuries ago, fleeing from the Voortrekkers, descendants of the Dutch settlers who migrated from the Cape and across the South African plains. They remained in the Maluti Mountains, a place that is now referred to as 'the Kingdom in the Sky'.

The car labours slowly up the steep hairpin bends, through the lofty mountain pass over 3,000 metres high while thin clouds flow down around us across the green-clad mountainsides. From here it is easy to understand why the country has always been closely linked to South Africa, and that South Africa will always have serious strategic interests here. Lesotho can best be understood as South Africa's water reservoir and water tower, for it is only here that South Africa has the possibility of obtaining a secure and adequate supply of water close to its financial centre. The national situation is so precarious that South Africa's leaders hold discussions about the possibility of bringing water all the way down from the Congo and Angola in the north.

At least half of South Africa's water comes from the rivers of Lesotho. The first governments of South Africa, and in particular those formed after the Nationalist Party came to power in the late 1940s, felt that Lesotho should be annexed. South Africa accused the British rulers in Lesotho (the country was never a colony but rather a protectorate) of limiting South Africa's use of the rivers and, thereby, the whole process of industrial development of the country, because they were not doing enough to prevent rivers that ran down from the mountains of Lesotho from carrying so much silt that they damaged South Africa's water system. London wanted to strengthen Lesotho's independence in the face of South Africa so that it could initiate the production of hydro-electric power for export to South Africa, but this was not successful. In fact, quite the opposite. After 1968 it was South Africa which sent electricity to Lesotho. Additionally, the water projects of Lesotho ended up being pure export projects – not of water power but only of water – untreated and unused water going to the province of Gauteng and the city of Johannesburg.

The only significant sign of modernity I saw in the verdant but bare, treeless alpine landscape – with its clusters of round mud huts dotted here and there with wafts of heavy smoke rising above them – were the roads and the dam sites built by South Africa to facilitate the large-scale export of water. As long as Lesotho remains a poor country without any realistic water plans of its own – and equally important, without economic strength needed to make use of the water within its own borders – and as long as it is content to live from the export of its labour and its water to the neighbouring country, it is an ideal neighbour for South Africa, the regional big power. These two countries signed a treaty in the 1980s according to which Lesotho has a responsibility to send a large proportion of its water to Johannesburg, 300 kilometres to the south, as part of what is called the Lesotho Highlands Project.

Only a short time after the first drops of water from the Katse Dam reached the parched and thirsty plains of South Africa, and after Nelson Mandela had attended the inauguration of the dam in January 1998, and said that the project expressed 'a new spirit of cooperation in Africa', serious political intransigence broke out in Lesotho. The Lesotho opposition condemned the water treaty with South Africa as a cheap sell-out of the country's resources. South Africa struck back. In September 1998 they sent their military forces into Maseru, the capital of Lesotho and to the Katse Dam, where they killed sixteen of the guards. The message was clear: nobody should believe that South Africa would allow anyone to threaten the water on which it was dependent. The Lesotho opposition called it 'an invasion' and demanded an apology, but South Africa's leadership described it as 'an intervention' in defence of a decision made by a legally constituted government in keeping with the charter of SADEC, The Southern Africa Development Committee. The military operation was over in a flash. It was greeted by the wider world almost without comment and quickly forgotten, but inside Lesotho it is one of the epoch-making events of the country's short history.

26. Watchmen on the dam where I am walking in this photo were bombed and killed by South African armed forces in 1998. South Africa and Nelson Mandela wanted to send a signal to the people of Lesotho that would be impossible to misconstrue: the country would never give up its rights to the water from Lesotho's highlands – the lifeline for the Johannesburg region.

'My brother was killed here', said my local contact, almost in passing, as she showed me around the Katse dam site.

The giant dam is 185 metres high and constructed in a convex half-circle toward the holding dam, so as to withstand maximum pressure. What I see, standing on the edge of a mountainside that drops down into this artificial lake, as the light begins to turn blue, colouring both the sky and the surface of the man-made, controlled body of water, is what might become the future solution to the gap between nature's unfair division of water and society's need for it. Water will most likely become an item of international trade, not only in plastic bottles but also in pipelines crossing borders between water-rich and water-poor countries and regions. The historical paradox is that it is here, in a beautiful, empty alpine meadow 3,000 metres above sea level in an unknown little country in Africa, that this future is being initiated. Lesotho's water export challenges most theories of trade relations – it is a very poor country that survives by sending a completely renewable resource to a rich neighbouring country, and the only country in the world that lives by exporting water to an urban region in another country.

As water becomes an item of international trade, then the power relations in the world will change. The water-rich countries will in general gain in strategic importance. If those who are in control of the water find themselves upstream they will occupy a completely new type of geopolitical power. But if the water barons live downstream, then the politically weak 'water-tower and water-reservoir' countries will encounter obstructions to their further development. Instead of enjoying economic and social improvements, they will run the risk of ending up as hostages to their own water wealth.

27. This is the river that runs through Alicante, one of the tourist El Dorados on Spain's Costa Blanca. It is quite understandable that northern Europeans who have purchased apartments in the area are worried about the future of the climate and the water situation.

CHAPTER 7
A WATER FESTIVAL IN SPAIN

'Each year is drier, drier, drier. If nobody helps us, we will become a desert. A full desert. And you know, politicians are talking day after day and year after year, and nobody finds a solution.' The slight stammer to the English strengthens the impression of desperation.

Miguel, the managing director of the hotel in which I am staying on the coast of southern Spain, expresses the frustration felt by people in this part of the country. It gradually grows, as the long-term water situation is going from bad to worse. Spain can be divided in many ways, but one important division falls between water-poor and water-rich regions, and my journey to the south, east and northwest of the country will demonstrate that.

When the Moors conquered Spain and Portugal over a thousand years ago, the area was called Iberia, 'the land of rivers'. In relation to the dry Middle East and North Africa, both Portugal and Spain were an El Dorado of running water. Spain has 1,800 rivers, but most of them are small and short and many run dry in summer. As a result, Spain's whole process of modernisation for the last 150 years is closely linked to the extensive manipulation, utilisation and control of these water resources, and no country has more large reservoirs and dams, in relation to its total area, than has Spain. The Spaniards have built more than a thousand large reservoirs to even out the rivers' seasonal and annual natural variations and regional and local imbalances in access to fresh water.[34]

Broadly speaking, one can say that the Conservative party and powerful interest groups in the regions in the south have pushed in favour of continuing this hydro-strategy into the future, and argued that the need for this type of water control is stronger than ever due to uncertainty about the climatic future. The Social Democrats and the regions in the north, on the other hand, want to have a new water policy based more on saving, recycling and restructuring the economy in line with the possibilities and limitations of the existing water landscape. Spain is an example of a country where the future distribution and use of water,

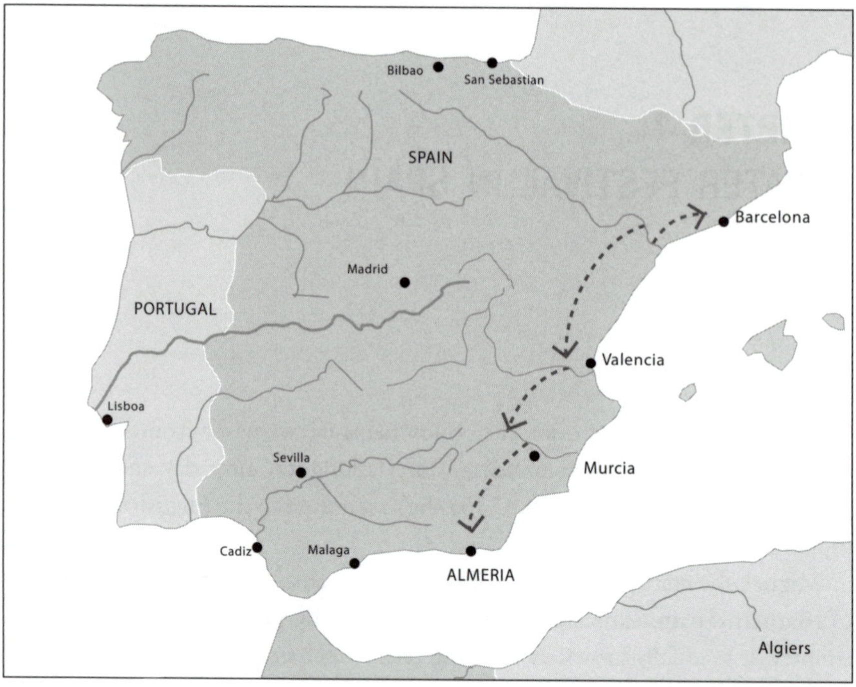

Map 2. A sketch of the plan that would take water from the country's largest river, the Ebro in the north, to parched southern Spain.

in a land where water is dramatically unevenly distributed by nature, is sure to become ever more central to internal national politics, driven by a growing need for water in the face of mounting uncertainties about the climate of the future. Recurrent droughts will cause people again and again to talk about a real and actual national water crisis, while the problem is long-term changes in water management practices and potential long-term changes in rainfall patterns.

For the sun-starved northern Europeans the southern parts of Spain have become a Mecca for modern mass tourism, precisely because it is a region of little rain. The sun-rich land of southern Spain, in the 1970s one of the poorest regions in the country and in Europe, experienced a very rapid growth the coming decades. But the intense building of hotels, golf courses and swimming pools, demands more water than is available in the region. Simultaneously there has been an extremely rapid growth of irrigated agriculture in the area, despite the fact that legislation has been passed to forbid the expansion of irrigated agricultural lands. But since the export of vegetables, especially tomatoes, to the rest of Europe had been most profitable, the expansion continued. The resort-building boom happened at the same time as many of its farmers switched to more thirsty crops. The combination put new pressures on the dwindling supply of water. Farmers stared to fight developers over water rights, and in a sign of their mounting desperation, they started to buy and sell water like gold on a rapidly growing black market, mostly from illegal wells. It has been estimated that there are between half a million and more than one-and-a-half-million illegal boreholes, sunk to bring up groundwater.[35]

The road I drive between the mountains and the coast is enclosed on either side by a dry dusty landscape; in many places there are signs of what has been called a 'creeping desert'; parts of what is Europe's garden are already desert-like. In Almeria, called 'a sea of plastic', there are rows and rows of hot houses, and black piping winds along like a snake, mile after mile, almost endlessly, it seems, radiating out among the plants. At the same time Almeria's authorities, according to the local press, have awarded building permits for 100,000 holiday homes and a large number of new golf courses. There is only one problem with this picture of bounty: the province is running out of water. Outside Alicante I try to find the river which – according to the maps – should bring water into the city, down from the mountains on the outskirts, between the houses and on out to the sea. Where it enters the city it is a river without a single drop of water. And at Vinalopó, still another of the rivers that are supposed to bring water to Spain's agriculture and growing tourist industry in the decades to come, children are playing in the river bed – they are kicking around a football, and I can run a race with one of them cycling there, because it is dry, absolutely dry. All the water is used, and controlled. The struggle over water scarcity has become so intense that the newspapers were reporting that the Junta de Andalucia, the Government of Andalucia, was using a completely new satellite system to monitor the restrictions on water use along the Costa del Sol, while other regional governments (for example in Castilla La Mancha) have used helicopters to spy on neighbouring regions to find out for themselves how much water their neighbours possess.

'There are fewer who want to buy apartments in Spain. Swimming pools are being built without water'. Such headlines in the press are becoming increasingly common after the waves of British, Scandinavians and other northern Europeans who for decades have fallen hungrily upon the Costa del Sol and purchased apartments there, become less. I travel around a tourist region where many of the swimming pools are without water and in some places the public fountains have been turned off. The newspapers were warning that millions of Spaniards will have to switch to buying bottled water in the future, due to shortages in the local supply of drinking water. Periodic drought and permanent over-consumption had led to a situation where the water reservoirs in some years were down to a mere ten per cent of their normal capacity. At the same time climate researchers are predicting that the temperature in the south of Spain will increase by 2.5°C before 2020 and by 5°C by 2050, and that, simultaneously, precipitation will fall off by 25 per cent. According to these predictions, the area will become even richer in sunshine and increasingly thirsty for water. There is a growing realization that there will not be enough water for everyone,

But despite an actual structural water crisis that reaches acute proportions in years of less rainfall than normal, the farmers continue to expand the extent of their irrigated fields, and the property developers have continued to build new houses and more hotels with swimming pools. In Murcia alone the authorities have made plans to double their tourist potential over a ten-year period, with a million hotel beds and 100,000 new apartments.[36] At the same time alarmist research published by the United Nations predicts that the North African desert will 'hop over' to Spain and a third of the country will become desert by the year 2050.

In the south the politicians and the local population argue that they simply must have access to more water, and since Spain, seen as a whole, has plenty of water resources, the northern regions should share with their southern countrymen. They are demanding that the government in Madrid distribute the country's water more justly than nature has done. In the 1990s, plans were circulated to pipe in water from the Alps of Austria and along the Rhone in France, to Barcelona. But the most comprehensive plan was to take water from the country's largest river – the Ebro – and run it south with canals and tunnels. The Spanish National Hydrological Plan was composed of two major components: the transfer of 1,030 cubic hectometres of water from the Ebro waterway to the water systems of Catalonia, Júcar, Segura and others in the south; and, second, a whole package of 889 other water management projects.

'Our Ebro must not be used to water golf courses and tourist complexes!' shouted the crowd in one of the largest demonstrations in Spain's recent history. At Zaragoza, which lies on the banks of the Ebro, official reports stated that 400,000 people marched and shouted slogans against the government's hydrological plans. They argued that it would herald a costly ecological catastrophe. As an alternative, the demonstrators wanted a new water policy; a blue revolution. They wanted to promote an entirely new blue philosophy, a water philosophy. 'Just like love', said some of the activists in favour of such a blue revolution, describing their relationship to water, 'it cannot be bought or sold'.

Despite the protests, Prime Minister José Maria Aznar turned the first sod in 2004 and set the Ebro diversion project in motion.

28. Demonstrators in Barcelona hold aloft a large water pipe in which they have tied a knot, as a sign of their opposition to the plan to bring water from the Ebro River to southern Spain. Altogether about a million people demonstrated against the plan.

'The canals from the Ebro will help everyone and harm no one', he said.

But the opponents of the project have a different opinion. When the Social Democrats formed the new government later that same year, they acted as they had promised. The first thing the new government did was to reject the whole plan. Instead, it backed a policy based on water conservation and large-scale desalination. This government maintained that 15 desalination plants would provide just as much water as the Ebro plan, but more quickly and more cheaply. It is more logical than sending water 3,900 kilometres through pipes and canals, they argued. The spokesman for Aznar's party, the conservative Partido Popular, maintained that from their point of view the new government had destroyed the dreams of the whole of southern Spain. Environmental activists in the south are also sceptical. They are afraid that many desalination plants will turn the Mediterranean into a dead sea. And while the Ebro continues to empty just as much water into the sea in one day as Alicante sees in the course of one month, members of the government from the south protested the cancelling of the plan by melodramatically emptying Ebro water from a plastic bottle into the bone-dry Vinalapó.

José, my companion and water expert familiar with the local situation, is in no doubt as we discuss the plan while walking beside the old irrigation channels around Zaragoza: 'The Ebro plan will never be carried out. People who still dream of this plan must literally have their heads buried in the sand.' This has to do not only with water but also with what kind of society the nation wants to be, he argues: 'Do we really want a Mediterranean coastline of cement and golf courses running from France all the way to Gibraltar?'

Yes, I think to myself, many seem to want precisely that. And the corruption scandals linked to the construction activity that many find so profitable also indicate that this is the case. As long as tourism and agriculture in the south develop, the demand for water will grow and the regional imbalance in water supply will remain an issue of conflict. Moreover, the water-poor provinces will, instead of enforcing radical local readjustments to the water they have, demand a strong central power that might help to convince the water-rich provinces to give up some of their water. As a counter move the water-rich provinces might demand greater autonomy from Madrid, among other reasons so as to gain more control of what they consider to be their own water resources, and which potential climate changes might reduce in the future.

Spain's present and future disputes and negotiations over water is steeped in a long and varied history of water management and water control. I travelled to Valencia, on the east coast of Spain, a city that tourists generally drive through on their way between Barcelona and the south coast, to Malaga and Marbella, in order to experience this past. Perhaps the 'hippies' stopped here on their way out to Ibiza in the 1970s, since it was known as 'the city of a hundred clock towers'. And for anyone on a water journey, Valencia is a 'must' because the city has Europe's oldest functioning court of justice; a water tribunal. The long history of this court is a telling empirical fact showing that conflicts over water are an integral part of Spain's history.

It is located in the middle of the old quarter of the city, and on the way there – if you get up early before the cars have had a chance to invade the early morning atmosphere – you can wander slowly around the narrow streets where the windows are closed off with shutters. One woman is obviously bawling out her husband; youngsters are fighting; someone is playing Mahler's *Das Lied von der Erde* loudly on the record player, or is it the radio? In a neighbouring house someone is practising on a violin. The crush of buildings opens out onto a square, and suddenly I am on Plaza de la Constitución – and there, the water tribunal.

Every Thursday, for more than a thousand years, outside La Seo, the cathedral, right before the clock in the church tower strikes 12 noon, there has been a meeting of representatives of the eight irrigation channels that encircle the city

29. Europe's oldest functioning court of justice. For more than 1,000 years there has been a meeting outside the cathedral every Thursday, when a tribunal is formed by representatives of the eight irrigation channels that have made Valencia one of Europe's most fertile regions.

and have made *La Huerta* (irrigated area) of Valencia one of Europe's most fertile regions. They meet to sort out disagreements arising from the use of water on this highly localised scale. The tribunal was first organised under the Moorish caliphate of Cordoba in the late 960s. When the Christians, under the leadership of James I of Aragon, re-conquered Valencia in 1238, the mosque was destroyed. A cathedral was built on the same site. Since this was not for Muslims, the peasants who had formerly met in the mosque, now met outside; that is, at the cathedral's 'Door of the Apostles'.

The proceedings are oral; the judges are chosen by the farmers themselves and decisions are always reached quickly so as not to cause destruction to the growing crops. The importance of the court has been reduced by the presence of an up stream dam, and the Turia River, beside which the city was first built, now 'runs' completely drily through the city, without water and thoroughly controlled. There are also fewer cases because, over the course of a thousand years, the court has evolved a strong position, and its judgements have been so clear that people choose to follow the law. The day I am there, a woman is requesting redress for her complaints against an entrepreneur who has reduced the quantity and quality of water she uses.

The black iron gate opens and the judges walk with dignity through the provisional hedge that marks the court's boundaries; they take their seats, on eight chairs arranged in a half-circle. They possess the deliberate movements provided by ritual; they stand for a kind of judicial embodiment of the unusual permanence of the water problematic in a society organised around the very management and distribution of water. The herald calls out, in the Valencian dialect of the Catalonian language, asking if anyone has any complaints to bring forward. He raises his staff, which is decorated with a symbolic rice plant. For more than a thousand years, in this way the herald has raised his staff into the air and asked the same question. The most frequent complaint has always been about people watering with 'forbidden water', that is, water to which others, often located further down the canal, hold the rights. Other common complaints are wasting water, or in other words, the farmer not using water at the correct point in time or else watering a tract of land that does not really need it.

The water system in *La Huerta* was an important economic condition for the independent Kingdom of Valencia. It was first developed under the Romans and had a second flowering following the Moorish invasion of 714. The small agricultural holdings, or *minifundios*, are criss crossed and encircled with narrow water channels. They create a system that for hundreds of years has made it possible to produce three or four successive crops in the course of one year. As a result of this water system, Valencia could serve as a sort of bridge or springboard for goods from the Middle East coming into Europe. Rice, which most associate with Asia, has for centuries been a 'national dish' of Valencia (*paella*, which stands for Spain in the eyes of many foreigners, is composed of saffron-flavoured rice, cooked with meat, seafood and vegetables). The rice plants were brought in from Asia by way of the Middle East. Citrus fruits have also been cultivated in the Valencia region for several centuries. The Arabs brought orange trees with them from India, first of all as an ornamental species. They believed the orange to be inedible, according to the great Arabian historian Ibn Khaldun, back in the fourteenth century. And this thinking held sway for a long time in Spain as well, but still it was from this region that the fruit arrived in Europe. And, when, at the end of the nineteenth century, the British colonial rulers and the American water experts wanted to introduce large-scale irrigation to India, Egypt and the USA, they went to La Huerta around Valencia in order to learn.

In a period when politicians, state leaders and the United Nations Secretary-General are talking about the potential of water wars and water conflicts, La Huerta and the local water court have important stories to tell. The one thousand year history of the water tribunal demonstrates how the question of apportioning the water is a question that is 'eternally' with us and cannot be solved once and for evermore. The water tribunal itself will go down in history as a proud tradition, but one that is an increasingly anachronistic institution and is now more or less only a rather exotic tourist attraction.

'It all started a good ten years ago after a long dry period – the faithful had prayed for rain, and it rained. The festival has been held ever since.'

I find myself in an overcrowded apartment in Vilagarcía de Arousa on the northwest coast of Spain to attend the annual water festival held there every year. I have travelled here to see a part of the country where the water landscape is very different indeed. The festival begins on the sixteenth day of August, the hottest month. The level of noise is almost more than I can stand, but through it all I can hear the authoritative voice of the young lady who is obviously in charge of the apartment and who let me in. People tramp across the sitting room

30. The water festival in Vilagarcía de Arousa on the northwest coast of Spain.

floor and out to the balcony with buckets of water and newly loaded water pistols; they are all wound up and determined to spray somebody walking along the street, three floors below. Of course I know that the festival is held and that is why I have come here, but the enthusiasm with which the young woman tells the story is contagious, not only to me but also to everybody in the room.

On that day it was very risky to walk around in the city centre. Everywhere one might venture, people are throwing water down from balconies and rooftops. The fire engine is standing in the town square spraying all and sundry. What you might take for an elderly couple on a quiet afternoon walk, might well be water warriors who, when you least expect it, will dump a bucket of water over your head! The town is celebrating its water riches, for even though the rains can fail here as well, it is the people of northern Spain who are the water lords of the country. Typically enough, on this particular 16 August, it rains and it is cold and blustery.

This water festival is a lively illustration of the fact that Spain's water is unjustly distributed. The conflict between the thirsty south and the more water-rich north over the division of the country's water resources, and who has the right to manage them, will surely become part of the mix of conflicting values, party antagonisms and other questions of structural discord between the regions and Madrid.

31. Egypt is a desert country where everything depends upon the Nile. Over 50 years ago Winston Churchill compared it to a deep-sea diver with a long and vulnerable air hose formed by the Nile. This shows the river as it runs down from the deserts in the south of the country.

CHAPTER 8
TO THE NILE

Every time I fly up the river to Cairo I press my forehead against the window to get the best possible view of the monotonous desert ecology. I have to admit that what surprises me is that my experience is always the same: I am yanked out of my northern European water blindness. I am once again overwhelmed, stunned – as one who is used to living surrounded by a profusion of water in both society and nature, where water is seldom remarked upon unless as a comment about too much rain – for there, beneath the plane, is an endless sea of grey lifeless desert, and a river glistening in the sun's reflected rays from an almost eternally cloudless sky. Beside the river is a long thin band of civilisation. The value of the journey is thus confirmed; I feel an indefinable joy at again being able to see concrete and materially manifested the importance of water, sketched here with extreme clarity against the surrounding sands.

Whenever I come to Cairo, or the 'mother of cities' as Ibn Khaldun called the Cairo of the Middle Ages, I always go straight down to the banks of the Nile. Everything else has to wait – Giza with its superhuman pyramids steeped in megalomania; the fabulous, filled-to-bursting but somewhat shabby Egyptian Museum with over 120,000 items from the time of the pharaohs to the Greco – Roman period, including treasures from the tomb of Tutankhamun; and the bazaars of Khan el-Khalili – about as close as it is possible to come to the West's image of the oriental bazaar in this the age of mass tourism – a chaotic diversity of shops that sell everything, and with sellers who know all the old bargaining tricks. I come here because the Nile is Egypt – the premise on which Egypt has rested, rests, and will rest in the future. The Nile and Egypt, the river and the desert, nature and civilisation, destruction and creation – for thousands of years they have both enjoyed a unique aura of adventure and mysticism. During the solemn and ceremonious festivals celebrating the annual arrival of the flooding of the Nile, the Egyptians greeted:

Offerings are made to thee
Oxen are slain to thee,
Great festivals are kept for thee,
Fowl are sacrificed to thee,
Beasts of the field are caught for thee,
Pure flames are offered to thee.

When I now sit with a cup of Turkish coffee and with one or another book open in my lap, with the high buildings of Cairo that crowd along the river, reflected in the waters of the Nile, I ponder the significance of its route, flowing as it does from the great lakes of Central Africa, the seat for centuries of old

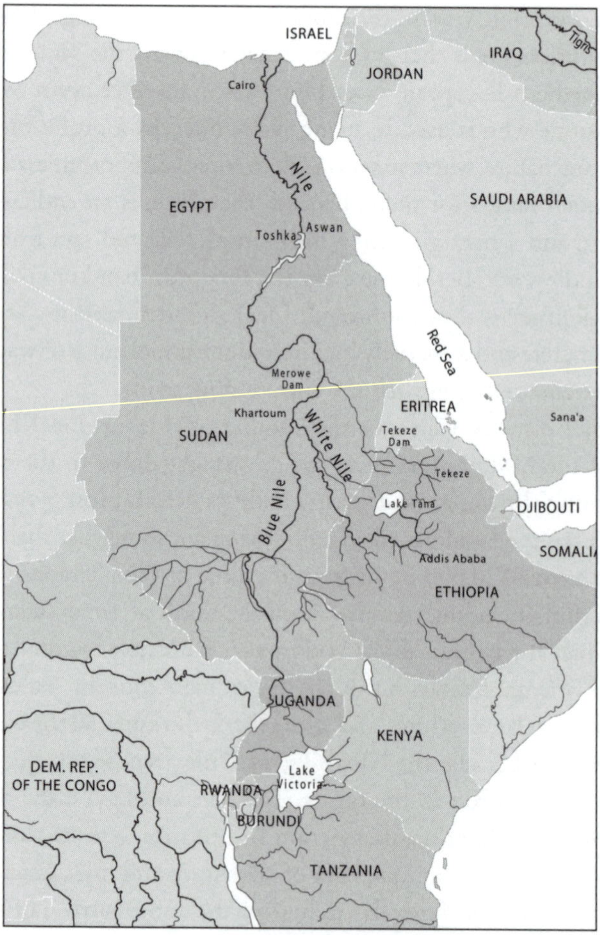

Map 3. The Nile runs through ten countries and three climatic zones but carries no more water than the Rhine.

African kingdoms; the alpine country of Ethiopia where one of the main tributaries starts not far from the stone church of Lalibela, a centre of Orthodox Christianity; past the semi-nomadic Nilotic pastoralists and their herds of cattle in the swamps of the Upper Nile area – people who developed neither state societies nor chiefdoms; past the pyramids of Sudan and Egypt on its way toward Alexandria and the Mediterranean Sea. The whole atmosphere creates a remarkable, physical – intellectual proximity to what, in both metaphoric and material terms, is the historical current of the region, a current of history that is neither produced nor created, but which exists in its own right.

Indeed, the Nile is a current that will continue to form the axis on which the development of Egypt and the whole region will depend as far into the future as it is possible to think. In Arabic, Cairo is called *Masr*, which means both 'capital' and 'country', a sort of primal city that recreates and regenerates itself in an eternal process, a kind of societal parallel to the river that created it and which continues to provide its soul. For millennia, all social life in Egypt has centred on the Nile. Even though major parts of this desert country has practically not seen rain in the last 5,000 years it was, thanks to the Nile and to irrigation, the breadbasket of the Roman Empire, and the cotton plantation of the British

32. This is one of the canals excavated in relation to the Toshka Project, not far from the border with Sudan.

Empire. Egypt's dynastic glory days would have been inconceivable without control of the Nile, and when the river failed them, the position of the rulers was weakened. The situation remains today as it was in earlier times: discussions about Cairo and Egypt's future are about the Nile. Egypt presents an unusually clear example of the geopolitical permanence and importance of rivers.

Today's political leaders are forced to recognise that they are in the same water management stance as their ancient antecedents. However, they are facing challenges of a completely different magnitude. Somewhat over a century ago there were four million people here. The flood irrigation system of the pharaohs could not provide food for more. Since then, the number of Egyptians has increased twenty-fold. Egypt now has almost 80 million inhabitants and it is far from self-sufficient in food production. Every fourth Arabic-speaking person in the world is Egyptian. According to predictions there will be 140 million Egyptians by 2050. If one can say about Europe that it has created conditions for its own disintegration by means of a sinking birth rate, one can say that Egypt in the last hundred years has been overtaken by its own fertility. What has made this growth possible has been the building of a comprehensive system of channels and dams that water fields year-round from the Nile, and thereby make three harvests possible each year instead of one. But can Egypt continue to rely upon the Nile for help in the future? In Egypt the dominant mood is as it always has been when I have visited the country: its future depends on the country being able to go on receiving this proportion of the waters from the Nile. But even this is insufficient now, because the government maintains that they need 30 billions cubic metres *more* water than they are currently using.

It is at Aswan that one ought to stand and gaze out over the Nile if one wants to understand how this life line defines Egypt's position. Here geography speaks unusually clearly: it underlines how correct British Prime Minister Winston Churchill was, over 50 years ago, when he compared Egypt to a deep-sea diver whose long, vulnerable air tube was the Nile. The river runs into Egypt under the eternally cloud-free desert sky, having crossed three main climatic zones and flowed more than 5,000 kilometres. This vulnerability – Egypt's location farthest downstream in the water system – is a physical reality that not even the strongest will can repeal or change, and it will have even greater geopolitical importance in the future, because the demand for water is increasing along the whole length of the watercourse.

There are few places where the struggle for water will take on more epic proportions and involve more countries than in the Nile Valley. In simple percentage terms, the populations in the Nile Valley are growing more rapidly than in other parts of the world. By 2025 around 600 million people will be living in the countries along the Nile.[37] But there are also global political dimensions to this struggle for water. The world's longest river runs from the heart of tropical Africa, through the Sahara Desert to the Mediterranean Sea, and through countries that are centres of both Islam and Orthodox Christendom. Here, as with the Ganges, Brahmaputra, Indus, Euphrates and Tigris, the water question will be woven into religious and cultural conflicts. And while the Nile system is one of few watersheds in which there are agreements in place about how the water is to be allocated, there is a problem because it is these old agreements that many of the upstream countries have campaigned to make obsolete or change. They see these agreements as a vestige of the colonialism of the past.

In 1929, London entered into what was later considered an agreement with Egypt on behalf of its East African colonial territories, in which Egypt was granted a right of veto on upstream water control projects, and which also stated that the water needs of the upstream British colonial regions were marginal and therefore without importance when it came to sharing of Nile waters. In 1959 Egypt and Sudan signed an agreement in which they divided all the waters of the river between them. Egypt got 55.5 billion cubic metres a year, and Sudan 18.5 billion cubic metres. There is at present no more Nile water to divide up because 10 billion cubic metres evaporate from the artificial Aswan Dam. The other countries along the waterway find this situation unreasonable and intolerable, and they have also been provoked by the fact that the agreement is called 'The Agreement for the Full Utilisation of the River Nile'. The big post-colonial question has therefore been how long the power structure for sharing the waters of the Nile, of which the Nile agreements are the legal reflection, will continue to survive intact.

In the coming decades, Egypt's relatively undisputed, millennia-long position as the water power of the Nile will increasingly be challenged by states located farther upstream. New technology will make it possible to use the water in ways and in upstream regions that were unimaginable a short time ago. The populations of these upstream states are growing rapidly, and Egypt's proportion of the total populations making up the Nile basin countries is being radically reduced. Economic growth and political stability in several of the countries upstream will create demands and conditions for embarking on new Nile projects. The countries along the course of the river have plans for water utilization that added together require more water than the Nile carries during its long journey from the tropics to the Mediterranean. In the long run it will be impossible for Egypt to prevent upstream countries from using increasing amounts of Nile water, however justified Cairo's claim might be that due to Egypt's vulnerable position and historic rights to the Nile, they should maintain their share.

At least since the days of Mohammed Ali – the Albanian soldier who seized power in Egypt in 1805 and wiped out his rivals in 1811 with one of history's great plots (he invited 500 of his enemies to a party and had them all killed the same evening), when profitable cotton production along the banks of the Nile was introduced and Sudan was invaded in 1821 (mainly due to a desire for gold, ivory and slaves) – Egypt has considered itself the natural ruler of the Nile Valley. Egypt controlled parts of Uganda until the British assumed power in the 1890s; and when the British, together with Egypt, also occupied Sudan in the late 1890s, the Egyptians called it a 're occupation' to underline what many in Egypt felt was their historical right to the country. As late as the 1940s the Egyptian king maintained that he was 'King of the Nile Waters', and in keeping with a large part of the Egyptian nationalist movement, he regarded Sudan as a natural part of Egypt. Many Egyptians continue to view Egypt as the natural and indisputable leader of the Nile Valley, and they are thus not prepared, nor would they accept, the adaptation of their needs to the demands of less developed and more unstable African states which, besides, enjoy more rainfall than they can utilise.

It is not difficult to have sympathy with Egypt and its fate as a state totally dependent upon a resource it does not control. I meet an Egyptian water expert in a little cafe at Aswan. I have met him before and we talk about Egypt's vulnerability as a downstream state in a large, multi-nation watershed. I do not know him well enough to understand what he really thinks, but when I meet him again, I get the same feeling: I am sitting across from a man who is marked by the loneliness that affects only those who have insight into fundamental and ill-fated historical processes that he neither can, nor will, share with others, either now or in the future. He has, I think, realised what Egypt's downstream position will involve in the long term, and is painfully aware of the fact that not a drop of this water comes from Egypt itself. He knows that the Egyptian government or the Egyptian public do not welcome such a potentially depressing national debate, and that he therefore cannot talk openly about it, because the moment he does so he might contribute to the awakening of an aggressive nationalistic wave that must be contained if Egypt's future is to be secured.

From the mighty Aswan High Dam – a construction project that Nasser thought would make Egypt into Africa's Japan, and would ensure full national independence from the British, whom he feared would use their role as an upstream power during the 1950s to pressure Egypt into compliance with Britain's interests – I gaze out over the 500-kilometre-long artificial lake that has guaranteed Egypt's water security for almost fifty years. It converted the Nile into an irrigation channel in Egypt. If there was a drought in Ethiopia or a flood in

Sudan, the Egyptian engineers here made sure that the Egyptian farmer could cultivate the soil without further worry. In the future less water will reach the dam because upstream countries will use more Nile water before the river reaches Egypt. The question is how much the flow will be reduced, and how Egypt will manage to adapt to this new situation and to what extent mutual projects for the benefit of all can be developed and implemented.

33. Here, in Khartoum, the White Nile, from the great lakes of tropical Central Africa, meets the Blue Nile from the highlands of Ethiopia. In the future, Sudan will increasingly make use of its geographical position right in the middle of the Nile river system.

CHAPTER 9
WHERE THE BLUE NILE AND THE WHITE NILE MEET

'Whoever controls Sudan determines the fate of Egypt.' The British strategists agreed with this statement, right from the time of Queen Victoria, when they took control over the Nile, all the way from its equatorial sources down to the Mediterranean. And this view continued into the reign of Queen Elizabeth II, when in the 1950s and 1960s the British had to give up all their possessions in the Nile Valley. What defines Sudan's geopolitical role has been its location in the Nile basin.

From the out-of-bounds roof of the Hilton Hotel in Khartoum, to which a friendly watchman has escorted me, I see clearly how the water from the Blue Nile, coloured by the mud and silt it carries with it down from the Ethiopian highlands, and the water of the White Nile, which runs out of the heart of Africa, meet and run slowly onwards through one of the hottest deserts in the world, down to Egypt and the Mediterranean Sea in the north. Later, looking at the river in the sunset from a small river boat while the muezzins are calling the faithful to prayer with a scratchy sound tape broadcast from the minarets, I ask the skipper to set a course to the precise point where the two rivers meet, in order literally to cross this current of history. These two rivers and their special character have had great significance, not only for the partition of Africa but also for the collapse of the League of Nations, the Suez crisis and the collapse of European colonialism.[38]

It is also fascinating to see how Khartoum is now undergoing a furious development, financed largely by petroleum earnings. The foreigners one meets in the new business centres that are springing up like mushrooms are not the Western aid workers and university teachers, who predominated when first I was here in the early 1980s, but rather technicians from Malaya, China and India. Following my old habits, I stay at Hotel Akropole, a place where everything is the same: the place is run by the same Greeks who ran it when I was first here; George looks just as young as ever, ready to help, and the waiters who shuffle slowly across the floor in their sandals appear to be just as friendly and to be just as old as they were the first time. For many years this has been the place where aid workers and consultancy people meet. Viewed from here one can get the impression that Khartoum too has stood still in recent decades, although the internet service functions irreproachably. In the streets outside there is the same heat, the same sand and the same yellow taxis that look as though they had been decommissioned yesterday, and the only obvious difference is that part of the hotel has been blown away by Islamic radicals. But this impression of economic stagnation is an emphatic lie, for parts of the city are being modernised under the austere gaze of the Islamic regime and the country as a whole has an average growth of almost 10 per cent per year.

'No matter what the character of the regime, the country's elite wants to realise their ambition of the 1970s to become the breadbasket of the Arab world.' The professor of social anthropology is in no doubt. I have just given a lecture about the history of the Nile and the role of Sudan in British foreign policy strategy during the 1950s. We are standing in the shade of a tree outside the brick-coloured buildings at the University of Khartoum, discussing Sudan's Nile strategy for the coming years. Although the goal of becoming a breadbasket to the Arab world might still appear somewhat unrealistic, I agree with him. Indeed they do have a unique potential, with almost endless plains, and millions upon millions of acres of arable land, given that they are able to obtain water. Today Sudan has 16 million acres of irrigated agriculture, and can profitably double this area, and in a short period of time. The problem is that this will require about 25 billion cubic metres of Nile water, or 6.5 billion more than they are allowed according to the terms of the 1959 agreement.

The Sudan Government has already taken what they consider to be the first great step in a new hydraulic revolution. A new gigantic dam has been rising across the Nile, not long before the river reaches Egypt. The Merowe Dam at the Nile's Fourth Cataract is being celebrated by the political leadership in Khartoum as the nation's future, and as the country's most important development project ever. It will produce hydro-electric power for the nation as a whole, but the dam will also gather up water that can potentially be used for irrigation.

Only a few years ago most experts predicted that this dam would never be built due to the World Bank refusing to lend money for its construction. But Khartoum went ahead, with Chinese help, just a few years after their religious leader Turabi had threatened Egypt with using the Nile weapon against them in a row over borders. And as if to underline the fact that water always has a dual role, the dam also has a positive effect for Egypt: namely, it will slow down the silting up of the Aswan High Dam, because the silt will build up behind the Merowe Dam instead. It is, on the other hand, obviously alarming for Egypt that this enormous colossus of stone and cement could hold back the waters of the Nile right before it reaches Egypt and enters Egypt's own water bank: the Aswan High Dam. But what most underlines Egypt's vulnerability in the long term is that Sudan – a country that has been Egypt's ally on the question of the Nile – has demonstrated that it both can and will build up its water installations without Egypt being able, or allowed, to control the process. Rather, Sudan has shown Egypt that it is in Egypt's best interest to be friends with Sudan.

For the regime in Khartoum this geopolitical aspect has probably been less important than national development and hydropower. But this is the core of the geopolitics of the rivers: when upstream countries want to develop the Nile to improve their own economies, this will have immediate diplomatic and strategic implications, whether intended or not.

The Chief of Information for the Merowe Project roots around a little on his desk before he brusquely pulls out a book of photographs of Sudan. The book is a classic in the art of photography – German photographer Leni Reifenstahl's famous book, *The Last of the Nuba*, with its themes from the Nubian mountains of Sudan. He pounds the book with his fist. 'They call this culture, we call it poverty!' He says that he has become thoroughly fed up with the Western media's criticism of all the construction projects in Africa – the West wanted Africa to remain underdeveloped. I try to get in a counter-argument but he continues his monologue and comes back to his criticism of the West's aesthetically motivated cultivation of 'the primitive African'. He is a big man with a square face partially hidden by a long black beard, and is an influential man in the governing Islamic party. He refused to allow our visit to the Merowe Dam, to my great astonishment, overriding his own minister, with whom I had just spoken, and who had given me written permission; a document that even had the official stamp of the ministry on it. He spoke with the assertiveness of someone with a one-dimensional worldview, but despite the fact that he spoke to me as though I were a child on a wild goose chase, I sympathised with his arguments. I was in conversation with a staunch defender of economic modernisation, a builder of society, a man showing an attitude toward the world that could contribute to explaining why the Islamic regime has managed to remain in power since 1989. Animated by a similar drive for modernisation, the regime in Khartoum has literally rolled over all local opposition to the Merowe Dam and moved 50,000 people away from the low lands where the water will take over.

When I left Khartoum and drove along the endless arable region between the Blue Nile and the White Nile and looked out across the vast narrow fields, like a huge patchwork quilt spreading out in all directions, I caught a glimpse of what might become the future scenery in large parts of Sudan.

In South Sudan the river boat winds its way slowly through the world's largest swamp, first toward the north, then toward the east, a little swing to the south in order to set the bow toward the north again. The only thing I see is papyrus and sky, everywhere. Now and then I glimpse a bird or, off in the distance, a grass fire. The swamp is as large as the Benelux countries together and it takes a couple of days to cross. It is this swamp, or *sadd* as it is called in Arabic, meaning 'barrier', that prevented Caesar's centurions from finding the source of the Nile a couple of thousand years ago, and which stopped European exploratory expeditions in the nineteenth century. In the middle of the day the heat and humidity are intolerable even though I am standing on deck in the shade of a roof, in an attempt to cool down a little by catching the breeze caused by the forward motion of the vessel. Here the daylight is a dazzling white and I see no signs of life; I even miss the crocodiles which guarded the river further along.

In this swamp area almost half of the water of the White Nile evaporates. The endless monotony of the swamp gives the impression of belonging to another world, being very different from other parts of Southern Sudan, where I have walked in the jungle, run away from elephants near Nimule and met lions on the road in Upper Nile State, navigated my way across the bumpy roads, drank my beer with Sudanese and other expatriates in the pubs of Juba, and above all, have sat on the veranda of the house, evening after evening, to watch the sun go down. The British strategists considered, and treated, this whole region as a kind of ineffective aqueduct for conducting the waters of the Nile toward the north. Millions live along the river, but I do not see them. The point is that the Sudd Region is not an interminable waste of useless swamp and water inhabited by hippos, crocodiles, and shoe bills, as it might appear to be from the view point of a steamer traversing its waterways at high-water season. Except along its khors and winding river channels, where real swamp occurs, it is a vast area of alluvial grass flats, flooded in the rainy season, bone dry for the rest of the year. It is, moreover, strange though it may seem, probably one of the most, if not the most, densely populated districts in the country, the inhabitants being chiefly Dinkas owning vast herds of cattle, but also large number of Nuers, Shilluks, and sub-Dinka tribes. They are semi-nomadic pastoralists. When the waters of the Nile draw back within their banks and the dry season comes, people leave on foot, driving their cattle before them. During the flood season the waters irrigate a huge area of pasture land, or *toich*, which even in the dry season has sustained, and continues to be the foundation for the whole society. Here the Dinka and the Nuer live along the banks of the river in their round kraals, and as they have done since they first came here hundreds of years ago, they often go naked while they are looking after their cows. Many British colonial administrators in southern Sudan were critical both of the Nile strategy and the local consequences of the planned canal advocated by London and Cairo, and they stated, not without irony, that the only thing they had managed to achieve was to preserve the region as 'an African zoo for anthropologists to study'.

The boat slowly makes its way past Fashoda, desolate and abandoned, surrounded as it is by vast plains on all sides. Almost exactly 100 years ago this was the centre of the big powers' struggle over Africa. It was here that Great Britain and France collided militarily. In Paris, people demonstrated for war with Great Britain, and they shouted 'Fashoda!' in the streets. But the French were too weak militarily. France had to give in. London milked the issue for everything it was worth, in the face of British and Egyptian public opinion. The British had managed to get the Egyptian taxpayers to finance the military campaign which now finally, circa 1900, made Queen Victoria ruler of the Nile, from Uganda in the south to the Mediterranean in the north. But why was Europe on the verge of a big war over a region in southern Sudan? When one looks over the region one might well consider this crazy, as an expression of blind European expansionism in an era when the idea of colonisation had invaded the public consciousness of Europe.

The big power politics of the day have been interpreted as if they were based upon ludicrous ideas, on fantasies about the vast quantities of gold and ivory to be found, or misconceptions about the Nile – that for example it would be possible to build a dam across it at Fashoda, and so forth. But such analyses underestimate the understanding the British strategists had of the Upper Nile in the 1890s, and also the implications of their understanding of the Nile as one hydrological entity; and that they conceived it as one river basin, constituting one political – economic region. Historical sources show that the policies of the British were both colonial and rational. London's Nile policy was a clear example of its understanding of the political significance of the water. They had one overriding Nile strategy that with tactical adjustments continued right up to the collapse of the Empire about 50 years later. And they had one regional aim: To excavate a new Nile outside the swamps so as to increase the yield of the Nile in the north.

South Sudan is also today at the very heart of the struggle for the Nile. My journey up the Nile had some years earlier brought me south from Kosti, toward Bor and Juba, and since there were neither buses nor trains, I hitched a ride with a lorry and sat, packed tightly together with about 20 southerners in a open, over crowded lorry bed. We lumbered and bumped across the endless flat plains. Here and there in the landscape the brown savannah was broken by trees, by compact villages where everybody, including the women, seemed to smoke pipes, and we saw a number of ostriches run past, somewhat arrogantly, with only their heads and upper necks visible above the grass. This is the territory of the Nilotic peoples during the rainy season. I went by lorry this way with one aim in mind: to see the canal trench that Sudan and Egypt started to excavate in the early 1980s, and to watch the enormous bucking wheel in operation. It dug 120 metres of canal every day through black cotton soils! I talked to the French engineers and the Pakistani workers, and they were very, very proud of their work. It was supposed to be 360 kilometres in length. A couple of weeks later the SPLA kidnapped some of the workers, killed them and the work stopped. Now it sits there, half finished and in danger of being overgrown and destroyed.

But once again – 110 years after William Garstin, the British officer in charge of harnessing the Nile went around the area measuring water flow and documenting topographical conditions to come up with his canal proposal – Egypt wants to put the canal back on the agenda. Technologically it is possible. Ecologically it is problematic. But in the end it will be politics in Juba, Cairo, Khartoum and regionally that will decide.

34. Ethiopia has utilised only a little over 3 per cent of its hydro-electric potential, and Africa as a whole only about 7 per cent. The pressure to build large plants on Africa's rivers has never been greater than it is now, and in Ethiopia future generations will demand a more ambitious water policy.

CHAPTER 10
DAMS AND BAPTISMS IN ETHIOPIA

It is a January night when we shove the boat away from the bank and move out into Lake Tana, the main source of the Blue Nile. We are completely alone and it is like being out at sea, for the morning light has still not begun to reveal the contours of the land (at its widest the lake is 66 kilometres, and it is 84 kilometres in length). We steer for a point of land where one of many monasteries is located, and which stands as isolated proof of the strong presence of Orthodox Christianity here in the highlands. The boat comes to rest on the shore. We are met by a group of men, all wrapped in cloaks of white cloth. They speak quietly to one another as they light the way between the trees with electric torches, making it easier to balance on the stones made wet and slippery by the dew.

The Timkat Festival is celebrated here: the annual celebration honouring the baptism of Jesus. In the pitch dark, and with candle in hand, the priest and the monks chant a monotonous prayer, and while the morning cold and the atmosphere send shivers through my body, they prepare for the ceremony on the shore of Tana Lake. With his face turned toward the lake, over which the sun rises slowly and throws off gleaming rays of red-gold light, the priest blesses the lake and fills a brass kettle with water. Row by row, people come forward, old as well as young, bend down under the spout of the kettle and are christened anew by a stream of running Tana water.

The remains of the morning fog lie like a soft veil over the completely red lake, and while groups of the faithful slowly break away and begin to get on with the tasks of the day, I remain standing among the stones on the shore, thinking of the countless metres of secret documents I have read about utilising the waters of Lake Tana, both in terms of hydrology and greater politics, and which were at the core of relations between London and Cairo, between the fascist Benito Mussolini and the English government during the whole interwar period; between Washington and London over the struggle for influence

35. The Timkat Festival is held in Ethiopia every year to commemorate the baptism of Jesus. Here, the faithful are being baptised in Lake Tana as the sun rises. Abbay, as the Blue Nile is called in Ethiopia, is known locally as *Gihon*, after the river running out of the Garden of Eden in the Bible, and its source is considered sacred.

in the region between 1927 and 1956; and between Moscow and Tel Aviv. In contrast to the timeless ritual I have just witnessed beside a lake that is still under the suzerainty of nature, the workings of geopolitical thinking seem almost childish and the stuff of farce. Yet I have no doubt that in the future the Nile will need more than a blessing to ensure that it does not become a source of conflict in the whole region.

Ethiopia is the water tower of the Nile basin. About 90 per cent of the water in the Nile comes from here. But still only a few per cent of Ethiopia's landmass is irrigated. The country has utilised only a fraction of its water power potential. Ethiopia, world famous for its long-distance runners, but above all for the severity of its droughts, now has more inhabitants than Egypt, and the internal political pressure to take water from the Nile system for irrigation will thus become stronger and stronger if, other things being equal, the country continues to develop economically and remains relatively stable.

'A significant proportion of our country suffers from recurring droughts. If we had the resources we would be able to dam up the water, irrigate the fields and provide our people with food.'

The Ethiopian Prime Minister, Meles Zenawi, speaks with sparkling clarity when it comes to Ethiopia's plans for the Blue Nile. He continues:

> 'And the country, which generates 85 per cent of the water in the Nile at Aswan, is not provided with one single litre of water. Now that obviously is not equitable, it is not sustainable . . . If and when we get the resources, we will use them, and are using them. Although our resources are limited we are building a few dams in the Nile basin and we continue to do so. Hopefully we will do so with the understanding, support and cooperation of downstream countries. But in the end it is a question of our own survival and we have to look after our own interests.'

We meet him in a well-guarded prime ministerial building on a height of land in the centre of Addis Ababa. He also takes up the historical 1902 agreement between Great Britain and Ethiopia, to which I have devoted so much time while trying to understand the background situation. Meles Zenawi insists that this agreement will not stop Ethiopia's development plans for the Nile.[39]

Ethiopia is in the process of implementing one Nile project after the other, each greater than the previous one. Lake Tana is the main source of the Blue Nile, a river that provides about 80 per cent of the Nile's total water flow in Egypt. The British tried to get a dam built here without succeeding, due to the complications of high-level politics. Now the government in Addis is building a dam at Chara Chara, across the Abay River, at its outflow from the Tana, and has established Tis Abay II Hydro-Electric Project. Tis Issat Falls – one of Ethiopia's greatest tourist attractions – has been reduced to an insignificant dribble of impotent water, devoid of the sound and the fury it possessed before the hydro-electric plant was built in 2003.

Yet between 2005 and 2009 what was happening on the Tekeze River, called the Atbara in Sudan, a large tributary of the Nile situated far into the Ethiopian plateau, was of much greater geopolitical significance. It is in 2007, and through the window in the cockpit of a small plane I am able to see how the river has carved its way deep down into ravines, beyond the realm of human control, for thousands of years. The aircraft lands at Aksum, where the Ethiopians maintain that Moses' original stone tablets are preserved and are carried around in colourful processions once a year. After almost a day's journey by car from Aksum we reach the construction site. The 4,600-metre high Simen Mountains stand in the distance. In the clear morning light, with the sun shining on the tops of the mountain chain, I had no trouble understanding why Emperor Haile Selassie, choosing the appropriate locale for an aristocratic picnic, brought Queen Elizabeth II here.

Across a deep canyon that holds the river in its narrow grip, a wall of concrete is in the process of rising to a height of almost 200 metres. The dam will provide storage for about four billion cubic metres of water. I am taken on a tour by car deep inside the mountain to see the power station itself. With Chinese assistance, the Ethiopians were building both the power station and Africa's highest dam, signalling a fundamental change in the relative power relations of the region. The Tekeze is important because it was a testcase, because, as long as the Ethiopians were able to build this dam, they could also, in principle, build others. Technological developments have meant that fresh cards will be dealt out to the different players and the rules of the game will also change. A new situation will arise because what upstream states have found it impossible

36. In this gorge in Ethiopia's high plateau, Africa's highest dam is being built. The same Chinese company that has built the world's largest dam, the Three Gorges Dam over the Yangtze in China, is building this dam across the Tekeze River (called Atbara in Sudan). It is being financed by means of a loan from China.

to do for thousands of years – and which has allowed Egypt to have the waters of the Nile to such an extent that it has in effect been Egypt's river – can now be accomplished by the upstream countries.

I stand there and lean over the railing that separates me from the 200-metre deep gorge where the foundations for the dam have been laid, while the Chinese engineers point out features on the project drawings and discuss technical details. The image demonstrates that in the coming years Ethiopia will be damming their Nile tributaries, and very little can stop them from doing it. A new era has arrived in the Nile Valley, and the Ethiopian workers gliding across the ravine in the aerial tramway symbolise it.

In the long run the water question will strengthen Ethiopia's political – strategic position in relation to Egypt. Africa's water tower will stand on its own two feet, so to speak, and the position of downstream nations will be weakened. The Nile Valley will become one of many multinational or international watersheds where relations of relative strength between the countries sharing the watershed will lead to continual power struggles about who will control and manage the water and who will decide what it will be used for. It will be difficult to adopt binding international laws regarding international or transboundary rivers in general because the countries that set the tone have such conflicting and fluid interests (some of the most central international players are both upstream and downstream countries like the USA, Brazil, India, Germany and Russia). The rights of the strongest, therefore, will have the greatest scope and effect in the various waterways. In addition, the general uncertainty over climate and the future water flow in the rivers will create a state of turbulence making the struggle over water a primary issue in many large and small river basins.

Institutions of multinational cooperation have been set up on some waterways to deal with the utilisation of water courses and to prevent conflict. In some cases they have worked. We can only hope that they will prevent hydrological anarchy and conflict between all the countries of the Nile basin.

37. Låtefossen in Hardangafjord is one of the most photogenic and photographed waterfalls in Norway.

CHAPTER 11
ON THE SCANDINAVIAN RAIN COAST

'You see, we've got a bit of an extra industry in the villages around here. Of course it's for the future, eh? It's uh, you know, for the next generation.' While he tells me this, the farmer sits on a stone directly below his own waterfall and points to the hydropower plant he is building. He talks about his own power plant with the pride that one might expect; but also, I think to myself, he speaks as though he were describing the obvious, as though this were a normal, everyday phenomenon in the world. In reality what is happening here – and in other small villages and farms in the Norwegian countryside – is extremely unusual.

I am meeting these farmers in a little valley right under the largest glacier in Scandinavia, Jostedalsbreen, for centuries the traditional symbol of remoteness, but which became famous as a result of the story about Jostedalsrypa (when the Black Death struck in the 1300s the prosperous who were living in the sparsely populated Sognefjord area moved up here to get completely away from other people and hence from the danger of infection). The two small-scale farmers own a barn with a handful of cattle in the stalls and a few acres of land; but most importantly, they own the rights to a waterfall that crosses their land. And therefore they are now building a small power plant to harness the waterfall with the aim of generating electricity they can sell on the international market. They represent the first generation of what could be called 'hydropower farmers' in Norway.

As I watch them gaze at their new power station – a square clump of grey brickwork standing on their own property – it is easy to understand their feelings, their optimism regarding the future; their sense of being pioneers. But what will happen to the water landscape if all the farmers in Norway who have waterfall rights do the same thing?

The more I travel, the more certain I become that few places are more beautiful than the Scandinavian rain coast in springtime. I had driven over the mountain pass from the southeast of Norway, from Østlandet, with metre-high banks of ploughed snow on either side of the road, even though it was the month of June, and on down toward Sognefjord in the west. The west coastal region, Vestlandet, is a unique mix of natural wilderness and a culturally created landscape; a meeting place of fjords, waterfalls, lakes and wild streams. The water rushes down the mountainsides from snow-capped peaks in torrential currents pouring over mountain ledges and right into the sea; or it gurgles its way through forested bottom land and runs into rivers and streams through the emerald green fields and lawns at the very edge of the North Sea. This mix of untamed water and controlled water, of untouched nature and societies built on water control, created what is increasingly rare in the world today: a kind of world heritage: namely, untouched nature and villages side by side, created at the point where the sea meets the eternal motion of fresh water. A combination of new technology and a unique form of private proprietorship regarding water is beginning to transform this Norwegian waterscape and add a new dimension to the environmental struggle.

As these regions take up the new bonanza of small power stations they will also have to tackle one of the dilemmas of the future, which fundamentally is a cultural dilemma. On the one hand, the small communities in Vestlandet, the western fjord country, as well as those along the rest of the coast, have had a modern and extremely successful history of development linked to different ways of utilising water as a source of energy. But on the other hand, and from a global perspective, the unique character and charm of the whole area rests upon the fact that the rivers and waterfalls continue to run wild, as nature intended, untouched by human hands whilst remaining at the same time part of society. Thus the Scandinavian rain coast is home to a landscape of increasing rarity in the present world.

Here one still can find untouched natural water – a natural waterscape that is at once within but not controlled by society, a phenomenon very different from that natural water one finds isolated from modernity in protected national parks. This will become ever more rare in the wake of coming decades of gigantic water projects around the globe. And while water is an item of scarcity in other parts of the world, a fact that sets country against country, as well as region against region, the allocation of water for the most part is still a non-question in Norway. The country has seven of the 13 highest waterfalls in the world and more than 3,000 river basins of which almost all run within the borders of the country. Norway is, in fact, a country that is increasingly unique in relation to the situation in the rest of the world: it is an El Dorado of year-round flowing water.

Norway's history is one that has been one shaped both by its waterscape and by human action in relation to features of its water, right from the first people who lived there, as they migrated northwards in the wake of the melting ice. What has formed society in Norway has not been the building of irrigation canals but rather the digging of ditches to drain off the water. In fact, the first large farm in Norway was called Sanner (Sand) because the waterlogged soil was transformed into drier, sandy soil. If I think back to a visit to Jæren, on the southwest coast near Stavanger, my memory is not accompanied by the sound of the wind and the larks singing in the heavens above the dry-stone walls, but rather the sound of water draining from the fields, hissing and gurgling through pipes, down into the drains, because these were the physical conditions that made Jæren's soil arable.

Norway's rivers were both transport arteries and sources of energy for the country's timber-centred trading and export businesses from the 1500s to the end of the nineteenth century. The rivers carried the timber and drove the gate-saws and made possible the foundation of many of the towns along Oslofjord, as well as many settlements in Norway's valleys. It was the rivers and waterfalls that made it possible for Norway to join modernity at the end of the nineteenth century, as people discovered that the waterfalls were 'white gold'. The country's status as one of the poorest countries in Europe was suddenly history and Norway became the first country in the world to be electrified. A whole series of industrial sites, glowing red with energy and based on power from waterfalls, laid the basis for the modern welfare society. But even here there is proximity between nature and culture, for in Øvre Årdal, not far from the Årdal hydro-electric station, whose pulse beats with the power of the snowfields, with mountains and glaciers on every side, one can walk in to the first protected waterfall in Norway: Vettisfossen, with a drop of 275 metres. It was given protected status in 1924.

The waterscape has also deeply affected social relations in Norway. Since the rivers run everywhere, and since the rains fall on everyone who lives in Norway, the country had, for example, established between 20,000 and 30,000 mills by the 1830s, and there were more mills per capita than in any other country. Many of them were farm mills, something that gave peasant farmers more independence from the authorities than the degree of independence peasants usually enjoyed in Europe, and they were not forced to subjugate themselves to the whims and the wishes of the large landowner or the *seigneur* every time they wanted to mill their grain. In the twentieth century, the thousands of local power stations, both large and small and owned by municipalities, have given political power and economic heft to the municipal sector *vis-à-vis* the state, particularly during the period when the production of hydro-electric power has been the motor driving the national economy. To travel through the Norwegian waterscape is therefore to journey through what has formed the long trajectories of Norwegian history, the relations and structures that the water landscape has helped to create and recreate day after day, year after year, generation after generation.

Since water runs everywhere, there has never been a need for, or the possibility of undertaking, large water transfer projects. On the other hand, the country is one of the largest producers of hydro-electric power – it varies between 90 and 150 terawatt hours per year. (One terawatt hour is one billion kilowatts per hour.) But now there is agreement that the era of the grand hydro-electric project is over: they belong to history and not to the future. From a global perspective, this is a most unexpected agreement, and Norway is among the few industrialised countries in the world where water continues to run in channels made by the water itself.

Since almost 400 waterways have been saved from large-scale encroachment, it is the farmers with private waterfall rights, in alliance with hydro-electric firms, who will become the lords of water in the future. It will not be gigantic projects that will be the mark of the future but, rather, small-scale power plants. This is

38. It has provisionally been estimated that 4,600 small power plants could be established in Norway. If they were built, the water landscape of Norway would be radically changed and the pristine nature of many waterscapes would disappear for ever.

Map 4. This map shows the 4,600 small power plants that could be built according to an estimate made by Norway's Watershed and Energy Directorate.

profoundly connected to a national feature of Norway: water is privately owned, an unthinkable situation in many other countries, where water belongs to God, Allah or the state.

'Do you own a river? Ring 03870.' This is the text on the poster of Norway's Småkraftverk A/S (Small Hydro-Electric Industries Inc.) that I find on the wall in a small shop in a remote village north of Bergen. What will the consequences be for the landscape of Norway if everyone who sees such posters and owns a river, or part of a river, actually wants to build a power plant? I have travelled back and forth through Norway, from Kirkenes and Hammerfest in the Arctic and Lindesnes on the southern tip, from Finnskogen, the Finnish Forests, in the east to Statlandet in the southwest, and everywhere one finds small streams running – modest rivers, water falling over a projection of rock – and everywhere this is distinguished in different ways by the distinct beauty of the waterscape, its light and its surroundings. It is this waterscape that may now be changed in completely new ways by all these small power stations, and hence the sound we may hear in an increasing number of settlements may soon be the steady drone of a small power plant. Formerly only plants with an installed capacity of less than one MW were exempted from the national plan, but now this has been increased to 10 MW, that is to say, all small power stations. The laws have been relaxed now so that it is also legal to build mini- and small power stations in protected waterways, and the processes for application and processing of applications has been simplified. Owners of large tracts of forest and arable lands also have strong economic interests here. For example, the state Church of Norway has plans to build generating units on 30 waterways in order to strengthen the economic position of the Church.

As things now stand it has been estimated that building 4,600 small, micro- and mini-hydro-electric plants is possible. In the next few years about 50 will be constructed annually, and at the present rate, within a generation almost 1,500 will have been built.[40] The potential for small hydro-electric power generation has contributed to a sort of Klondike atmosphere in many Norwegian farming communities. Norway, in contrast to much of the rest of the world, will be changing the face of nature and the waterscape by means of small hydro-projects, while the Norwegian state, in reversing its former role as the biggest construction corporation, will become the protector of the waterways, yet it will be a very restrained and laid-back protector.

Landowners holding rights to waterways, sometimes backed by strong economic interests, are now being let loose on the waterfalls with renewed energy. It is obvious that this might lead to parts of Norway's unique water-centric natural scenery, where untouched rivers exist side by side with the human cultural landscape, disappearing forever. This new conflict between conservation and development will determine the ease with which one is able to experience authentic waterscapes – or water in a genuine state of free-fall – in the future.

'We're doing it for the coming generations', says the farmer, and it is not difficult to understand his viewpoint. But for the country as a whole, values other than the individual economy of the farmer, or the increase in the municipality's tax base, will be in play. Once an encroachment has been made, one can never return the river to its pristine nature: the untouched waterscape will be lost forever.

I walk into the forest, deep into the woods, and sit down on a slab of stone beside an untouched lake and read the text of American naturalist, Henry David Thoreau. 'A lake is the landscape's most beautiful and expressive feature. It is the earth's eye, looking into which the beholder measures the depth of his own nature.' What will the Norwegian society find in the depths of its soul, as water in its state of nature, free from human control, is ever more frequently sacrificed on the altar of economic growth? For the rivers and watersheds, the waterfalls and the lakes, are not only the carriers of energy that can be lost; they are the bearers of cultural and social values and are at the core of the very identity of the landscape.

39. The combined impact of the monsoon and the character of the river systems has, throughout history, shaped development possibilities and constraints in large parts of India. To this day a bad monsoon can, according to the Indian government, affect the GNP by up to 5 per cent.

CHAPTER 12
DETHRONING THE POWER OF THE MONSOON

The traveller can easily be blinded by stereotype and subjective experience. I am standing, hour after hour, for several days at a stretch, on the banks of the Ganges at Varanasi, trying to understand, as a total outsider, what is going on, and to make sense of all the books I have read about Hinduism and its relationship to the Ganges and the other holy rivers. As early as almost 3,000 years ago the wording of the famous Sanskrit text, *Mahabharata*, summed up the position of water in this religion (XII.83–4): 'The Creator first produced water for the maintenance of life among human beings. The water enriches life and its absence destroys all creatures and plant-life.'

The cultural and religious significance of the *ghats* are played out before my eyes: the families who arrive one after the other carrying a dead mother, a father or a child; the act of submersion in the Ganges to give the deceased water for their journey; the fires in which the bodies are burned before the ash is cast into the river; the *sadhus* seated cross-legged in meditation on the riverbank; all the believers who in the midst of this chaos of sounds and smells bathe in the holy river in a state of profound concentration; and all of them, as millions have done before them, mount the steps, away from the river and walk through the back streets of Varanasi carrying holy water that they have scooped out of the Ganges. A celebration of a kind of mythic geography is carried out on the *ghats* of Varanasi – a landscape conceptualised in a way that it is simply not possible to comprehend from a rational scientific perspective. This adoration of water at Varanasi has been regarded and described as the very essence, the very illustration, of exotic India.

But this well-known touristic image of what is often called 'timeless India' cannot anymore obscure the ferocious modernisation that large parts of the country are undergoing. This economic development has occurred with fantastic speed. What is interesting about the rapid modernisation that is taking place in India, not least in relation to its water systems, is the parallel existence of water that is subject to the power of the engineers and water which is carefully carried up through Varanasi's narrow back streets in small gilded pots.

India is one of the classic river civilisations, and the history of the whole Indian subcontinent can be read from a water perspective. Rivers like the Ganges, Indus, Brahmaputra and Yamuna, and the regular but uneven pulse of the monsoons, have provided the framework and the form to India's development. This water system has laid the basis for agricultural civilisations and trade routes, and has provided one of India's unique features – 'the abandoned cities'. Cities have disappeared from history because whatever river they were founded on either meandered from their course or was 'captured' by another, greater river. The British colonial rulers saw the advantages of irrigation and canal-building: they used more money on dams and canals than on the more famous railways. After the British left, sovereign India continued to erect water works, and since the 1950s they have built more than 3,500 large dams. The country's legendary Prime Minister, Jawaharlal Nehru, was not exaggerating when he called them

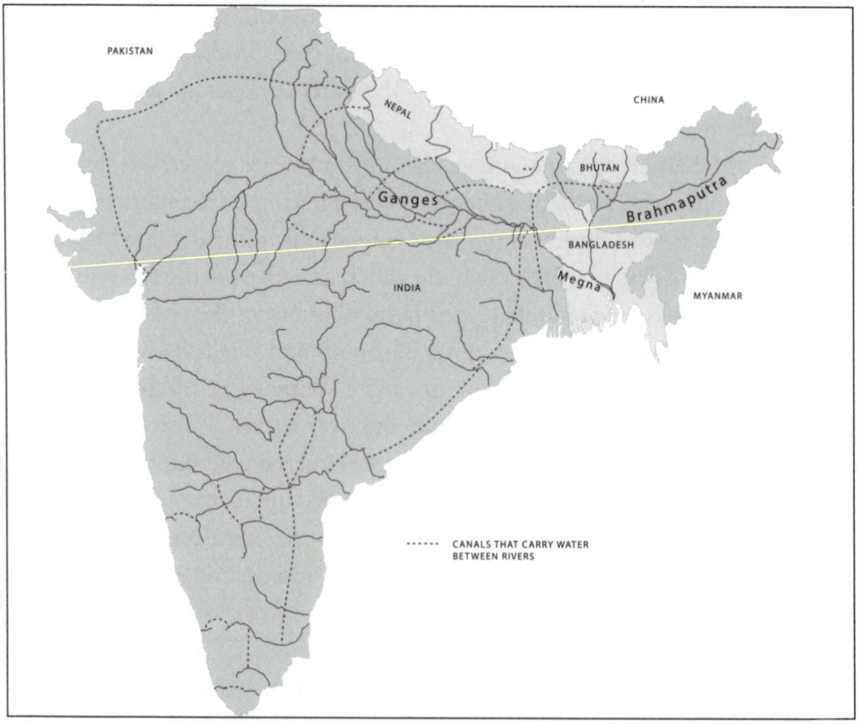

Map 5. With the River Link Plan, all 37 rivers from the Himalayas would be joined together in one human-controlled system; moreover, they would also be linked with the rivers of southern India. When the project is completed, the waters of the Himalayas could reach the southern tip of India.

the 'temples of modern India'. They were not only intended to have pure economic goals: they were also intended to have nation-building goals. The water works were meant to bridge existing regional and social contradictions; they were considered very important in a country where a *paraiya*, a member of a certain low caste (whose name gave rise to the English word *pariah*) still had to shout out a warning that he was coming, wherever he went, so that no passing high-caste Brahmin would suffer the pollution of having looked at him. The dams stood for visions of a modern, united nation-state, based on a secular development ideology. This engineer ideology has existed in tandem with an intense religious veneration of water, especially along the banks of the Ganges, and for millions upon millions of people the flow-controlled rivers continue to be at the centre of ritual practices.

The signs of growth are easy to see in the capital, New Delhi, and the country's economy is expected soon to surpass those of France and Great Britain to become the fifth largest in the world. Some even believe that by 2050 India's economy might be larger than that of the USA. Sections of the economy are among the most modern in the world, and the country's population is already more than one billion. But almost everywhere one goes in India, there is a problem of water, either for agriculture, urban water supply or efficient sewage systems.

Delhi has many faces reflecting the region's turbulent past. Compared to the rest of India there are few noteworthy monuments, apart from the Birla Mandir Lakshmi Narayan Temple, the Qutub Minar and the Red Fort, but as a capital city it is interesting from a water perspective. Even though the country's economy as a whole competes with that of Great Britain in terms of size, its basic infrastructure is extremely poorly developed. It is possible to bump into middle class men in water queues at a water tap in Delhi, dressed in suits but carrying a bucket or two in their hands. At the same time, the richest and most prosperous members of the middle class use more water than do the rich in Paris or Sydney, and they pay less for the water than the costs incurred in bringing it to them. The queues in front of the water pumps for the millions living in the illegal slums are so long that many choose to buy from what are called 'the water mafia'. One day's water consumption can cost about what a middle-class citizen pays for about the same amount of water for a whole month. Inequality of access to water is becoming one of the country's greatest structural problems.

The political leadership has seen the writing on the wall. The lack of water is acute in many places. The authorities in India's western state of Maharashtra have informed the producers of crops with a high water demand that they will not receive more water for irrigation if they have more than two children. The water minister in this state has said that this policy is a necessity in order to limit water consumption. According to reports, hundreds of farmers commit suicide every year. Some historians who published reports in 2005 argued that the minarets on India's most famous building, the Taj Mahal, have begun to lean to one side because the water level in the Yamuna, one of the major tributaries of the Indus and which runs past the Taj Mahal, is so low that it has destroyed the balance in this world-famous symbol of love.[41] Other investigations reject the claim and say that nothing has changed.[42] But the discussion in itself expresses a widespread feeling that the country is on the way toward a water crisis, and that conflicts over water use will escalate. Reports come from everywhere, and from all possible regions, about such conflicts. Some years ago an Indian water minister maintained laconically, 'I am not the Minister of Water Resources but the Minister of Water Conflicts'. Since ninety per cent of India's territory is drained by rivers that cross two or more states, the potential for national conflict exists. Water is also at issue in many of the regional movements for independence, from Assam to the Punjab. The Punjabi Sikhs for instance linked their demands for an independent state with their disagreements over the ownership and distribution of river water.

In the long run the greatest political importance arising from the unequal regional water situation is uneven development in the various states within India. This will threaten the unity of the state built up by Gandhi and Nehru. Some have predicted that the country's western and southern regions will become more and more like California, while the north and east will become similar to the traditional image of Africa south of the Sahara. Regarding the 12 largest and 40 medium-large rivers in India, the government predicts that by 2025 there will be water shortages in the Ganges, the Subarnarekha, Krishna, Mahi, Tapi, Cauvery, Pennar and Sabarmati Rivers, and that this will hit hundreds of millions of people. And this calculation was made without taking into consideration possible climate change or the fact that China has plans to take water out of the rivers before they reach India. At the same time the potential for the expansion of agriculture in India is enormous, according to the government, with the help of irrigation. The government maintains that 40 per cent of all arable land in Asia is located in India and therefore the development of Indian irrigated agriculture is in the interests of the whole hemisphere.

'Every budget is a gamble on the monsoon', India's Minster of Finance has declared. The monsoon rains constitute one of the great and eternal uncertainties in India. The rains begin late in May in Kerala State in India's southwest. Six weeks later the monsoon reaches Rajasthan, if the rains are willing. This movement, sometimes unstoppable, sometimes half-hearted, has been celebrated by a whole range of poets bewitched by India – from Kipling to Tagore. The feelings are always the same: if the rains fail to appear, all will be black, indeed. Water is very unevenly distributed in India. In some parts of the country it rains more than anywhere else on the planet – more than 11 metres a year in Cherrapunji in Meghalaya. Other areas are almost without water and receive only 100 millimetres annually, such as western Rajasthan. As a result, India's pre-modern history is a cavalcade of drought and flood catastrophes. The really huge catastrophes killing millions of people have become a thing of the past due to increased water control, the Green Revolution and better communications. Even so, the trend is unambiguous: despite all the dam-building, water stress has increased dramatically over large parts of the country. Food-production is not able to keep pace with the growth of population.[43]

In order to counteract what has been considered a profound looming water crisis, threatening India's development and unity, Delhi is working on one of the most comprehensive water transfer projects in human history. It is called

40. At Allahabad in central India, where the three sacred rivers – the Ganges, Yamuna and the mythical river of the Hindus which comes down from heaven – where they mingle, and where up to 20 million Hindus gather because the water is more holy than at other places, here the water flow will be severely subjugated to the regime of the water engineers. Both rivers are intended to play a central role in the River Link Plan. How can the devotion of the faithful be reconciled with the fact that the flow of the water in which they take their sacred baths is to be determined by hydrological engineers?

the River Link Plan; based partly on a British colonial idea from the latter half of the nineteenth century, this project was launched in 2002.

The idea was first put forward by the foremost representative of the Empire, Arthur Cotton, but it has now been resurrected and enlarged: 37 large rivers coming from the Himalayas are to be linked to the country's large southern rivers to form a man-made river system. A central water command will then be able to determine how much water the various regions on the subcontinent will be allotted. According to the 2002 plan the project would achieve the following aims: Every year 170 billion cubic metres of water will be moved between different watersheds. Some 12,500 kilometres of new canals will be built, some of them in the neighbouring countries of Nepal, Bhutan and Bangladesh. 60 million acres of land will be brought under irrigation. Between 30,000 and 35,000 megawatts of hydro-electricity will be produced. The cost was estimated to be between 65 and 140 billion dollars. The comprehensive, detailed technical reports published by the government, their assessments of future water needs in agriculture and industry, and their various prognoses about the population of India, estimated to become somewhere between 1.2 and 1.8 billion by the year 2050, give a good impression of the overwhelming size and complexity of the project.[44]

India's leadership wants to redistribute water with the River Link Project, from water-rich to water-poor regions. The aim is to reduce the negative consequences of the vagaries of monsoon precipitation, and at the same time also reduce the enormous variation in the various states' water situation. Hydrological engineers want to 'dethrone the monsoon' from its position as the arbitrary and dictatorial ruler of the continent. In this context, the age-old fatalism in relation to the power of nature has been abandoned. In effect, they want to recreate India's geography, and draw a new map of the country. This is aimed at solving the problems caused by two-thirds of India's water resources being confined to the Ganges and Brahmaputra while at the same time one-third of the country is located in drought-stricken regions.

The most spectacular part of the project will be sending water from the Brahmaputra through tunnels and canals, right across the whole Indian subcontinent – from the border with Bangladesh in the east to the border with Pakistan in the west. The water will be carried to the desert state of Rajasthan, one of Asia's most classic desert landscapes. They will feed more water into the Ganges by means of a 457-kilometre long connection channel, a dam across the River Manas, and a dam and embankment over the Sankosh River in neighbouring Bhutan. And the mystical river of Sarawati in Hindu mythology is going to be resurrected after 3,500 years, with water from, among other rivers, the Sutlej and Brahmaputra, which both come from the glaciers of Manasarovar in the Kailash Mountains of Tibet. If Kanyakumari river reaches the southernmost tip of the Indian subcontinent with waters from Himalaya, grand history will have been made. About a thousand years ago when Rajendra Chola – one of the greatest rulers of the Tamil Chola dynasty of India – invaded the Ganges region, he asked not for gold or more land, but rather a golden cup of Ganges water to bring to Kanchipuram, to be mixed with the sacred springs in front of the temples of Kanchipuram. It is this cultural heritage that will be resurrected with the plan to carry water from Lake Manasarovar in China to the southern tip of India.

According to some observers, the debate about this plan has become 'a shouting match devoid of scientific analysis'.[45] Environmental activists and water-rich states are against the whole plan. Indian environmental activists believe the project will have destructive consequences, and they do not believe that India has the resources necessary to mess with nature on such a scale. Water-rich states do not believe they have anything to give away because they feel their needs will become greater. West Bengal's water minister calls the plan 'a potential threat against West Bengal', while in Assam party leaders maintain it is 'a deep rooted conspiracy to deprive the people of the State their due share of water'.[46] People and politicians in West Bengal consider the Brahmaputra belongs to them. Indeed, the more extensive the project becomes, the more difficult it will be to distribute the water in a balanced manner between the different states and consumers. Constant conflicts about the apportioning of water will therefore put to the test relations between the central government and India's 25 states. The success of complicated water projects has always been predicated on a strong central state. If this project, which exceeds all others in terms of complexity and the need for cooperation, is to be a success it will demand a strong state at the centre.

The visions inherent in the National River Link Programme will never die, although different governments might decide to temporarily bury it. As long as different states discuss large-scale measures to narrowing the gap between demand and supply of water, it will remain an idea; and by many seen as a possible option or the solution. President Abdul Kalam, who came from the very dry Ramanathapuram District, and who had a technical background (as did Nehru), was the driving force for the idea of linking the rivers of India. Opponents of the plan claim not only that the project is a conspiracy to hide the ineffectiveness of the national irrigation bureaucracy, but also that the plan for many has become a sinecure. The proponents of the plan argue that thousands of engineers have studied the project and support the plan, and in the future, therefore, the country's rivers are to be linked together in one system.

From the Red Fort, Lal Qil'ah, built by Shah Jahan between 1639 and 1648, and which acquired its name from the red sandstone used as building material for the 16-metre-high walls, I look out over the Yamuna, considerably reduced in summertime by increased upstream use. Some populist politicians use or make use of such alarming events to advocate the implementation of the River Link Plan, while other, equally populist politicians, argue that the uncertainty about the future water landscape should be one reason for postponing or scrapping the whole plan. What is certain is that elements of the plan will be implemented, and that discussions about it will continue in decades to come because it goes to the heart of India's problem; water security and national unity. The water flow in Yamuna, as in the other big rivers, will remain on the top of India's political agenda.

41. Bangladesh has 150 million inhabitants packed together on a low river delta of only about 150,000 square kilometres, and it is estimated that there will be an additional 100 million inhabitants in four decades' time. It is a powerless downstream country at the outflow of the Ganges and Brahmaputra watersheds, and an innocent victim of a potential rise in sea level.

CHAPTER 13
THE FLOOD PLAIN CAUGHT IN THE GRIP OF WATER

I do not know of any other country where population density feels so claustrophobic, so directly, physically overwhelming as it does in Bangladesh – almost 150 million people packed together in what is little more than a river estuary of almost 150,000 square kilometres. And the capital, Dhaka, a classic river city, steaming humidity, suffocating heat, with cars standing in relentless queues, hundreds of thousands of bicycle taxis or rickshaws, and the unmistakable smell of sweating men as they put their shoulders to the wheel and push what appears to be an endless line of *thela gaari*, or pushcarts, loaded with coconuts, shoes, barrels, buckets and everything else to be found between heaven and earth. After a few hours here it is easy to accept the most common theory about the origins of the word 'Bangladesh'. It has been derived from 'Vanga' and was mentioned for the first time in the Hindu script *Aitareya Aranyaka*, and comes from the Tibetan word *bans* that means 'wet and humid'.

One reason for visiting a city of almost ten million people that lacks not only hills but also a real urban centre and any classic tourist sites, is precisely to experience directly and without remove a seething world of sounds, and the noise and bustle bursting from the chaos of overpopulation. The way to do so is to take a rickshaw, the means of transport often considered a typical feature of Bengali cultural tradition – even though they first appeared under the British Raj about a century ago.

When you let yourself be pulled through the narrow streets, assailed by the impression that tens of thousands of human beings and bicycles are bearing down on you at the same time that thousands more are about to overrun you from behind, you are startled by the realisation, or rather seized by the gut feeling, that population density can be experienced as a physical threat. In a rickshaw you feel completely vulnerable and helpless. I mumble to myself that I should have stayed at home, as we are unable to move either forward or backward. The thin canvas gives no protection. We are imprisoned by the crowd

– not in an abstract way but rather by an enormous mass of humanity from which there seems to be no means of escape.

While my rickshaw cyclist tacks his way forward and I sit in a state of angst, afraid of being run over from behind by motorists who might suddenly lose their cool as they feel unable to put up with the traffic for a moment longer, I come to think of an old Bangladeshi myth, which I had learned while in Sylhet in the hills, toward the north of the country. Hazrat Shah Jalal's temple is located in the city of Sylhet. Six hundred years after his death the faithful are still going there. Legend has it that Shah Jalal came from Delhi to spread Islam. He won over the Hindu king, Raja Gour Govinda and those who believed in the king's Hindu powers, he transformed into lumpfish. Their eternal fate was to swim round and round in the water cistern beneath the holy sanctum, where even today one can find the ruler's sword, clothing and his gift of the Qur'an.

We are stopped by a new mass of human beings. The traffic has come to a complete standstill. People have crowded forward to catch a glimpse of three men who are beating a defenceless dog. The wild howling and the desperate eyes of the dog haunt me all the way through Dhaka's overcrowded narrow streets. At the same time I am well aware that the fundamental reason the country is so densely populated, and why Bangla is the seventh most spoken language in the world, is the unusual fertility of its soil, composed as it is from millennia of silt washing down the big rivers Brahmaputra and Ganges to the delta lands.

In my experience, those moments when one is suddenly overwhelmed by an intense enjoyment of nature and beauty tend to happen when one least expects them, when one is least prepared. Now I found myself again overwhelmed by – of all things – the beauty of the twilight on the Padma River in the middle of the humid, overcrowded Dhaka, in a little rowboat I had hired. From the river, which together with Brahmaputra and the Ganges have created Bangladesh, Dhaka looked both charming and busy.

The country is the drainage area for much of Asia. It comprises one river plain with a delta, and as other major river deltas in the world, it is extremely heavily populated. This country will have another 100 million inhabitants by 2050. There are also predictions that maintain Bangladesh will have a larger population than the USA by 2050. The Netherlands is Europe's major drainage area and it has the highest population density in Europe. Along the Yangtze and Yellow River deltas in China, and along the Niger in West Africa and the Nile delta in Egypt one finds again extremely dense concentrations of the world's population. To date there have been no comparative historical studies undertaken with regard to the development of large deltas but there can be no doubt that all these areas are facing great challenges – yet none has such poor odds for solving them as does Bangladesh.[47] If the climate changes, and if the glaciers in the Himalayas melt and the ocean rises, Bangladesh will be lying in the cross-hairs of two sharpshooters – or, so to say, imprisoned in a trap from which it simply cannot escape. Bangladesh finds itself in an extremely vulnerable position that is a result of an unfortunate combination of social and natural conditions. It is located downstream on major waterways, and it lacks the power to determine or control the flow of its rivers.

Bangladesh has 230 rivers, 57 of them international. When there is no flooding, the rivers cover 13 per cent of the surface of the country. In a normal flood, which occurs annually, around a third of the country is inundated, and from the air it looks like a nation consisting of small islands. When the flooding is extensive up to 65 per cent of the country can disappear underwater. The flood of 1998, for example, lasted for more than two months and the government was forced to find food and shelter for about 20 million people. The society and the state face structural problems of a magnitude that most states in the world do not have the necessary experience to tackle, and Western governments have never been faced with having to solve such challenges.

I heard the same stories everywhere I went: living by a river in Bangladesh, as most people do, means that one is prepared to regularly submit to the power of water. Such has been the case in the past, such is it today, and most assuredly such will it be tomorrow. The extremely rapid growth of population and settlements has meant that many low-lying flood plains have been developed with roads, houses and asphalt. As early as 1988, the country had more roads per hectare of land than any other country in the world.[48] Canals and small river tributaries that formerly carried water away, have been sealed up. The country has thereby gradually made itself more vulnerable to flooding, almost keeping step with the danger from increased water flow due to the melting of the ice in the Himalayas.

The water question, and the sharing and utilisation of the Ganges and the Brahmaputra, both affect and reflect the political relations and relations of trust between the states of the whole region. In this geopolitical and water-political game, Bangladesh is certainly one of the Lilliput nations, a rather powerless player faced by the big powers of India and China. India is criticised in Bangladesh because Bangladesh asserts that India takes more water from the Ganges at those times when it is experiencing a shortage of water. As a result, the water supply crises deepen in Bangladesh during periods when there is already water scarcity. Dhaka also maintains that India reduces its flood problem by simply sending the flood waters on down to Bangladesh, thereby enlarging the floods downstream. Bangladesh has tried to work out a water agreement with India, but has only been partially successful, and then only with regard to certain areas.[49]

In general it is reasonable to assume that the flow of water in the rivers running through Bangladesh will decrease in future due to the increased use of water as the rivers pass through India, particularly in the states of Uttar Pradesh, Bihar, Haryana and West Bengal. India has also signed agreements with Bhutan to conduct water away from the Sankosh and Manas rivers, tributaries of the Brahmaputra which run it into the Ganges watershed, so as to be able to distribute it to some of India's water-poor regions. India has built control structures across the Teesta and Mahananda and plans to construct a reservoir on the Barak, which is the main source of the Meghna River. The gigantic River Link Plan will, if implemented, take water from the Brahmaputra and conduct it directly west to the desert lands of Rajasthan. The River Link Plan involving the Brahmaputra river will, according to the political leaders of Bangladesh, therefore have catastrophic consequences in this downstream country. It is argued that India's water project will destroy Bangladesh's water resources, and thereby the country's economy and ecology. Less water in the Brahmaputra will lead to less water in the River Meghna, which again will mean that the sea will eat its way further and further inland through the low-lying country of Bangladesh. The River Link Plan exposes and threatens Bangladesh's geopolitically precarious position: a downstream country without power and influence.

And of course the higher the sea levels rise, the more vulnerable Bangladesh will become. The oceans do not have to rise very much before millions of people will be forced to pack their bags and head for the country's few ranges of low hills. If the sea level rises half a metre, six million people will lose their arable land. If the ocean rises one metre, 15 per cent of the country's total area will disappear, a land mass where at present more than 15 million people live. Rising seawater will seep in and contaminate the ground water. And above all, this will make the country even more vulnerable to acute natural catastrophes. The 10 metre-high wave driven in by a 240 km/hr gale-force wind which pounded the coastline here on 12 November 1970, took the lives of about half a million people in the course of a few hours. It was one of the great natural catastrophes in history.

A research colleague, a Bangladeshi economist, tells me as we eat our chicken curry at the Hotel Golden Gate, about the dismal future prospects for the country's economy if the water systems are altered, be it due to climate change or upstream human interventions, or both. When he searches for comparisons with Bangladesh's situation, he cites the 5,000-year-old epic of Gilgamesh that described what was said to happen in old Mesopotamia:[50]

> The evening came; the rider of the storm sent down the rain. I looked out at the weather and it was terrible. [. . .] With the first light of dawn a black cloud came from the horizon; it thundered within, where Adad, Lord of the Storm, was riding [. . .] Then the Gods of the Abyss rose up; Nergal pulled out the dams of the nether waters; Ninurta the Water lord threw down the dykes [. . .] The God of the Storm turned daylight into darkness.

Along with the ravages of nature, he says with resignation, there comes the upstream countries' utilisation of the rivers.

Out on the low-lying flood plain near the edge of the Bay of Bengal there is a Sisyphean struggle underway, marked by the conflict-ridden aim of holding the sea at bay. Bangladesh uses river water for irrigation, the river for transportation; and it is a necessity not least when it comes to standing up to, or preventing, the sea from making constant inroads into the land. But while the silt enriches the earth and makes it amazingly fertile it also makes the bottom of the sea ever shallower, making the situation increasingly dangerous. The delta regions become ever more vulnerable. And there are fewer and fewer of us who recall that this was once the jungle where, 'The Phantom' – that 'walking spirit' of comic book fame from the 1930s – was said to have washed ashore on the coast of Bengal in 1536; and which subsequently provided spice to Rudyard Kipling's *Jungle Book* about Mowgli, Shere Khan and the other famous creatures of his story.

Uncertainty about future sea level is creating general insecurity and anxiety. Where should people settle? Who will invest in a country that many believe will soon disappear?

When I stand at the edge of the Padma, while overcrowded boats shuttle people back and forth from one bank to the other, and as youngsters are jumping, from everywhere it seems, into the water to cool themselves off – from boats, from bridge, railings and buildings – and as I gaze at the houses on stilts that raise them up barely above water level, it is not difficult to understand that societies can come to a point where they stand still, and that civilisations have collapsed due to changes in the waterscape. On the basis of historical experience one thing is clear: future surprises are unavoidable.

42. For more than 20 years since 13 April 1984, thousands of soldiers from India and Pakistan have conducted a war – the 'War of Heaven' – on the world's largest non-polar glacier. Here we see Pakistani soldiers on the Siachen Glacier. The conflict over Kashmir is also a conflict over water and, not least, the disbursement of the waters of the Indus watershed.

CHAPTER 14
TO THE HIMALAYAS AND THE 'WAR IN HEAVEN'

Immediately before I journeyed to the Hunza Valley in the far north of Pakistan on the border with China, I came across a modest little volume published between the two World Wars and entitled *Das Geheimnis der Hunza oder wie Hunza das sagenhafte Alter von 145 Jahren erreichen* (The Secret of the Hunzas, or how the Hunzas live to the the incredible age of 145). I took it with me as a reminder, and as a warning, about the power of perspective; about how one tends to see what one wants to see. The land of the Hunzakuts was described as an earthly paradise – indeed, as nothing less than Shangri-la. They were referred to as 'the world's most fortunate population', as 'complete masters of their own thinking' and they lived in a state of absolute harmony with nature. This little volume found itself a solid place at the centre of the the kind of literary Orientalism that distinguished the travel descriptions of the era. It frequently took on a metaphysical and religious character and the writers were adept in poetically fleeing from themselves and their own society – a literary tradition that gave rise to such evocative titles as *Take Me Away to the End of the World.*

This literary tradition was a concentrated expression of both the attraction afforded by cosy folktales and an ardent desire to rediscover the true self alienated by Modernity. The *modus operandi* at the time was to journey to places where the influence of the West was still not noticeable. The Hunzakuts' isolation – behind the mountain peaks of the Himalayas – made them well-suited to be the objects of European fantasies about the good life. Their way of life was set up as a counterpoise to the unnaturalness of the industrialised West. It was here that Europeans projected their longing for a Faraway Land.

We filled our four-wheel drive vehicle with provisions in Islamabad and drove north, up the Karakoram Highway, built by the Chinese in the 1970s and which opened up the region for development. The highway winds its way up narrow rocky benches between the foaming rush of the Indus's brown waters and the precipitous mountains, past villages where the women never escape from within the walls of their houses and where the street scenes are unbelievably homogeneous: men adorned with beards on their way to or from the market, or men adorned with beards sitting around a table laden with glasses of tea, as well as a good number of children, although almost none of them is playing. We pass Chilas, where the tremendous alpine massif of Nanga Parbat thrusts upwards, perpendicular, like a wall, rising 7,000 metres almost straight up from the bank of the river. After a couple of days on the road and a good 20 hours of driving, the car struggles up the hairpin bends to Karimabad. This 'capital city' of the Hunza Valley opens out quite quickly into a green, friendly-looking oasis surrounded by the jagged peaks of the Himalayas, with the intractable gray Hunza River in the valley bottom below, digging itself deeper and deeper down through the porous geological strata, while the Himalayas continue to grow higher.

Karimabad is a strikingly beautiful village and women (without the *hijab*) are part of the street scene here, and I grab the chance to buy myself a cold beer while I am in Pakistan. The relatively liberal Ismailis are predominant here – in the West they are probably best known for the fact that their former leader, the Aga Khan, married Hollywood star Rita Hayworth. The oasis, which has provided the basis for an almost self-supporting agricultural society, is not the work of nature itself, nor a result of the Hunzakuts having lived in passive 'harmony with nature'. From nature's side, the Hunza Valley is very arid and barren, and even though the region is honeycombed with rivers they cannot be utilised because they often run hundreds of metres lower than ground level. They are a barrier both to trade and communication rather than being a sign of economic well-being. While the Indus is the life-giver on the dry plains of southern Pakistan and India, here the river runs in such a manner that it is both irretrievable and almost unbridgeable.

Living in an inhospitable desert climate 3,000 metres above sea level, the Hunzakuts have nonetheless created, laboriously and over many generations, a green oasis, surrounded by a grey barren alpine landscape. Their solution to the water question has been ingenious. From a burgeoning apricot orchard – the Hunza people are particularly known for their cultivation of this fruit, and traditionally the apricot has been the summer diet – I look through the branches of the trees at long stripes that seem to be scratched across the surface of the precipitous mountainsides. These are water channels in the mountain side, several kilometres long. They carry melt water from the glaciers. They are what makes all agriculture possible here.

I tag along with some of those who are going up to repair the channel that feeds water down from the glacier lying at the foot of Mount Ultar, 7,388 metres high and quite certainly still not climbed by alpinists. On the way up we pass a complicated network of lesser channels that distribute water to the various villages, and at the division point there is a guard hut for the man who makes sure that no village takes water that is not allocated to it. We climb onwards, ever upwards, until finally, with a view out over the whole valley, and as I nervously balance on the edge of the channel which is paved with stones and crosses the mountainside, I see that every green patch in Karimabad is fed with and nurtured by water from these channels – visual confirmation of precisely what I have read.

The canals are even more impressive when I stand in the middle of them – an artificial shelf along the mountainside with a stream bed varying in breadth, in some places under half a metre and at others, more. They are large enough to walk in, but wherever there is a lot of water I have to balance with my feet against the outer wall of loose stones, while with my arms I manage to cling, certainly without much grace, to the mountainside, at least wherever this is possible, for we are without ropes or attachments. In many places I am forced to bend down low since the channel has been hewn out beneath a rocky overhang. When I peer carefully over the edge of the canal and glimpse the steep cliff face we are crossing, or when the eye follows the narrow water artery that carries melt water from the Ultar Glacier, and is the lifeline of the society and which in its flight curves across the steep mountainside, I have no doubts: this is the most doggedly tenacious and monumental example I have ever seen of a society's struggle to obtain its daily water. Without any tools other than stone, the horns of goats and ibex, and homemade blasting powder, these channels had been excavated, often by men roped together and hanging from the mountain face to carry out this obligatory communal labour. And the canals have to have the proper incline. If they are too steep they will be destroyed by the stones carried down with the water from the glacier. If they are too gentle they will quickly fill up with silt and mud. The glaciers are always pulsating with activity. They are moving all the time and there are frequent rockslides and avalanches. Thus constant repairs are crucial to keep the channels open. Since the same long canal can provide water to several villages and to absolutely everybody who lives there, and since they are their only source of water, the building, management and maintenance of this system compels a kind of cooperation that is quite different from what a rain-based agriculture will normally develop.

The building of this water system was predicated upon a strong central power. It is thought that this revolutionary water system was initiated when Thum Silum Khan III (1790–1824) came back from exile in Badakhshan in present-day Afghanistan. Prior to this time, the Hunza Valley's rulers had obtained their daily bread by raiding merchant caravans along the Silk Road, which in some periods led through the valley, or by selling slaves. The technique introduced by Thum Silum Khan was by and large simple, but it demanded organisation, perseverance and the ability to read the landscape. There is a story told in the Hunza Valley about this. It recounts how the ruler of a neighbouring valley told the ruler of Hunza, 'You rule over three small villages that are the size of my penis and testicles'. Instead of doing what rulers usually did in these parts, which is to attack the neighbour's town, take prisoners and sell them as slaves, the ruler of Hunza had a better idea: build water canals. Canals enabled the villages to expand. Tax revenues increased. He was able to attract allies by giving away newly arable land. And the Thum, who perhaps could be best likened to a local, petty king, gradually increased his power. Since a parcel of land without access to melt water was completely without value in Hunza, and the Thum, in popular belief, possessed the power to manage the melting of the glaciers, the local population simply had no choice. If they wanted to live here they had to subject themselves to his regime. This system of more or less autocratic petty kings in northern regions of Pakistan was only dissolved by the Bhutto government in the early 1970s, when these regions, including Hunza, were for the first time placed under direct control of the central government.

The constant need for more water is reflected in the local conceptions of nature. At a dinner given by the technical leadership of the local waterworks, I heard the engineers maintain with the greatest conviction that it was possible to mate a male glacier, which is black and full of stones, with a female glacier, which is white, in order to breed new glaciers. By covering 'the child' with carpets and suchlike, the gestation is given the possibility of success. As we fly back out of the highlands, the small aircraft follows the valley depressions between the ice-capped mountain peaks, and without seeing any tracks of the Abominable Snowman, I think to myself, 'That mating theory was an optimistic theory for a region so dependent upon melt water'.

I see it the moment the plane comes in over the plains of the Punjab Province: a network of canals criss-crosses the country in all directions. This is the greatest unbroken area of irrigation in the whole world. More than 60,000 kilometres of irrigation canals have been excavated, and all carry water from the Indus system.[51] Punjab means 'the land between the five rivers' (an appropriate designation). Colonial rulers and water engineers from Great Britain transformed the Punjab which is now in Pakistan, and part of which is in neighbouring India, into one enormous cotton farm. The rivers have been tamed and linked together with other rivers. In many places the dry Indus Plain has been converted to oases. Agriculture here is the backbone of the country's economy; the artificial watering is itself the central spinal cord to the nervous system that is the Green Revolution.

It is an unequivocal historical fact that without the Indus and its tributaries, agricultural Pakistan, as we know it, could not exist. But this main artery in the country's economy is not a national river: it comes from China. Still more importantly, both China and Pakistan share it with India. The struggle over water in this river system will determine the state of war or peace between the two new atomic powers of Pakistan and India, and will also to a great degree affect the resolution of the Kashmir question.

I have driven by car from Multan into the irrigated countryside surrounding the city. I am crouched down on my haunches and I draw my hand across the uneven surface of the earth. I get a fistful of thick, grainy salt, and around me there are vast areas as white as snow . . . I have seldom seen anything more alarming. But nowadays there are many huge, white areas like this in Punjab and Sindh. The Indus carries with it enormous quantities of salt from Tibet and the Himalayas. Millions of hectares are threatened or already destroyed by the process of salination, poor drainage and ineffective irrigation. Pakistan also has many lakes that from a distance appear to be the usual idyllic bodies of inland water, but when you come closer you see that they are completely dead, spookily devoid of life. For the water in them comes from below. They are fed by salt-retaining ground water that rises due to the artificial supply of water leaking from irrigation channels.

'Almost 40 per cent of the area is water sick, and 15 per cent is seriously water sick. The salts in the earth are the cause of a 25 per cent fall in productivity'. The researchers I meet at one of the research institutes in Multan are in a state of dejection. They have this development over time, and the attempts to do something about it, but they also know that the problem is longstanding, as can be seen in Mohenjo-Daro.

When archaeologists found Mohenjo-Daro in 1922 it became necessary to add to our knowledge of earlier human history. It became possible to form a picture of the level of development reached by the Indus civilisation, and it was revealed, to the great surprise of many, that in terms of development, the Nile Valley and Mesopotamia had a parallel on the Indian subcontinent. People at Mohenjo-Daro cultivated wheat, barley, groundnuts, melons, sesame – and cotton (they found a fragment of cotton cloth coloured with plant dye, and this turned out to be the oldest in the world). The Indus civilisation was also based on trade. Caravans crossed the desert, and boats conducted trade and commerce up and down the Indus. They had dogs and cats, cattle and buffalo, and possibly pigs, horses, donkeys and camels. And they may well have tamed the elephant. It is estimated that about 40,000 people lived in the city. While the Egyptians were building the pyramids, and while along the Tigris and Euphrates craftsmen were building monumental temples to venerate their gods and their rulers, the Indus civilisation was marked by more modest and standardised buildings, where even 'the man in the street' could have decent housing. This civilisation occupied an area that stretched in circumference from Badakhshan in northern Afghanistan, south, then along the coast of the Arabian Sea and all the way to the west coast of India. Permanent settlements sprang up all along the lower reaches of the Indus waterway. Nomads arriving from the west must have seen the advantages of settling down on the alluvial plains, but how this led to a developed civilisation remains a mystery to this day.

One very hot morning in June I am in 'the Great Bath' in Mohenjo-Daro, almost 5,000 years old, pacing out its 8 by 12.5 metre dimensions. The rising sun playing back and forth between shadow and golden light brings life and sparkle to the old walls, and I am eager to finish the visit before the thermometer soars to more than 54°C and before the camera we are filming with succumbs to heatstroke. The bath is the most prominent building in the archaeological centre of Mohenjo-Daro, in Sindh Province. It is located on a man-made platform about ten metres above the Indus and its flood plain. It is the most famous building left behind by the Indus civilisation, which arose in this region about 5,500 years ago.

No one knows precisely what the function of the Great Bath was. It may have been used in purification rituals, or perhaps it was the arena for a similar religious veneration of water that later became so important in Hinduism. Be that as it may, every house had its bath and sewer system. The baths were filled from hundreds of wells. Since no city can exist without tackling the problem of human waste, and since this is particularly important in a hot and humid climate, the sewage system is just as fascinating. Even today one can follow it, where the trenches, lined with specially-made brickwork, down the length of the streets are as straight as arrows. The drainage system, better than anything else, reveals the level of organisation of this civilisation. Waste materials were more effectively removed at that time than they are in the surrounding villages today, some 4,000 to 5,000 years later.

Approximately 3,700 years ago the Indus civilisation disappeared, gone from history. The city was attacked and overrun by foreign troops, and among others, by Aryan immigrants. Some believe that a series of great floods sapped the society of its life force. Others believe that the Indus was dammed up by nature itself, a little to the south of Mohenjo-Daro, due to a combination of shifts in the crust of the earth and build-ups of silt and sludge from the Indus. Still others believe that what happened here was the same as in Mesopotamia 4,000 years ago, the same as is happening today on the Indus plains. In brief, the fields are being ruined by artificial irrigation, with rising groundwater levels and increased salination of the soil caused by evaporation and a lack of sufficient quantities of water to flush the salt away. Mesopotamia and other ancient civilisations collapsed, according to many archaeologists and historians, due precisely to this process.

Now Mohenjo-Daro, or 'the city of the dead', is being threatened once again by water. In 1922 when the excavation started, the water table was 7.5 metres below the surface. Now, during my visit, the distance is less than 1.5 metres. Not far from the Great Bath there are flakes of newly produced salt on the ground. The ancient ruins are ringed with pumps that are in constant action, not to produce drinking water but rather to save the old buildings, which are decomposing since the rising water leads to the formation of salt crystals that react with the clay brickwork. The international community and the Government of Pakistan are making a great effort to save this monument but the rising groundwater is an insidious opponent.

In order to understand Pakistan's present geopolitical situation it makes good sense to leave the flat, overheated Indus plains and return to north Pakistan. There, perhaps more than anywhere else in the world, the mountains soar with the most terrifying beauty, like enormous monoliths of granite, rising almost vertically thousands of metres, almost perpendicular the valley bottom and the banks of the river. Tirich Mir, on the border with Afghanistan, and Nanga Parbat, which soar in lonely splendour as the last part of the Himalaya Massif, separate the fertile plains of Kashmir from the tremendous canyon of the Indus. It is through this region that Pakistan's life-giver cascades downwards, before it and its tributaries broaden to form the agricultural country of Pakistan.

And so I am travelling north once again, this time by small plane from Islamabad to Skardu, where I hire a taxi driver for less than $100 a day and get to experience the most frightening car trip of my entire life. The price reflected the fact that the car was old, with worn tires, and even the driver had seen better days. It began as a calm drive along the windy road that follows the sand-covered river plains of the Skardu Valley, surrounded by the same glaciers that the local population believes know how to breed. After a few dozen kilometres we reach the road that closely follows the course of the Indus. We drive along, beside the river, hour after hour. Sometimes there is a vertical drop of several hundred metres down to the seething cauldron of the river, while above us, enormous mountains tower and seem to lean over the road as though to envelop us. We cannot drive along hugging the mountainside because stones break loose all the time; nor are we able to drive too close to the precipice on the other side because the shoulder of the road is indistinct and composed of loose gravel. At the same time, every bend brings with it the danger of collision, with vehicles coming from the opposite direction, often driving much too fast, and for whom my driver is undoubtedly unable to brake for in good time. After many hours, and as darkness is falling, I feel myself completely given over to fate, and in this condition, in a state of fatalistic tranquillity, I arrive at my hotel in Gilgit. Nanga Parbat is bathed in the cold light of the full moon as we arrive.

Here in the far north of Pakistan, on its way down from Tibet and the Himalayas, the Indus carves out deep, almost impassable canyons. To say that they hinder communication is a gross understatement. In many places people have to ease their way across from one bank to the other, swaying across ropes and cables suspended several hundred metres above the surface of the water, on their way home from their jobs in the evening. Every morning and every afternoon the same activity unfolds along the stony ledges on the forbidding mountainsides bordering the river. People fasten themselves to the line, jump out from the rock they are standing on and drag themselves hand over hand above enormous gorges, inconceivably small beings compared to the massive mountains they pass between.

43. Pakistan has the largest contiguous area under man-made irrigation in the world. Some 60,000 kilometres of water channels have been dug out. The country is completely dependent upon the Indus, which Pakistan shares with India. Some 90 per cent of the water of the Indus comes from glaciers in the Himalayas.

What has been called 'The War in Heaven' has been taking place not far from here. At 6,000 metres and 7,000 metres above sea level, it is the highest battlefield in the world. Thousands of soldiers from India and Pakistan have conducted a bloody war since 1984, for control over the world's largest non-polar ice-cap, the Siachen Glacier. It is an area long by 78 kilometres. However, the death-toll of the two sides has been 4,000 soldiers and they have died from cold and avalanches rather than from actual fighting. Temperatures can fall to −50°C and lower. Although there has been a cease fire in place for some years, there is no settlement of the dispute. On both sides, in Delhi and Islamabad, politicians have said that they are prepared to continue this 'war in heaven' for as long as necessary.

The roots of the conflict over Siachen lie in the non-demarcation of the cease fire line on the map beyond a map coordinate known as NJ9842. The 1949 Karachi Agreement and the 1972 Simla Agreement presumed that it was not feasible for human habitation to survive north of NJ9842. Prior to 1984 neither India nor Pakistan had any permanent presence in the area.

But the battle for an unpopulated glacier also points the way toward a possible future, for the glaciers are vast water banks. Almost all the summer water in the Indus comes from glaciers in the Himalayas. They are of such hydrological importance that Pakistan's military leadership discussed the possibility of getting more water out of them by using lasers or dumping coal on them to expedite the melting. Their aim was to lessen the water crisis on the hot plains of Pakistan. The plan was dropped. The mountain war at Siachen (Siachen is the glacier that provide water to the Nubra River, which runs into the Shyok River, which in turn enters the Indus) has to be understood also from this water perspective. In a situation where the Indus question is, has been, and most certainly will continue to be, a serious bone of contention in the conflict between the atomic powers of India and Pakistan, the glaciers become important. So important, that India, for example, has built the world's highest helipad on this glacier at a place called Sonam, which lies 21,000 feet above sea level, to serve the area and ensure that her troops are kept supplied via helicopter support. The war demonstrates therefore how relations between political power, the importance of fresh water and conceived national interests are intertwined. The irony is that research has shown that the Siachen Glacier has been melting alarmingly more due to military activity of India and Pakistan than global warming. As it has been said: 'Siachen is weeping, tomorrow the world will cry'.

The water crisis will be worsening in Pakistan in the long run, both due to possible climate change in the Himalayas, the likelihood that Kashmir under Indian leadership will demand more water, and growing water demand in Pakistan.

Pakistan's ability to use more of the waters of the Indus than they do, or the possibility of them continuing to use the share they have, is more than anything else dependent upon what happens in Kashmir. Since many of the tributaries of the Indus run through Kashmir, then whoever controls Kashmir will control the future of water on the subcontinent. Few observers ever raise this question, but the water issue will affect, if not determine, the outcome of the conflict.

Under British rule, naturally enough, the Indus waterway was regarded as one whole planning unit. When India and Pakistan were separated and made independent in 1947, both the river system and the irrigation system were also divided between them. Conflict over the Indus rapidly became a central issue. To force Pakistan into compliance, India quite simply closed the water tap to Lahore in 1948. Lahore was Pakistan's most important city at that time. After 18 days the Indians opened the water mains and thereafter the two countries signed an 'Inter-dominion Agreement' which led to ongoing negotiations to solve the water contradictions.

In reality, what became the Indus Agreement, signed in 1960, was a tripartite accord between India, Pakistan and the World Bank, which had carried out a most important job in bringing about the Agreement. This was hailed as a victory for peace and friendship and held up as a model for agreements on other international waterways. The Agreement, however, was not based on water sharing and cooperation on the Indus, but rather on dividing up, so to speak, the whole Indus watershed. India received exclusive rights to the three eastern rivers, the Sutlej, Beas and Ravi, while Pakistan got the western rivers, the Indus, Jhelum and Chenab. Thus, according to the 1960 Agreement, Pakistan has rights to all the water in the Jhelum, the river that feeds water to and creates the heartland of Kashmir. The government in Islamabad argues that Pakistan needs this water more and more.

Kashmir, which is still an unsolved problem in the relationship between India and Pakistan (Kashmir is a disputed territory administered by India, Pakistan and China), has no rights to the waters of the Indus, nor does it have rights to its tributaries running through Kashmir. The predominant Hindu myths about Kashmir, and which are the basis for the Hindu rights to this area, are closely linked to the Indus. Hindu myths describe Kashmir as an enormous waterscape surrounded by mountains. One Sanskrit text from around the year AD 700 (the *Nilamatapurana*) describes how the valley grew up out of the water under the protection of gods called the Nagas, who were synonymous with the source of life. The text describes the whole of Kashmir as the material manifestation of Uma Parvati, as the sacred form of Vitasta, or, to use the river name that appears in the Indus Agreement, the Jhelum. It is a tributary of the Indus running today through Pakistan. Hindus even celebrate the birthday of the River Vitasta; people offer their prayers and present milk and flowers to the river. Thus it is this land, which according to the myths of the Hindus was created by Vitasta or Jhelum, which has no rights to the water of the Jhelum, since Pakistan holds the water rights under the terms of the Indus Agreement.

In 1984 India proposed building a small dam across the Jhelum. The declared aim was to make the river more navigable at those times of the year when it naturally contained little water. But the government of Pakistan protested and got its way. In reality Pakistan possesses the right of veto; the question is, however: will they have the power to use it and would it be wise to do so? The problem is that Pakistan then will be seen as a force opposing Kashmir's development. In Kashmir also pro-Indian politicians criticise Delhi for not doing enough to secure more water for the region. They say: 'The government in Delhi has sacrificed the resources of Jammu and Kashmir'. The leaders of Kashmir argue that Kashmir needs water from the Jhelum, and should have the right to use some of it. The diplomatic reality is such that they cannot get it without the diplomatic support of New Delhi against Islamabad, because it will be Pakistan's agriculture that is impacted if Kashmir takes water out of the river in Kashmir. India points out a proviso in the Agreement that allows 'economic use' as long as the volume is not reduced and argues that this gives Kashmir some possibilities. But there are many in Kashmir who regard the Agreement as a straitjacket stifling all development, since it gives Pakistan all the waters of the Jhelum. Comprehensive development plans for Kashmir tend to come into conflict with the Indus Agreement. The demand for a new Indus agreement is growing stronger and stronger in Srinigar, the capital of Kashmir. The Legislative Assembly has officially undertaken an evaluation of the Agreement and demands that Kashmir be compensated for losses they have suffered as a result of the Agreement and that it is only natural that Pakistan must pay.

The government in Kashmir criticises Delhi for not making more forceful demands in relation to Pakistan. On several occasions India has considered bringing the Indus Agreement to an end if Pakistan is not willing to cooperate. Every time the situation between the two countries becomes more tense than normal the politicians bring out such proposals. But Indian politicians cannot, even if they wanted to, simply annul the Agreement because the consequences would be fraught with untold complexities. Not only would the international community most likely object to such a behaviour, but also it would open a Pandora's Box in terms of the complex internal balance of interests between different states with regard to the sharing of water. In the long run, however, it might well be that the Jhelum does the diplomatic job for India in relation to winning Kashmir over to the Indian side. Over time, restrictions on the use of the river will cause contradictions, particularly between Kashmir and Pakistan. By supporting some of Kashmir's plans, Delhi knows that its position in Kashmir will be strengthened, while Islamabad will appear to the world as being opposed to the economic development for Kashmir.

The Indus Agreement of 1960 was a diplomatic triumph and it has been crucial for maintaining peace between India and Pakistan. There can be no doubt that the expected growth in the population and the development strategies of the two countries are predicated on more water than they have, or on a completely new and more effective use of water than that which is in effect today. Moreover, a third actor has accordingly marched on to the stage – Kashmir, where increasing numbers demand that the Agreement be scrapped. Uncertainty over the fate of the glaciers in the Himalayas and Tibet also casts long shadows over the Indus Agreement's future. There are tremendous possibilities to save water in both countries, so the water crisis ought not to be overrated, but politicians might come to play out and make use of the water card as part of a wider political – strategic game. Whatever the reasons and motivations; there could be unanticipated consequences.

The Indus Agreement will most certainly come under growing pressure and this will increase the threat of mounting instability in an already unstable region. Since hundreds of millions of people are dependent on the water they get from this river, which will continue to provide the lifeblood of these countries, the disagreement between them has an enduring, rational and very real background that will not disappear even should the climate of cooperation improve at certain times. The struggle to control and make use of the Indus will continue to have great significance for the future of power relations in the region, and all the participants as well as the relevant international institutions have a lot of work to do if they are to succeed in establishing agreements and arrangements that can limit the open danger of further conflict.

44. The Bagmati, at the Pashupatinath Temple right outside the capital Kathmandu, is the most holy river in the country. Hindus come here for their purification baths and each year they throw the ashes of 5,000 to 6,000 corpses into this little river, which scarcely manages to wash away the bone fragments.

CHAPTER 15
WHERE THE MOST SACRED RIVER IS TOXIC

Every journey has its high points, and they are often unexpected. I travelled to Nepal and Kathmandu to see and take part in the celebrations for the birthday of Shiva, or in more cosmological terms to commemorate the day that Shiva appeared on earth, taking the visible form of the lingam or phallus at the Pashupatinath Temple just outside the capital city of Kathmandu. But what was to make the prime impression on me that day, and put the whole religious festival in a new light for me, was the sight of a middle-aged man running around in a t-shirt on which is written 'Do not touch the water'. He stands at the top of the stairway that thousands of the faithful will use when they descend to bathe in the waters of the holy river, right here at the most sacred place in the country. 'Don't touch the water in Bagmati! It is poisoned!'

I do not believe I have ever seen a clearer or more concrete expression of how economic development and rapid urbanisation can create conflict between faith and modernity. The man in the t-shirt personifies a simple act saturated with meaning and symbolic power.

The previous day I had walked along the river to the flat plains stretching toward Kathmandu. This most holy of all the holy rivers in Nepal flows 36 kilometres through the Kathmandu Valley before it joins the Ganges and runs on into India, past Varanasi, through Bangladesh and out into the sea in the Bay of Bengal. The topography at the top of the river makes it possible to understand the ecological background for the Hindu story of the creation of the river. It is told that the river was born when Shiva laughed and the river burst from his mouth.

The river runs pure, beautiful and clear for a great distance between the rocks it has borne down from the mountains. On the hillside above the northern bank is a Tibetan monastery. At the edge of the river, I pass by a whole series of Hindu temples with their altars and their *lingas* (or *lingums*). The combination of emerald-green fields, clear air, monotone Tibetan monastic music and Hindus throwing flowers into the sacred river create an aura of innocence and harmony, of rural holy peace.

And yet the closer I come to the capital the more the river changes character. The relationship between nature and society becomes more obviously out of balance with every kilometre I walk. The river does not become especially larger, yet it has been converted in a spectacular and rapid manner into something that, without exaggeration, becomes an artery of poison. Factories for dyeing carpets are placed along the river, one after another. Almost 100 have been established in recent years. Untreated chemicals from these factories run directly into the river. The waste of other industries, as well as the city sewage and excrement, are dealt with in the same way. Bagmati is derived from a word meaning 'mantra' or a 'current', a current of words bearing a story. The story it bears at the moment is a story of the costs of modernity.

Pashupatinath is located some kilometres upstream of the city. It is both a temple complex and the most holy of the holy sites in the country. The faithful stand in mile-long queues as they wait to enter the temple square. Holy men, or *saddus*, from India have achieved their goal of wandering all over the Indian subcontinent, and thousands of them have come here to bathe in the holy river, which is supposed to wash away all their sins and secure the fulfilment of their desires.

I remain in the temple square for two long days.

'I have consumed nothing but milk for the last ten years.' Paramahamsa Ram Krishna Das, the Milk Baba, an ascetic who lives for a great part of the year in one room at Pashupatinah, meets his disciples and swears that it is correct to take no other nourishment than milk (but for the additional nutrition of a vitamin pill and one glass of tea a day). A pale woman in her twenties, from the Netherlands or Germany, is sitting on a cushion in a corner of the room, not very communicative but listening. She told me that she finally had found her guiding light, the Milk Baba. The *saddus* sit or lie in groups around small fires on the temple square, smoking hashish and talking quietly to one another.

I speak with the holy men who had wandered miles and miles across the dry plains of India to this mountainous land about the state of the Bagmati and the role of water in Hinduism, while I gaze out over the blue-grey smoke of the funeral pyres and at people throwing ashes and bits of bodily remains into the murky shallow river.[52] Veneration of the water, which happens here, is a concrete expression of the non-material role played by water in many religions and cultures.[53] Here, as one finds in other major world religions, water is a symbol both of God and the divine, of paradise, and yes, of life itself. Almost all over the world, with its many different cultures, water has been accorded a central place in the cosmologies, myths and rituals, from baptism in Christianity, where water links people to God, to Hinduism where humans can escape from the eternal cycle of rebirth by being burned and thrown into the sacred rivers. When I see with what sensitivity the believers place lotus flowers on the dirty water, it becomes even more interesting to learn about how the art, music, poetry and the metaphors of language have been inspired by the shifting character of water, by its role as a fluid elixir that is in constant motion, not least because it is at the same time naturally and socially created, and thus has offered itself as a rich reservoir of metaphor. From such a perspective one is able to understand why Hindus in Bradford in England have wanted to convert a little stretch of the River Aire into a kind of English Ganges, where those who could not afford to visit India could still manage to throw the ashes into a busy river. In the words of their leader, 'It will be a sort of Ganges in Bradford'.[54]

It was on the birthday of Lord Shiva that the man in the t-shirt broadcast his message. There was a striking contrast between the significance of the river in the country's religious and spiritual life, and the stinking sewer that ran past the temple steps. Nobody bathed in this sacred river that day. The authorities had set up some water taps on the river bank, where water was piped in through plastic hoses from another source, so that people could at least wash themselves, but this had no religious function or dimension. The power of mythology or the concept of the sacred cleansing Bagmati could not, in this case, transcend realities. Even though the Hindu faith insists that by bathing in the Bagmati one is freed from the eternal cycle of death and reincarnation, and even though the faithful had walked and walked for days and weeks to reach the temple and pay respects to he who is lord of all living things in the universe, and this on Lord Shiva's birthday, they did not bathe. The man's shirt and his shouts symbolised a global conflict between rapid modernisation and traditional values, and more particularly, between the form that development has taken along Nepal's Bagmati River and the significance of people's religious symbols and rituals, and the core beliefs invested in it. To me, the Bagmati at Pashupatinah represented a kind of cultural outcast, one of modernity's losers. If Bagmati is a stream of words, a narrative, as Shiva described it, then today the river is telling me a depressing story.

'It is a catastrophe and a shame.' The old engineer, who had decided to use the last of his strength to save the river, is dispirited. I understand his frustration: the river is actually being used as a flowing rubbish dump. The glorious morning sun only serves to accentuate the misery and sorrow in the large eyes behind the engineer's thick spectacles. One does not have to travel very much in Nepal before one finds that the Bagmati is atypical of the Nepalese river system. Thousands of rivers with an enormous total volume of water (the total water flow is around 225 billion cubic metres) are streaming across the country, almost untouched, and on into India.[55] Indeed, this is why it is a popular country among rafting enthusiasts. The large rivers – the Karnali, the Kali Gandaki and Sapta Koshi – are all trans-Himalayan waterways. Together with small tributaries like the Bagmati they thus make up approximately half of the water flowing into the Ganges in India. Nepal has the potential to generate 83,000 megawatts of electricity. It is calculated that 42,000 megawatts of this potential could be developed.

Nepal is thus an upstream state to India, in contrast with Bangladesh and Pakistan. Increased water control in Nepal would be an advantage in many ways for the 600 million people living in the Ganges watershed. Electricity could be exported to a North India that has a large and growing demand for electrical energy but which is unable to satisfy these needs locally. Bangladesh would be happy to see water plants built that reduced the water in the river during large-scale flooding and that increased the flow of water during periods of drought. For its part, Nepal would like to sell hydro-electricity and improve the waterways such that they can become transport channels to the sea. In the dry season, the water flow in the Ganges is too low to cover the needs of India and Bangladesh. By regulating reservoirs in Nepal, the water flow could be increased by four times what it is at such periods today. This regulated flood could be used to water many millions of acres, more particularly in India and Bangladesh since Nepal itself possesses limited amounts of arable land.[56]

But the political power implicit in water control makes such rational solutions to the subcontinent's water problems highly unlikely. India will not build large dams in Nepal that might give a future anti-India Nepal possibly more power over India's life line rivers. And Nepal is not eager to undertake collaborations with India if India is not prepared to make concessions to Nepal, both economic and political. The prevailing attitude is that *no* agreement is better than a bad agreement.

Tensions increased between what were, at the time, the Hindu kingdom of Nepal and the Hindu nationalist government in India after India built the Tanakpur Dam across the Mahakali River in 1998, a river that runs along Nepal's western border with India. The political parties inside Nepal have criticised each other for selling out national interests cheaply to India; also because the project involves the relocation of more than 50,000 people. The River Kosi was known as the sorrow of the Indian state of Bihar, due to the flood catastrophes it produced, but now according to many in Nepal, it has become one of the sorrows of Nepal because India has shoved all the negative consequences of the project onto the weak upstream country. But it is a low-key criticism and has seldom been made official, with the notable exception of King Birendra who, before being shot in his own palace in June 2001, said that Nepal had been deceived by India.

I return once again to Pashupatinah. I sit on the stone steps that wind their way down to the river. The day after the festival the sight is even more depressing. With so much water flowing through the country, why is it that they cannot clean up here? I think of the pictures I have seen of posters about the River Thames in London in the 1850s, with the text 'A Cup of Death'. The Thames now runs clean.[57] Will the same thing happen to Nepal's most holy river? Nepal's development and stability are dependent upon India. In India both the implementation of the River Link Plan and the possibility of obtaining enough electrical power and extending it into the least-developed regions of the country are dependent upon Nepal. A burning question for the development of Nepal will certainly be the ability of the countries in the Ganges watershed to cooperate on the question of water.

45. Since the Tibetan Plateau is the water tower of not only Asia but also China, Beijing will always seek to exert control and influence over Tibet Autonomous Region.

CHAPTER 16
THE DARK HORSE ON THE ROOF OF THE WORLD

'Have you heard that the Chinese have built a dam over the Sutlej, across the Zada Gorge, or Lang Chen Khambab, in the western part of Tibet?' I met the well-informed Dutchman at the Yak Hotel in Lhasa. He told me the news, knowing my interest, and was obviously just as astounded as I am. No, I had not heard about this, I answered him, although it was a development of great geopolitical consequence. Could such a thing be true? What would the Indians say? I made my way immediately to one of the many internet cafes in Lhasa and checked it out. It was not mentioned in any of the news bulletins in the available international newspapers, but it turned out, I found out later, that his account was true. Satellite pictures have indicated that the dam is finished.[58] Perhaps China had informed its downstream neighbour, India, in advance, but in any case, they had said nothing publicly. And the Indian government was not speaking openly against it because this would only underline their weak downstream position. The challenge for India is that there is not even an agreement about sharing hydrological knowledge between China and India, even though almost all the large rivers on which India is absolutely and totally dependent, come from their great neighbour China.

China has great plans for the rivers and waters of the Himalaya Region and the Tibetan Plateau, including in Tibet Autonomous Region.

After some hours of driving from Lhasa I reach the high mountain pass; or rather, our driver's steady hand has brought us safely through an almost endless zigzag of hairpin bends and up so high, that the lake of Yamdrok Tso comes into sight. The lake has a deep turquoise colour that resembles nothing I have ever seen before, and at a height of almost 5,000 metres is nestled amid grass-clad hills and mountains with their light dusting of snow. Rather than an actual natural landscape, I am surprised to find it is looking more like a painting in which the artist has not been very careful with his selection of colours. Every summer, flocks of pilgrims come here to pray and receive blessings. They believe

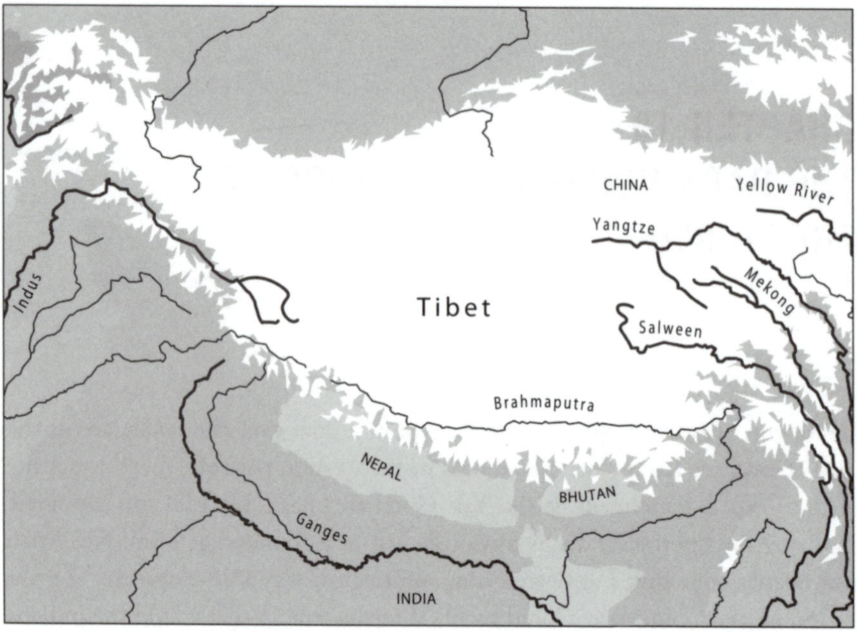

Map 6. Tibet is Asia's water tower, and the glaciers of the Himalayas are the water bank of Asia.

that the waters of this lake make the old young and the young wise and that this lake is where the actual life force of the Tibetan nation resides. Tibetan nationalists believe, and many exiled Tibetans also consider, that the lake must be protected in order for the nation to be protected. Before 1950 it was common for Tibetan leaders to come and place offerings in the waters of Yamdrok Tso. The Chinese have now begun to make use of the lake's water as a source of power. They have not been able to dam this turquoise lake because it has no outflow. Instead, they now pump water into tunnels, ten metres below ground level, which carry it through turbines and on down into the Brahmaputra. This is one of many projects that show the Chinese mean business when it comes to utilising the water resources of the region. Several of the state-owned hydro-electric giants have signed agreements with the government of Tibet regarding enormous hydro-electric projects, but so far they have moved slowly, partly because the local power needs have been rather modest. Many argue, and prominent among the opponents are exiled Tibetans, that building dams in Tibet is risky because the local ecology is highly vulnerable. They have already accused China of committing 'eco-murder'. China's political leaders counter this designation by arguing that they are modernising and developing Tibet.

In Tibet's Brahmaputra Valley, northwest of Lhasa, the distances are great

46. Yamdrok Tso is almost 5,000 metres above sea level. Every summer, flocks of pilgrims come here to pray and be blessed. They believe that the water in the lake makes the old young and children clever, and that this lake is the home of the life force of the Tibetan nation. The Chinese have now begun to harness the lake as a hydro-electric power source. They do not have to dam up the water because it has no outflow. Instead, they are pumping the water into tunnels, ten metres below the surface, and leading it through turbines and on down into the Brahmaputra.

between settlements, in contrast to the Brahmaputra watershed which, as a whole, is home to a population of 600 million. The sky has a milky blue colour here and some of the clouds are quite special, or rather the tails on the clouds are special, because they are formed by rainwater within the clouds evaporating into the atmosphere without ever falling to earth.

We stop by a suspension bridge across a river; it sways in the strong afternoon wind that sweeps through the valley bottom of this isolated landscape. The bridge is decorated with brightly-coloured traditional Tibetan prayer flags, packed tightly beside one another. My official guide, who has been detailed from the Chinese Foreign Ministry, has at last shown a few signs of enthusiasm. He, too, has to take pictures of the river from this vantage point.

'Our river looks small from here, but beautiful, don't you think?'

Backlit by the sun, between the flags standing almost on the perpendicular, the river shimmers like real gold, and appears to be a powerful artery of life-giving water rushing toward the dry plains of the Indian subcontinent. The

Brahmaputra, or Tsangpo ('the purifier') as it is called here, is one of many rivers running across the Tibetan Plateau – this great desolation – indeed, the completely rural, apparently bucolic atmosphere is made more poignant as I realise that this river is today, and will become even more so tomorrow, a player of world historical importance.

Brahmaputra, or 'the son of Brahma' as the river is called in India, as though to underline its religious, cultural and economic importance in the country, runs more than 1,000 kilometres across Tibet before it reaches Arunachal Pradesh in eastern India, and almost as far again as it crosses India and reaches the Bay of Bengal through Bangladesh. The volume of water is dependent mainly on the glaciers further inside the Tibetan Plateau as well as precipitation in northern parts of India and Bangladesh.

Until now the downstream states have had little to worry about in regard to developments in Tibet. The terrain itself, in league with technology and economic abilities, has combined to create a limited field of action. India has certainly expressed its worries; China's hydro-electric plans will impact the profile of seasonal water volumes. But now the situation is beginning to change. Beijing is giving increased priority to the dry regions of northwest China such that bringing in water from the Tibetan rivers becomes increasingly attractive. Experts at China's Academy of Sciences have conducted feasibility studies with regard to blasting away a mountain beside the Brahmaputra and thereafter building a gigantic dam project. The day that China decides to use more of the river for its own purposes, people living on the vast plains down toward the Indian Ocean will discover, perhaps to their great surprise that China is their water baron. If such a plan were to be implemented, India would certainly interpret it as an aquatic declaration of war, and for those planning to implement the most ambitious aspects of the National River Link Plan there, it would be a devastating setback.

China's upstream position in relation to India and other smaller countries in the region is potentially the trump card that no nation could expect it to surrender – either from threats of conflict or by appeals to good neighbourliness – and especially given that China is an economic superpower and that it will increasingly require more water itself. Beijing will most certainly continue developing the rivers as though they were national resources, just as they have developed the upstream Mekong without agreements of cooperation with other countries in that water basin. The international community will neither be powerful enough, nor have sufficient interest to pressure China to designate these waterways to be international rivers. Nor is it realistic to believe that the downstream states will be strong enough to challenge China. Thus, while they hope for a climate of political cooperation, or for increasing internal political discontent within

China to moderate her unilateral actions, what is most likely is that they will be forced to live with both the man-made and the climatic changes to the water volume of the rivers.

Tibet Autonomous Region and Himalaya Region, regions totally without historical traditions in terms of water control, will become a global focal point in the future of water management. Those who rule these areas will be the water lords of the continent. Today, for the first time in history, it is possible to utilise the rivers before they reach the Indian subcontinent. The potential of water as a means to power and as a source of conflict, and – in the best scenario – as a source of cooperation, will become ever more evident. There is no escaping the fact that downstream from where these rivers run across the Tibetan Plateau and Himalaya, lives half the world's human population. Ninety per cent of the water in the Tibetan rivers runs into India, Bangladesh, Nepal and Pakistan. Therefore, the struggle about how to share and make use of the waters of the Tsangpo or Brahmaputra, and the other rivers rushing down from the Roof of the World, will affect the future of the whole continent. China will not give up at any price the idea that Tibet or Tibet Autonomous Region is part of the greater nation, particularly if the rivers in the future are to contain less water because the glaciers have melted. Those who continue to dream about a Tibet independent of Beijing will be disappointed. For as long as Chinese state power is largely built around the taming of the waterways and the rivers flowing from the glaciers up in the high mountains, such a goal will remain unrealistic. Tibet is not only a water tower of Asia, but it is also that of China as well.

I return to the Yak Hotel for a dinner of Italian pasta, as well as a cold beer on the terrace, where I am able to sit undisturbed and watch Lhasa's street life below. I have also come here to look for the Dutchman who told me about Sutlej: I forgot to ask him if he knew anything else about Tibet's water sector. I do not find him. He is probably on his way to Mount Everest.

47. Grotte Massabielle, Lourdes.

CHAPTER 17
'COOL' WATER – PARIS AND LOURDES

It is Saturday morning, very hot, and I am almost alone on the boat that carries tourists along the Seine in Paris. The Eiffel Tower, Notre Dame Cathedral, and the Louvre. (I had been to the Louvre the day before – one among six million other tourists to visit annually – and among other things, I saw the stone tablet of Hammurabi, emblem of the Mesopotamian civilisation from the thirteenth century BC because it contains the first known laws about how water was to be entered into jurisprudence.) These world-famous buildings located along the banks of the Seine help to emphasise the river's natural place in the history of the city.[59]

I fall into a state of calm, thanks to the baking sun and feel that the present is slipping away, a feeling that only travel gives rise to. I have seen these buildings before, and in my half-asleep dream state I can clearly comprehend how Napoleon built the Arc de Triumph together with Jean-Paul Sartre. I am suddenly brought back to reality by a Swedish couple some rows of seats behind me. The man is delivering a long, irritating tirade in a loud voice about a football player. I scramble ashore at the very next jetty.

In one of the small streets not far from the Garden of the Tuileries I find what I am looking for: Europe's first water bar, Le Colette. It is located in the basement of a trendy boutique that sells music, designer jewellery, designer books and designer clothing. Guests in the minimalistically furnished premises can choose between around 100 different brands of bottled water.[60]

'This place is very popular among the fashion slaves', says the barman, holding aloft a bottle from New York. The water waiter makes a presentation of the waters in various different bottles as though they were vintage wines. While I look over the premises and examine the various bottles, I am asked to taste the different brands, although each time I have tasted one, I am faced with a problem, a big problem: that of identifying the differences between them. As I listen to the water waiter's monotone assessment of the relative merits of the various brands, what I find easier to understand is that the struggle to control pure untouched water will increase all around the world. Bottled water has become more expensive than oil. It can cost 5,000 times as much as tap water and is normally 3,000 times more expensive.

The bottled water industry is growing rapidly, not only in the West but all over the world. While Le Colette is a pure water bar, many classy restaurants today have water menus in addition to their wine card. These menus are frequently long and include both national and imported brands – highly exaggerated examples of what is a new historical phenomenon – drinking water is being sent millions of kilometres from one specific source where it occurs in nature, to the customer's cafe table in one large city or another around the world. This new social and global phenomenon has spread with monstrous speed and has most likely come to stay. Along with the growth in both the popularity and the price of bottled water, a new and potentially lucrative competition is intensifying over the control of particular water sources.

At the same time, there is an increasing cultural struggle over bottled water and its social significance. For instance, the largest Protestant Church in Canada has initiated a large-scale campaign to get people to stop drinking bottled water. They see it as one of the most important ethical questions of our time. As they put it, a gift from God must not fall prey to market forces. The pragmatic argument is the price. In Canada, they argue, bottled water usually cost 3,000 times more than tap water. The Church argues that even if it tastes the same and is not more healthy than tap water, bottled water has become a fashion statement, leading to a few large companies making a great deal of money, while poor families will waste their money on unnecessary products. But this moral fight seems to be a losing battle. Precisely because everybody must have water, and because the drinking of water is the most normal of all normal activities in the world, it becomes a particularly powerful marker of social well being and social inequality. The absurd price differences are paradoxically one reason for the current market success.

As I cast a glance along the bar I ponder over what Pierre Bourdieu would have said about this. This French sociologist was famous for his work on taste and how people in the course of their everyday lives choose between what they consider aesthetically pleasing and what they consider to be unattractive, either fashionable or bluntly put, ugly. He concluded that snobbery was an integral part of bourgeois being. The various choices that are made are always undertaken in opposition to choices made by other social groups or classes. Taste is not pure or neutral. Bourdieu discovered a world of meaning within this social sphere which – and here it becomes interesting – at the same time functions as a system of power relations and as a symbolic system where small differences in taste become the basis for social reputation and social evaluation.

But what strikes me when I look around this water bar is that Bourdieu's theory of taste might be too subtle and of too fine a mesh to explain what is happening here. To me, a bar such as this functions as an intellectual insult with a repulsive self-aggrandising affectation, where the whole point is to initiate the drinking of water as a field where social difference can be demonstrated and practised in what is seemingly an ordinary social setting.

Of all the places I have visited around the world, there are few that so bluntly and unsentimentally celebrate the differences, not between the West and the rest, or between civilisations, but between the rich and the poor. Waters of distinction are carried thousands of miles so that I and other guests are able to fill our mouths with what everyone on the planet must have. While they play techno-jazz in the background and as the bar acquires a mixed atmosphere of the eternal lightness of being and the hectic nature of the modern style of life,

48. More than a billion people have no fresh water piped into their dwellings. The UN says that 80 per cent of the hospital beds of Asia, Africa and Latin America are occupied by patients with water-borne diseases. Millions of women spend many hours each day obtaining the water their families require in order to live. The pipe in the photo is called a 'Life Straw', a personal water cleanser that the producers hope will help millions of people.

I see in my mind's eye the 2 billion people who do not have running water and must forage and scavenge to get it wherever they can, because I have certainly seen them, these women in Bangladesh or Ethiopia who themselves, thanks to television, have become a cliché of underdeveloped countries. And indeed, the longer I sit here the more real do these women become, walking and walking, hour after hour in the heat, to get water for their families – a sick child perhaps, a dying mother. Because 6,000 people, most of them children, die every day as a result of drinking unclean water.

The way water is distributed in many large cities in Africa, Asia and Latin America makes it more expensive the poorer one is. The slum-dwellers are not linked to the network because they are not good at paying their bills. As a consequence, they are handed over to the 'water mafia', who lay waste to the poor quarters of the cities. The poorest in the world have no choice. In order to survive they need just as much water as do the richest. Many find themselves in the grip of a poverty from which they cannot free themselves because they have to use a large proportion of their income – in the cities as much as one-third – to obtain enough water, without which they could not live. This is one of the reasons why a solution to the water problem will be fundamental to solving the problem of poverty in general.

At their summit meeting in Johannesburg in 2002, world leaders adopted a statement that agreed clean drinking water was one of the century's most important development goals. By 2015 the proportion of people who do not have access to clean drinking water and decent sanitation must be cut by half. For this to come into effect, 300,000 people have to be brought into grids of piped water every day, at a cost of $25 billion per annum. It is a grand goal but it is hopelessly unrealistic. The problem is not simply that such pious goals create a rather inflated impression of a 'world society' that takes action on such issues; it is also about what it is able to achieve: the lack of realism about these good intentions exposes and expresses a definite way of conceptualising development making the world incomprehensible.

'I don't let anything upset me', he says with determination. The man who wants to talk to me is immaculately dressed and has travelled in from Lyons for a conference in the capital on the subject of the pedagogical computer games. 'And I have never tried to find out where I come from, or anything about myself. It is action that interests me.' That is one way of putting it, I think to myself, looking down at the designer bottle of Voss water.

Not far from the left bank of the Seine and the trendy restaurants of Paris, one is able to step into a world where discussions about secular modernity and postmodernity are replaced by the cultivation of the 'water of life' and faith in miracles, confirmed by the actions of millions of people every year. The myopia of our modern industrial culture easily creates the impression that the worship and cultivation of water is something that belongs to the past, or to more 'primitive' societies. But despite the fact that the past century has seen the transformation of the river landscapes around the world, and that the governments of Israel, Australia, Saudi Arabia and the USA are sending aircrafts up to spray the clouds, and that the water has been run through pipes, and in many places the rivers that flow across the landscape are arteries of poison, despite all of this, there have never been so many people cultivating water as is now the case at the beginning of the new millennium.

Every year, between 3 and 5 million people come to Lourdes, at the foot of the Pyrenees with its holy waters. With the exception of Rome, more pilgrims are be found in this small French town with its holy water than at any other place in the Christian world. The shops that ring the basilica are completely commercialised. Here it is not the pushy, garish religiosity that catches my attention but rather the mercenary spirit. Large and small water bottles are hanging everywhere on display, some in the form of a Virgin Mary figure, others as normal water casks, roughly like the ones nowadays found on ordinary campsites all over Europe. What is slightly absurd is to see people wander down the crowded modern shopping streets, with a cigarette or an evening edition of *Le Soir* in one hand, and a little bottle of Virgin Mary water in the other. But within the gates, in the square in front of the basilica, in the midst of the noisy mass of people from all nations of the world, where one is surrounded by thousands of the afflicted in no condition to walk on their own, and who have been brought by their assistants from the holy waters to the holy baths, it is hard not to be moved by their silence during the procession, the choral hymns rising into the air; indeed, the song with its prayer for help seems to envelope the whole place. I witness an expression of the strength of faith and prayer, a collective action to help the thousands upon thousands who hold onto an obvious and sincere hope, perhaps a last hope, that the curative water shall restore them to health.

Here at Lourdes, in the country where the rationalism of modernity made its breakthrough, water is making a come back as 'the water of life', not only as a religious symbol but also as an affirmation and a medium of God. I have stood, all told, a couple of days in the patient queue of the hopeful, in front of the water that trickles out from the many taps installed right below the basilica, and some metres to the left of the sacred spring. Here, everyone carries a bottle of water (or several), whatever the design. The mood in the queue exudes at the same time seriousness and normality. People are not in the least bashful about filling their bottles with water, or of displaying their faith in the efficacy of this common substance. No one makes fun of themselves or what they are in the process of doing, namely, filling bottles with holy water to take home with them, to Sydney or Zagreb. What is taking place before my eyes is at one level a quiet and perhaps unarticulated protest against the idea of the triumph of scientific rationalism, using water as its medium.

The status of Lourdes comes from a very simple, and some will say, rather moving story. On 11 February 1858, the Virgin Mary appeared for the first time in the Massabielle Grotto, in front of 14-year-old Bernadette Soubirous, the asthmatic daughter of a miller. She was the eldest of nine children in a poor family. An event happened four days later that put Lourdes on the map and assured it a foremost place in Christendom, and which at the same time made the place so interesting from a water perspective. According to Bernadette's later accounts, the Virgin Mary said, 'Go and drink at the spring and wash yourself in the water'. Bernadette did not see any water when, as commanded, she went off to the grotto. The Virgin Mary pointed her finger as to where Bernadette was to look, in under the large stone that hung over the entrance to the grotto. She found a little water, more like mud. It was such a small amount that she could scarcely get a little into her hand. Three times she threw it away because it was so dirty. The fourth time, she managed to drink it. People who had heard rumours of the visitations streamed to the site and continued the task of clearing away the muck. The water became clearer and ran more and more. That very first day it was possible to fill two bottles with the water collected from the grotto and to carry them to the nearest town.

Stories arose immediately about how, by drinking the water, people were cured of serious illnesses. In March 1858 the first of seven miracles occurred, which the Pope would declare authentic in 1862. A pregnant woman stuck her hands in the water of the grotto and her two paralyzed fingers began to move as they should. Some years later the Pope decided that the Virgin Mary had indeed revealed herself to Bernadette, also because research had shown that the water did not have any special physical or chemical properties. When in 1933, about 70 years later, Bernadette was canonised, Lourdes became world-famous. Sixteen baths were set up in 1955. Hundreds are bathed every day. The assistants stand on either side of the bather, lean the patient backwards, hold the body submerged under the water for a few seconds, and then, next, please!

Europe's most sacred water runs from the many taps of Lourdes. People come from all over the world to drink it, and to take it home, just as for thousands of years Hindus have taken home water from the Ganges, bearing it right across the Indian subcontinent on foot, or similarly, as Muslims carrying water from

Mecca for centuries, on pilgrimages by camel across the African savannah, all the way to Mali and Mauritania. Millions believe that it is precisely this water that accomplishes miracles, that its miraculous properties can cure illness, wash sins from the soul and extend one's life on earth.

Many attempts to comprehend the history of human ideas have presented this as a straight line of development from primitive magic via modern religion to science. According to this paradigm, primitive peoples use rituals in a mechanical and instrumental fashion. Magic is reduced to an expression of primitive people's lack of ability to distinguish between one's own subjective associations and external objective reality. The processions at Lourdes are an expression of these three forms: scientific methods have been employed in the search for evidence that the spring really works; the whole setting and atmosphere is deeply religious, and at the same time there is an apparent element of magic in play. Down through history there have been individuals, groups and movements treating sicknesses by non-medical means. Illness is viewed as one or another manifestation of evil. The journeys of pilgrims to holy places and the prostrating of oneself before a sacred object – these have long been an important means of healing. From the very earliest times such healing cults have been associated with sources of water. For example, there is evidence of Neolithic and Bronze Age practices held at a whole series of springs across Western Europe.

The basilica, the grotto and the crosses that hang from the ceiling above the sacred spring therefore represent a renewal of a long and deep water cult in European history. Lourdes is an example not of people throwing themselves at the mercy of water and its power, but rather of their perceptions of the power of water. The quiet processions of people rolling along in wheelchairs toward the sacred water can also be seen as a protest against the omnipotence of human beings over nature, carried out not while facing thunderous waterfalls, a rising ocean or the force of monsoons, but rather facing a modest jet of water in a spring.

PART 3
WATER TRANSFORMING THE WORLD

49. 'The wise man's transformation of the world arises from solving the problem of water', Lao Tze. This picture is of a geothermal plant in Iceland.

INTRODUCTION TO PART 3

The wise man's transformation of the world arises from solving the problem of water.
Chinese sage Lao Tze, 3,000 years ago

Man reaches ever higher, while water runs to the lowest point.
Taoist tract *Guanzi*

It is generally overlooked, but one of the deepest and most fundamental movements in world history has been the gradual liberation of human beings from the power exerted by springs, rivers and lakes in determining where they settle and build and what they produce. Whilst animals must still flock to waterholes day after day and year after year, humans have become increasingly clever at moving water to where they live and have need for it. Whereas the ancient city of Jericho could be established because the nomads found a spring in a dry desert area (the inhabitants built a wall to defend themselves and the city's very foundation, the water source), today's large cities and large-scale agricultural schemes can be located hundreds of kilometres from springs, large rivers and lakes because of modern societies' ability to build huge dams, dig long canals and pump enormous amounts of water up from deep underground aquifers.

This part of the book describes how gigantic plans are going to change the appearance of considerable portions of the planet, more radically and in a much shorter time than at any previous epoch in history. Humans moving water is nothing new: the evolution of state societies, or civilisations, has been predicated upon diverting and controlling water. It has been a decisive activity that has helped the creation of civilisation. When for the first time human beings conveyed water from the large rivers of the Middle East into the surrounding dry desert regions they thereby laid the basis for a kind of agricultural production that over the course of the years yielded sufficient surpluses to keep alive soldiers, artisans, administrators, artists and poets who did not themselves have to cultivate the land or hunt for food. In these ways, forms of state administration could be established and sustained. The moving of water is therefore an act that fundamentally binds together the past and the future. It expresses a deep continuity of our whole evolution as a species.

More than anything else, this journey in water shows that what Chinese sage and philosopher, Lao Tze, pointed out 3,000 years ago is more relevant today than ever: 'The wise man's transformation of the world arises from solving the problem of water.' Many people, particularly in Western Europe and the USA, have for some time tended to believe that the era of the mega-projects is over, because in post-modern societies such projects have become politically unpopular and are no longer carried out within the same sense of national urgency. But it is actually now, during this very same period, that we are able to witness the implementation of the world's largest ever hydro-projects; and in the coming decades they will not only change the physical appearance of large parts of the globe but also determine the development of central countries and regions, as well as the stability and authority of important geopolitical state actors. The growing fear of rising sea levels, flooding rivers and devastating drought will lead to a situation where the struggle to control water, in an increasing number of countries, will be given higher priority.

Parallel with the growing number of warnings about an impending global water crisis, increasing numbers of gigantic reservoirs of fresh water are being discovered underground and beneath the bottom of the oceans; and, in addition, desalination technology will come increasingly into play as time goes by. Many self-declared experts and international institutions have for years now been talking about the global water crisis – but there is no such global water crisis: there are regional and local water crises, partly due to the natural character of the water system that societies depend on, and partly due to the lack of ability to control, manage, utilise and distribute the available water. As has been the case throughout the whole of human history, the way that water will be used and moved, in the future will have a fundamental importance for settlement patterns, the relations between city and countryside, as well as for the power struggles between countries. In addition to all of this, water will become the fuel of the future, and at NASA they are talking about how discoveries of water on the moon and Mars could be our 'ticket to the universe'.

50. The USA is the breadbasket of the world but its agriculture is to a great extent dependent upon artificial irrigation. The western USA is an oasis civilisation in a climate that is naturally desert or semi-desert. It is only gigantic water-moving projects that have made large portions of the 'sun belt' inhabitable. It is no wonder that many look to water-rich Canada as the solution to the USA's water problem.

CHAPTER 18
CALIFORNIA DREAMING

The writer Mark Twain once said, 'In California whisky is for drinkin' and water is for fightin' over'. The governor of Arizona has charged that Nevada and Las Vegas have been stealing water from the Colorado River 'at gunpoint', but through the window of my taxi as I am driven down the Strip in Las Vegas I see no sign of this atmosphere of crisis, nor do I see a city suffering from lack of water. Rather, what I see is modernity fitted out in its most grandiloquent way, but also at its most seductive and fascinating, a kind of postmodern pilgrimage centre that can be conceived as Modernity staging itself. Like some enormous exotic plant of steel and concrete, this desert city stretches toward the sky as if it derives nourishment from the stars above. From being a dusty rest stop established by Mormons a little more than a century ago for people travelling through the desert, Las Vegas has been transformed into the world Mecca for gambling and the entertainment industry.

In the course of a few decades, this desert settlement was transformed into a watery Urban Neon Paradise. In the city-centre there are veritable cascades of water from huge fountains, shining and glistening in the neon lights all along the main streets, and acres and acres of swimming pools. The city's nostalgia is directed completely toward the present, underlined by weird imitations of Roman temples and fountains, by a pyramid-shaped hotel, and a complete hotel complex built as a model of Manhattan. The city *is* the present tense, surrounded by artificial objects and technology and it is precisely this that makes Las Vegas so brutally fascinating but also so interesting from a historical perspective. Nowhere else have I ever seen the belief expressed – so energetically, urgently and with such total certainty – that the battle against nature has been decisively won.

At the gaming tables and around the slot machines of these, the world's largest hotels, with 4-5,000 beds, and where Elvis held his farewell concert and where later Mike Tyson bit off the ear of Evander Holyfield, scantily-clad serving ladies provide drinks for those of us playing, each for himself and himself alone, pulling away at the one-armed bandits. The real game in Las Vegas, however, the one determining its fate, is taking place at the water negotiating tables and on the drafting boards of the water engineers. For in Las Vegas, a mental picture of show and illusion itself, the biggest and most widespread of all illusions is the idea that the city can continue to splash around in water.

In reality, the water crisis is already closing in on Las Vegas. In spite of the fact that the city is built on sand and surrounded by desert, the consumption of water per inhabitant is among the highest in the world. The city is located in one of the driest parts of one of the most precipitation-poor states in the USA. Moreover, like large parts of the USA, it is dependent upon the Colorado River, where Nevada is already using the maximum amount of water that is available. Sources of underground water in the Las Vegas Valley are being pumped up considerably more quickly than the water is able to filter back underground. Las Vegas over-uses its aquatic capital; its natural water bank account is inexorably overdrawn. The city is faced with importing water from other groundwater reservoirs or from sources farther away. The engineers have built a water tunnel at a cost of several billion dollars that brings in water from the man-made

51. The USA is a water-rich country but the water is unevenly distributed. Parts of the country suffer chronic drought conditions. This is Lake Mead, which was created by the Hoover Dam and is the reservoir that provides water to, among other places, the desert city of Las Vegas, Arizona and southern California. The white ring on the stone comes from minerals in the water. This photo was taken in 2007 and shows the effects of both seven years of lower than normal precipitation (and, therefore, lower water volume in the Colorado River) and steadily increasing water use.

Lake Mead. Otherwise, the authorities can try to renegotiate and exert pressure to get more water from the Colorado River than the existing accords allow them. The struggle for water is about to become just as turbulent as the river itself.

Las Vegas has been hailed as the capital of laissez-faire capitalism. The question is, can it continue to be, and if so, for how long? In the long run, water consumption has to be reduced, but who should bite the bullet and start the process? This is the question that will haunt the whole region in the coming decades. Las Vegas continues to welcome new inhabitants and new enterprises. No city in the USA has been growing faster. Without the government taking a strong stand in establishing and enforcing new initiatives and compulsory regulations, it is doubtful that the water crisis can be solved. Over time, will a persistent condition of scarcity – with regard to a resource so vital to the city's hotels, the inhabitants' gardens and the economy of the whole Las Vegas Valley – lead to the development of a stronger state at the expense of the scope that the market and the liberal institutions currently enjoy?

I have just returned from a drive through the scorching desert that surrounds the city. I walk through the door into the 'Mirage' hotel, only to be confronted immediately by an enormous artificial garden with streams, waterfalls and fountains that refreshingly embrace guests as they make their way to the swimming pools or gaming rooms. At this moment it strikes me that no other city, either now or in the past, could exude the same contemptuous disregard for the limits that nature places on society's development – or with the same careless matter-of-factness.

The pioneers of enormous modern irrigated agriculture in the western USA are the Mormons. For them irrigation has to do with making real the prophecies of Josiah, who predicted that when Jesus returns to earth, the deserts shall 'rejoice and blossom as the rose . . . for in the wilderness shall the waters break out, and stream in the desert'. Inspired by the Bible's description of the divinity of water, the nineteenth century Mormons were in the vanguard of a social movement that came to transform the American Great Plains and desert into the world's breadbasket. Mormon leader, Brigham Young, developed a religious – ideological project with enormous practical consequences. There have been very few who have succeeded as well in converting ideology into action. He practised polygamy – he had 27–56 wives and 56 children – but he also managed to spread fertility to the desert. His Utopia was not realised but by the 1850s they had founded a series of towns and cities, including Salt Lake City, or the New Jerusalem, which would become the world capital of the Latter Day Saints, and which was located beside a river that, inspired by the Bible, they called the 'Jordan'. By the beginning of the twentieth century, Mormon settlements stretched over one-sixth of continental America and consisted of more than 500 carefully planned towns.

The Hoover Dam, which when built across the Colorado River in the 1930s was the largest dam in the world, is perhaps the foremost symbol of the American state in the form of the US Bureau of Reclamation taking over what the Mormons had started, but on a completely different economic and technical scale. The dam, and the network of water utilisation plans it entailed, quickly became a paradigm for complete and monumental water control and management. It was copied all over the world. When I stand at the rim of the dam and look down into the deep blue river, surrounded as it is by the completely bare, red and wild mountains encircling the river, it is not difficult to understand the optimism that enveloped the latter part of the Depression. It was in itself the symbol of Franklin D. Roosevelt's New Deal politics. New canals, thousands of kilometres in length, were excavated. Cities like Los Angeles, Phoenix, Las Vegas and San Diego could become big cities and southern California could become a leading agricultural region. (The story about how Los Angeles got its water from the Owen Valley in opposition to the ranchers there was made famous by the film, *Chinatown.*) As if by means of a miracle, the dam made possible the biblically-inspired dream of the Mormons, only on a completely new scale.

But now both the dam, and the potential of the Colorado, have been realised and used up. The river is used to grow vegetables in California and grapes in New Mexico; it is an El Dorado for whitewater rafting in Arizona and for fishing in Nevada, and is used in the swimming pools and in the ice cubes of drinks served in Las Vegas. Everyone wants to have more of the Colorado, particularly the cities farthest to the south, in what is often called 'the sun belt', and they stick their guzzling pipes into the riverbed. But nothing more can be teased out of it. Nevertheless, many and growing demands are being asked of the river because needs are increasing.

The California River Aqueduct, through Arizona and into the cities in southern California, gives the impression of being a river as it winds its way through the desert for several hundreds of kilometres; but it is the work of technology not of nature. This 'river' stands for big business and big government, not for romance or individualism. In the middle of the desert, with my back up against the fence that protects the aqueduct, I hear the refreshing sound of running water: not the playful sound of water in a stream running over stones, but rather water controlled behind mile after mile of brick walls – and it is this canal that provides water to Los Angeles and southern California. In many parts of California there is no rain whatsoever between May and October – precisely when the demand for water is greatest.

Two-thirds of the states within the USA report that they will suffer serious shortages of water in the coming decades. The water crisis is particularly threatening in the southwest, where the economy and the population are growing most rapidly. Cities and agriculture are fighting over water. Farmers in California have been forced to accept that they are being deprived of water, which instead of coming to them is being sent to water-thirsty cities. 'I want to go and walk on water', I tell the farmer whom I have tracked down.

He does not immediately know what I am talking about. Do I look like a born-again Christian? I am in Bakersfield, and in this part of California farmers and large agro-industrial corporations have constructed vast underground facilities called water banks. These collect surface water in geological cavities underground. Since the thirst for water is so great in the state, they choose to save it in these water banks until they can sell it at the most favourable point in time to the nearby cities; in other words, when the need is great and the price is right.

'The water crisis', I say, about to tell him what I am looking for. But he interrupts me, suddenly understanding. 'Follow me', he says.

He shows me a large field. It looks like the ordinary fields to be found in other places but directly under the surface, is a water reservoir, albeit artificial.

The states are fighting over water, and in California and parts of the western USA the authorities are raising their voices in alarm.[61] Former US President George W. Bush with a career in the Texas oil industry, said that water is more important than oil. The rivers have been used up and the groundwater is pumped out more quickly than it refills. It has been calculated that agriculture in the USA is losing $400 billion each year due to the lack of water. California for long the world's fifth largest economy yet it is extremely precipitation-poor. Although it is known as 'The Golden State', getting this as the official state nickname in 1968, water has been its most precious resource. From the gold rush in the mid-1800s, when towns grew up wherever the rivers washed and exposed gold, and on up to the present, water and its ever more intense control have determined the settlement patterns and the landscape. As a society, California is barely 100 years old and in the course of this short period has radically altered the waterscape. Yet it has done so without finding a long-term and sustainable solution to its hydraulic problems, problems which hold it in a vice-like grip. Local newspapers are writing increasingly often about local water conflicts. It might well be asked whether California's water and irrigation system – one of the most costly water taps in the world – is indeed, as some have maintained, a painstakingly prepared set of blueprints for an ecological catastrophe?

From the man-made oases of California I travel to the north, to Chicago, Illinois and the extreme water rich parts of North America, drive along Lake

Michigan and on into Canada, where I stay overnight on a houseboat on Lake Erie, and wake to the golden September light over a calm, milky blue lake whose surface hides how polluted it is. I am on my way to the distant dream of my childhood – the Niagara Falls where I, like everybody else, am given a blue rain slicker as I catch the boat that takes us in under the falls. As we stand there, getting wetter and wetter, and I am thrilled by simply finally being there, a tall guy starts talking to me – or rather bellowing in my ear due to the noise from the falling water – about the economic and political actors who want to utilise the enormous up-stream lakes. They plan the greatest engineering project ever seen in the USA, he says. I tried to answer him, politely but almost screaming, that this was very surprising; I had thought this old idea was dead. A whole series of proposals for dealing with the water crisis have been discussed in the USA: everything from transporting water in gigantic plastic balloons from northern California, to towing icebergs down from Alaska, to pumping water through pipes from the Ogallalla Reservoir under the American Great Plain. Centrally placed politicians have said again and again that the USA also has to get water from Canada. The reason is obvious: Canada is awash with water, and although such figures are imprecise, it has been said that Canada has 20 per cent of the total water in the world. Thus Canada is in competition with Brazil to become the world's water giant. Many plans have been advanced. One of them is called the GRAND Canal: the Great Recycling and Northern Development Canal. Part of this plan is the proposal to send new water into the Great Lakes, and from there, on to the Sunbelt in the southern USA, and perhaps further, to Mexico. The plan was abandoned in the 1980s but now there are those who want to revive it, or at least elements of the original plan. There is very strong opposition to these plans in both the USA and Canada. There are many opposed to giving away water to their powerful southern neighbour. Others, however, say that in the light of the North American Free Trade Agreement, Canada's water has to be considered a continental and not a national resource. What is going to happen if the southern states and the government in Washington DC, from differing perspectives, come to push this issue forward with greater force in the future? And, even more to the point, if heavyweight actors in Canada consider both the building of these projects and the sale of water as economically (and not least politically) expedient? On our way back and before we disembarked I had received an update on American water transfer visions, which was useful although the conversation destroyed my experience of the power and nature of the Niagara Falls.

Ken Heard, the director of the Tampa plant, shows me around the water factory and tells me that the plant was planned to produce 37,000 cubic metres of water a day; and, if so desired, could produce up to 95,000 cubic metres I am on the southeast tip of the USA, in Tampa Bay on the west coast of Florida, facing the Gulf of Mexico. This is an area of powerful growth, where people are attracted to the good life beneath the palm trees and the warm sun. While there is now a population of 2.7 million in the Bay, at the time of the first census in 1850 there were 974 inhabitants. Out along the sea there are long rows of very large houses – almost palaces to the eyes of a middle-class European – with emerald-green lawns the size of a modest football pitch. There are definitely many reasons to be here, and not least for those who enjoy American football and the Tampa Bay Buccaneers. But my reason for being here is to see something that is less well-known but which is nonetheless more significant: I am visiting the largest desalination plant in the western hemisphere.

Hundreds of desalination plants, big and small, are built annually, with the largest located in Saudi Arabia and the United Arab Emirates.[62] Israel has the goal of being able to provide 15 per cent of its water needs from desalination by 2017; and in the Canary Islands a technological revolution is following in the footsteps of mass tourism, with most hotels there producing their own water. To date, the roughly 16,000 existing plants produce less than one per cent of water consumed worldwide. But the demand is increasing, not least because increasing numbers of water-thirsty cities with populations in the millions are situated on coasts and because two out of every three people on earth now live within 50 kilometres of the ocean.

Tampa Bay is a typical representative of such a coastal city, although a little more prosperous than most, and with more political will to investigate new technology in practice. At regular intervals over the course of the last decade, *The St. Petersburg Times* and *The Tampa Tribune* have written about local water wars and water shortage. The gap between demand for water and access to water increases. The urban area does not produce enough water to keep up with the increase in consumption and it is pumping up too much of the groundwater. The authorities say that the water situation is not sustainable in the long run and already the situation is perilous in dry periods. As a result, the authorities have begun building, right outside Tampa City, the largest plant in the western hemisphere to convert sea water into fresh water. The global desalination industry is following closely what is happening here at this plant, due to its size, technology and competitiveness. The process is based on a technique called reverse osmosis. Salt water is pressed through membranes at great force, leaving salt on one side and good, clean potable fresh water on the other.

The Tampa plant consists of the factory itself, with seven independent reverse osmosis systems and their respective components, an intake of sea water, a waste system for the residual brine, various chemical storage facilities and a 24 kilometre transmission network for the water produced. The fresh water produced is sent out to a 20,000 cubic metre tank near the plant, where it is stored before being pumped into the city's distribution system. He tells me that the desalination system is still facing a series of problems and as a result the start-up has been delayed. He tells me this with what is almost a haunted look, caused, I think to myself, by all the difficulties they have encountered, and which he lays out before me in persuasive detail. But in spite of these problems, or precisely because of them, his faith in the worthwhile nature of what they are doing, not only for Tampa Bay but also for all coastal places with water problems, is all the more convincing.

For he is correct – desalination is hardly a technological cul-de-sac. Uncertainty about the future patterns of precipitation and the fate of the glaciers and natural river systems makes desalination one of the more attractive solutions, since it can produce water independent of flood and drought. And since the price of water is generally rising, this relatively costly technology will more easily become competitive. As a spokesman for the industry, he says, he is quite sure that within a few years human beings will succeed in producing cheap water.

If the industry succeeds, it will have unimaginable consequences regarding where cities can be located and how big they can become. And the march toward the coast will increase. Air conditioning makes desert cities liveable. In the same way, coastal cities that can make their own water, will constantly draw more people to them, almost like a sponge – people who are, as some would say, environmental refugees from dry interior regions. Current attempts – from Israel to the Persian Gulf, and from China to the USA – to produce cheap drinking water from seawater represent the beginnings of a vision of a future where we can ignore the boundaries that nature's water imposes on the evolution and development of society. If the attempts succeed, it will put to shame predictions of a global water crisis, and will create a level of predictability, with regard to water access, that will make societies that are dependent upon the vicissitudes of nature for their access to water, appear to be almost prehistoric. There are even those who have seriously proposed that a multitude of desalination installations could be an appropriate human counter-move to rising sea levels: by pumping salt water out of the oceans at strategic places and converting it into fresh water for our use, the oceans could be held in check!

Great technological advances have been made in recent years. Anyone who has been on a modern sailing boat knows they have the facility to produce their own water. Aboard such a vessel one is amongst the first people in history to be able to move around free from the limits normally imposed on people by the

52. As they cross the world's oceans, these sailboats point to another future. The crews have escaped from the imperative power that the localising of fresh water has always exerted over human movement. They make their own water and therefore are free.

location of fresh water sources or by the necessity to carry water with them on their journeys. Crews on the modern racing sailing boats are in this sense the first free human beings: they have overcome a decisive factor that has always limited human mobility. When they head out to the open sea without tanks of stored water obtained from inland fresh water sources they are perhaps also setting course toward a completely different future, one where nature's available fresh water will no longer be a limit placed on other human activities.

53. The Mubarak Pumping Station, which uses electricity generated by the Nile, pumps Nile water out into the Sahara Desert so that a new Nile civilisation can be created. Speaking about this project, the Egyptian Minister of Water said that it is 100 times larger than the pyramids.

CHAPTER 19
A NEW NILE VALLEY IN THE SAHARA

I am on my way up the Nile in Egypt, from the pulsating metropolis of Cairo with its almost 20 million people in daytime, to one of the hottest places on earth in the southern desert, to take a look at what the Egyptian water ministry has planned as a turning point in Egyptian history. I once again make a stop in Aswan in Upper Egypt, this beautiful city on the eastern side of the Nile, with long promenades where men and young women sit on the green benches and speak to each other in low tones while they rest their eyes on the peaceful river. The traditional sailing vessels, the feluccas, glide just as soundlessly downstream as they have always done – their white sails highly visible against the desert hills that plunge directly down to the river on the western bank.

We drive to the local military base, and after taking the compulsory cup of tea with the chief officer there, we climb aboard an old Russian military helicopter with a crew of four. We fly, with the door open, up along the Nile to Lake Nasser behind the Aswan High Dam. Surrounded by the noise of the helicopter and the wind, and while my gaze follows the mighty curve of the Aswan High Dam that holds back a 500-kilometre artificial lake I have to contain my joy: having studied the history of the Nile for several decades and read metre upon metre of old books and archival documents about the hydrology of the river and the struggle to control it, this view from a low-flying helicopter is a high point, the realisation of what I had always thought was an impossibility.

The Aswan High Dam, or the Nasser Dam as it is often called, named after the man who was President of Egypt when the dam was built, decisively transformed many fundamental premises for the country's development. It also had direct consequences for the whole of the Middle East, the fate (and demise) of the European colonial system, as well as for developments in the Horn of Africa. Around 5,000 years ago, the primary task of the first Egyptian calendar was to inform the Egyptians when the flood would come. They discovered that Sirius, the dog star, became visible just before dawn some days prior to the annual Nile flood. Egypt abandoned its moon-based calendar and adopted a solar calendar of 365 days. With the advent of the Aswan High Dam, it was no longer of economic and political consequence as to *when* the flood would come in Egypt, but simply *how much* water the Nile was carrying. The country lost the historic day of celebrating the annual inundation, but it was freed from the despotic power inherent in the river's seasonal and annual fluctuations. The country got electricity, and millions of acres of new cultivable land thanks to this new Nile dam.

At the same time the Aswan High Dam brought home the eternal dualism of water: for the build up of water behind the dam hindered the dispersal of the natural fertiliser that the river brought with it in the form of silt. For millennia the Nile had brought the silt down with it from the Ethiopian highlands. Now it lay collecting at the bottom of the lake behind the dam, and, even though it has taken a longer than first thought, it remains an uncomfortable fact that sooner or later the dam will be destroyed by the build up of silt if Egypt does not manage to clear it away with technology that remains to be found, unless the country is saved from this disaster by countries building huge Nile dams upstream trapping the silt there. But today the Aswan dam is not able to meet the water demands of the Egyptian society, according to the Egyptian political leadership.

The government believes that the country must break through the natural limitations placed on it by the river if, in the long run, it is to deal with the growth of the population. Accordingly, we depart from the banks of the Nile and the helicopter swerves out into the desert – a barren Sahara spreading in all directions beneath us as far as the eye can see, where the heat creates indistinct contours and reflections. Then I see what looks like long narrow lines of life in amongst all of this: mile after mile of dead-straight waterways excavated by the government. We circle several times above the gigantic pumping station, where hydro-electric power generated by the Nile is to be used to pump Nile water out into the desert. The pumping station, which was named after the president who initiated it, Hosni Mubarak, is the very heart of the project. The goal is to be able to cultivate the desert from whence the first Egyptians came, when more than 6,000 years ago they migrated in from the Sahara, a Sahara which at that time was green, and where elephants and giraffes grazed round and about.

Wherever one travels along the Nile in Egypt one sees examples of how the Egyptians have made use of the river.[63] Not long after their migration from the desert, the people in the valley found ways to raise water up and out of the Nile and into the desert soils. For millennia they used the *saqiya* (an animal-driven wheel-and-axle system), the *shaduf* (a bucket, pole and fulcrum system) and what was known as Archimedes' screw (an inclined screw used to draw water up and out of the river), all of which provided some litres of water on a daily basis. Now, however, on the banks of the artificial lake, they have built an enormous pumping station. Its task is also to raise up Nile water for greening the desert – but on an infinitely greater scale. If this vision of creating a new Nile valley is ever realised, it will be the most fundamental revolution in Egypt's long history.

The pumping station stands only some kilometres away from Abu Simbel – one of the most famous monuments in the world, hewn out of the mountain-side of Upper Egypt 3,000 years ago. When the Aswan High Dam threatened to inundate it, its move was organised by UNESCO, and section by section it was cut free and relocated. It has now been reconstructed higher up in all its impressive majesty and resplendent self-glorification. It was Ramses II, the pharaoh, with six wives and 100 children, who had it hewn from the rock – one of the most self-glorifying edifices in the history of the world. Outside the entrance there stand four statues, portraits of the pharaoh himself, more than 20 metres high, and inside there are even more, while around the entrance there are *bas-relief* carvings of Nile gods who united Upper and Lower Egypt, and did so on the backs of African and Asian slaves. In Egypt they now talk about the Toshka project – as it is called – as Mubarak's Abu Simbel, or his pyramid. In any case, mankind has taken a step forward in unilateralism and civilisation, for there were no glorifying statues of the Mubarak erected at the pumping station bearing his name.

'I have never seen anything like it. The Mubarak Pumping Station is one of a kind.' The English manager of Skanska, the firm that has built the pumping station, cannot hide his sense of pride. I meet him in a pub that has been erected in the midst of the construction site, where the British building workers have done their best to recreate a feeling of 'Britishness' in the Sahara Desert, with billiard tables and satellite-transmitted Premier League games. He is the leader of an experienced group of 'expats' who move from country to country, building huge infrastructural projects, and he appears to be one who is not accustomed to boasting. The pumping station can pump a new Nile into the desert, he says.

The rectangular building, which was completed in 2002, is nothing less than a man-made midwife assisting the birth of an artificial river valley. It will have the capacity to lift five billion cubic metres of water into the desert annually. The power station by the spillway of the Aswan High Dam provides electricity to the 21 pumps such that the Nile is pumping itself up and into the desert. A 50-metre deep intake canal feeds water to the pumps. The main canal is 50 kilo-metres in length, 7 metres deep, 30 metres wide at the bottom and 58 metres

54. The main canal of the Toshka Project stretches mile after mile out into the hottest desert in the world to provide water for new cities, export-orientated agriculture and new residences for millions of people.

across at the surface. It is one component in a system of hundreds of kilometres of canals. The plan is to build cities, start industries and develop export agriculture. The dream is to make the desert bloom and build ten new industrial zones. The total arable land in the western desert is 7.5 million acres.

In its first phase, the goal of the project is to irrigate a million acres. The whole complex will stretch more than 300 kilometres into the desert. In Phase II, which is to be completed in 2017, the canal is to extend to the north, to the oasis region capital city for the whole complex: the New Valley Governorate. Then 400,000 additional acres can be cultivated. When the project is completed, a little before 2020, more than three million people are expected to live there and it will increase Egypt's arable land by 10 per cent. In all, 1,400,000 hectares of land will be put under cultivation, according to the most ambitious goals. At its most ambitious moments the government has talked about settling more than ten million people here, with supplementary water from enormous aquifers beneath the Sahara.

'Well, you know, if we compare, and if we consider the pyramids as the projects of the pharaohs, then this project is more than 100 times bigger than the pyramids.' The Minister for Water for many years, Dr Abu Zeid, is clear about what the Egyptian government was doing. Again and again he stressed to me when I met him in Cairo, the strategic importance of the project and that it for the younger generations represent hope for the future.[64]

When I balance on the edge of the canal, with the blue waters of the Nile surrounded by endless desert, I find that if anything is to be called a man-made artery of life, then this is it. Mile after mile of canals carrying water where there has been practically none for millennia.

So when a local worker drops to his knees at sundown to pray, and he turns toward Mecca, which is in the same direction as the pumping station, this coincidental weaving together of the sacred and profane mingles with another contrast that pervades the atmosphere of this place: the paradoxical mixing of technological optimism and desolation, of a potent pumping station amidst the total silence of the desert. And this is one reason why the project has come under heavy fire both in upstream countries and in Egypt, and many consider it a great vision that will never materialize.

55. The water crisis is acute in parts of China, and the Chinese government warns that this will hinder development. The man who is delivering water here has 39 plastic casks tied to his bicycle. Moving water has been a constant and central human activity since the first civilisations developed in the Middle East, right up to today's megaprojects. The water-moving projects of the future will change the appearance of huge portions of the globe and, more radically, over a shorter period of time than at any other corresponding intervention in nature during all of human history.

CHAPTER 20
HISTORY'S GREATEST ENGINEERING PROJECT IN CHINA

'Rainfall in Beijing, London and Paris is the same. But when you look at the distribution over the year', says the Vice-Minister, 'the picture is quite different. It doesn't rain in Beijing from May to July, August or September. For the most part, where you come from, the rain falls year-round, while we get no water for large parts of the year.' China's Vice-Minister of Water emphasises Beijing's particular conditions in relation to the situation in central European cities, and leaning over the glass table decorated with a beautiful wooden boat, he asks, from the perspective of someone living in a city of 15 million people, 'Don't we have to do something?'

The times we are living through will be summed up as the period when China's incredible growth changed the world. When I travel in China to large cities like Beijing, Shanghai, Zhengzhou, Nanjing, Kunming or Chengdu, the first thing that hits me is not the importance of water or the water crisis, but rather the frenetic building activity going on everywhere – the cranes outlined against the sky, the hectic tempo, the traffic congestion – in other words, all the indicators of a country in the midst of an economic development process such as the world has never seen. But the political leadership has long insisted, and continues to maintain, that the country is facing catastrophic water crises and that the lack of water is a ticking bomb that threatens to put the brakes on, indeed even undermine, the whole of China's development. Due to China's economic position, the manner in which they solve the water question will have global significance.

The reports regarding the water situation have been alarming for many years. The water table beneath the North China plains is sinking dramatically and more than 100,000 wells have dried up. The groundwater level in Beijing has undergone a rapid fall and the state leadership has discussed how they either have to move the capital to the water or bring the water to the capital. With increasing frequency the Yellow River fails to reach the ocean due to the number of large pipes that extract its water. At the same time, China has officially stated that 400 out of almost 700 large cities have serious water shortages. In nine out of ten cities the water is polluted, often because the groundwater has been over-consumed, and, in large cities near the coast, salt water has penetrated and takes the place of the fresh water.

It might be a surprise to many, and very difficult to understand if one travels around in the southern parts of China, but China has comparatively little water per inhabitant: they have 22 per cent of the world's population but only 8 per cent of its water. On average, every Chinese has at his or her disposal about one-fifth as much water as an inhabitant of the USA and about one-tenth as much as a Russian. In China, water is also extremely unevenly distributed, creating water-rich and water-poor regions. In the south there is much rain and frequent flooding; in the north it is dry and the water landscape there makes China one of the largest desert countries in the world.

The ability of the regime to solve the country's regional water problems will be decisive for its legitimacy and authority in the future, just as it was for the Chinese in the time of the emperors.[65] The political significance of water control has been given political-institutional weight by the doctrine of the 'Mandate of Heaven'. The 'Mandate of Heaven' is a traditional Chinese philosophical concept concerning the legitimacy of rulers. It is, however, according to my opinion only apparently similar to the European concept of the divine right of kings. Both sought to legitimise rule from divine approval, but unlike the divine right of kings, the Mandate of Heaven manifested itself very concretely, in the form of river discharge and rainfall, i.e. in their ability to control and provide water. A good leader held power on the sufferance of Heaven, for if the ruler governed badly, then Heaven would withdraw its blessing and show its displeasure by letting the water take revenge through 'droughts, floods and earthquakes'.[66] From such a perspective there is no doubt that until now the communist leadership has enjoyed the Mandate of Heaven, for never before has China experienced fewer serious flood catastrophes (even though they do regularly continue to occur), nor has the population been given as much water as now. But the fantastic economic growth, along with the population increase, nonetheless makes this unsustainable.

In China, the state has always acquired legitimacy for itself and expanded its power by exercising control over the rivers. The Chinese built the first large dam in the world, including both a dam and a canal system, as early as 250 years before the birth of Christ – the Dujiangyan Project in Guanxian, now Sichuan province. I went to see it, in a misty morning over the Chengdu plain, and it is still in place, spanning a tributary of the Yangtze and, with certain modernisations, still in use. The Fulung Temple is enthroned a little downstream from the dam, almost like a Buddhist pagoda, built in honour of the governor and the man behind the project, the famous Li Bing. The legend, which is reiterated on a small plaque in front of the temple, is that it was erected at the location where Li Bing vanquished the dragon of the river by building the dam.

On one hand China is a modern symbol of the influence that ideas can exert on historical development. On the other hand these great swings in ideology during recent decades can throw into the shade other, and perhaps more fundamental, characteristics of modern Chinese social organisation that will have still greater consequences in the long run. A common thread running through all the ideological conflicts is one activity to which the state has given priority: building dams, dykes and canals. On average, over the last 50 years the country has built three large projects a day. In 1949 there were eight dams. Now there are around 20,000! The constant expansion of such water projects, both in size and number, has made possible new cities, increased food production and rapid industrialisation. Thus, until now, these water projects have provided a fundamental condition, a real material basis, for modern China's continuous and incredible economic growth. All state formations share a set of common features, but they also have their own particularities that ought not to be neglected, and compared to all other countries China can be called a water-controlling and water-moving state. It is also a country that has developed aquatic warfare to a level (theoretical and practical) seen nowhere else on the planet.

The Yangtze is China's national highway, and the largest river in the country. It comes from Tibet and reaches the sea not far from Shanghai, having run through nine provinces. Altogether it drains one-fifth of China with its more than 700 tributaries, and it waters one-quarter of each acre of the country's arable land. For thousands of years it has created what has been called 'China's granary'. Much of what has been produced down through China's history has found its way to the river, which is 6,300 kilometres long. It runs through what today are many of the country's important industrial regions. Two-thirds of everything that is exported from China is carried along this water highway. It is navigable to a distance 2,000 kilometres upstream from the sea.

In China it is easy to be convinced of the idea that rivers are an old Taoist master teacher, which holds lectures on the great wheel of life, as Claudio Magris wrote in *The Danube*. The behaviour and development of the Yangtze have fundamentally affected the life of the people who live along the river system. Here, as in other places, people have suffered catastrophic floods and endured enormous suffering due to the vehemence of both the river and the monsoon precipitation.

One flood story dates from the summer of AD 813 when the T'ang Dynasty was hit by a huge flood.According to ancient Chinese tradition, women represent the fertile, the humid, the receptive element of nature. In mythology, humid earth, waterways and the great water cycle were symbolised as almost the quintessence of the feminine. Metaphysicians read into imbalances in nature a disparity between the two fundamental cosmic forces. Yin was the dark, earthly, humid, submissive female principle that ensured continuity in the great circular flow of both nature and water. Yang was the light, positive, heavenly and masculine principle. Such imbalances in nature reflected or revealed themselves in such human relations as the ability of women, by virtue of holding unnaturally strong positions, or their arrogance of power, to harm the established order. At the time of this flood, in AD 813, the reigning emperor, Li Ch'u (who after his death was known as Hsien Tsung), was convinced that the catastrophe was the result of too much yin in the cosmic relationship between yin and yang. But this imbalance could be put to right, at least in part, by human intervention, above all by the Son of Heaven – the emperor that is. Accordingly, the emperor sent away several wagonloads of women from his palace on 21 July that year. They simply had to be removed, because women represented metaphysical water in human form.

First I travel up the Yangtze from Yichang one ice-cold January night aboard a battered old hulk, and while I try to sleep, clad in two pairs of long-johns under a wool blanket, I think of the poem that Mao Zedong wrote back in 1956, after he took the first of his famous swims here across the Yangtze:

> Great plans are afoot:
> A bridge will fly to span the north and south,
> Turning a deep chasm into a thoroughfare,
> Walls of stone will stand upstream to the west
> To hold back Wushan's clouds and rain
> Till a smooth lake rises in the narrow gorges
> The mountain goddess if she is still there
> Will marvel at a world so changed!

The Chairman's poem provided a green light for the damming of the Yangtze. The leadership of the Communist Party of China decided to build the world's largest dam across the world's fourth largest river (China's first modern leader, Sun Yat-sen, proposed a similar but smaller dam back in the 1920s); the Three Gorges Dam. The banks of the river, crammed with historical memorials about the struggle of warlords to control the Yangtze, were inundated by the water behind the dam – including, among other things, the 'iron gate' that was built across the river during the Song Dynasty (960–1279). Two-metre high iron pillars and seven 250-metre long chains made it possible to control all military transport and to tax almost all the trade between the central parts of China for several hundred years. The river rapids where, as late as the beginning of the twentieth century one out of every 20 boats was wrecked, are disappearing. In the past, junks were drawn upriver by boat-pullers who balanced on narrow pathways that spanned the mountainsides, and shamans were paid to go on board with a yellow flag bearing the words 'Power of the Water' and they stood in the bow waving the flag with regular movements, all the while throwing rice into the river by way of pacifying the dragons and the spirits of the rapids. This is definitively history, but a history now drowned by the waters of the new dam.

Later, as I journey down the Yangtze in a speedboat, eating rice and chicken from plastic cups that are simply tossed overboard afterwards, the Chinese passengers cast lingering glances at the large cities and riverbanks that will definitely disappear and toward the gigantic construction works, a kind of technological anthill with bulldozers, lorries, cranes and ready-mix cement vehicles. I know that I am travelling a stretch of the river that will soon be completely drowned by the waters of the enormous dam; yes, this is the last chance to see the Three Gorges as nature made them. I look at the Chinese travelling with me; do their glances reveal a mixture of sadness due to the loss of cities and untouched nature and an optimistic view of the future? What do they think?: is the dam an example of human megalomania in the face of nature, or does it represent the final victory of human beings over the river, a monument to what modern technology can achieve? Will it prevent the repetition of catastrophes like that of 1954 when 30,000 people died and tens of millions of acres of arable agricultural land were destroyed? Some describe the silting problem as the project's cancerous tumour – what will happen when 680 million tonnes of mud and silt accumulate on the riverbed annually above the dam? In the long run, will it destroy the river as a transport route above the dam, because that is where the river will deposit more silt? And will the reservoir be able to withstand the great floods of the millennia? Looking up at the workers who build the dam, I know that these are questions that will always be debated, since the river will always be in flux.

The enormous wall of earth, stone, steel and concrete that was rising across the Yangtze will directly affect the lives of a large proportion of the people in the world's most heavily populated country. Indeed, more people live along the Yangtze waterway than live in the whole of Europe. 'This golden waterway', that the Chinese have sung about, revered and feared since time immemorial, is disappearing – as a river – for good: it is being transformed into a controllable canal.

56. The first of three gigantic channels is being built here, which will conduct 5 per cent of the water from the Yangtze to drought-prone regions in northern China. This largest engineering project in world history will cover half of China. It will be ready in 2050 and will cost roughly £100 billion.

The Three Gorges is a telling example of the global race for rivers that has been underway during our current era. In the last 50 years it is as though an extraordinary geological force has changed the fresh water landscape of the globe, but with the difference being that, in contrast to geological time, this has occurred overnight. Hundreds of thousands of waterfalls have been utilised to make electricity and tens of thousands of new lakes have been tamed; there are now 60,000 dams of over 15 metres in height that regulate the natural flow of rivers. If in the future, archaeologists from another planet were to pick through the remains of our civilisation, they would with good reason be able to claim that the true temples of our civilisation are our dam installations. Many of them are so massive, and constructed with such technical consideration, that they will stand much longer than our skyscrapers, mosques and churches. Our alien visitors would be flabbergasted by the numbers, and the durability would surely impress them. Technically speaking, even today only a fraction of the water power potential of the so-called developing countries is effectively utilised worldwide – still less than only 20 per cent. And the era of dam-building is not over. Rather, the projects are becoming larger and larger, while they encounter greater and greater opposition from environmental organisations and from the millions of people who are concerned with what they see as the hidden downside of the advance of Technical Rationality. When the boat docks at Yichang, right downstream from the Three Gorges Dam, I think to myself, 'Will the mountain goddess, about whom Chairman Mao wrote, be simply astounded? Or will she fall into a state of distress?'

Shanghai is at the downstream end of the Yangtze River basin. For most foreigners the name used to conjure up images of ocean-going ships and, as it were, the tang of saltwater. But the sailors who wrote apologetic letters home to wives and children were not shanghaied in a coastal city. The Huang-Po, a tributary of the Yangtze, and on whose banks Shanghai is located, is in effect an inland harbour. When the tide is high, however, ocean-going ships can sail up river to the city. It is early twilight as I walk along the quay, and freight boats as large as ocean-going ships, pass by; dozens and dozens of flat-bottomed river boats lie at their moorings, red flags fluttering – everything gives the obstinate impression of activity, anxiety and growth. From here it is easy to understand why the Chinese themselves do not use the name Yangtze for the main river, derived from the old Yang kingdom. Instead, in China they use Chiang Jiang –

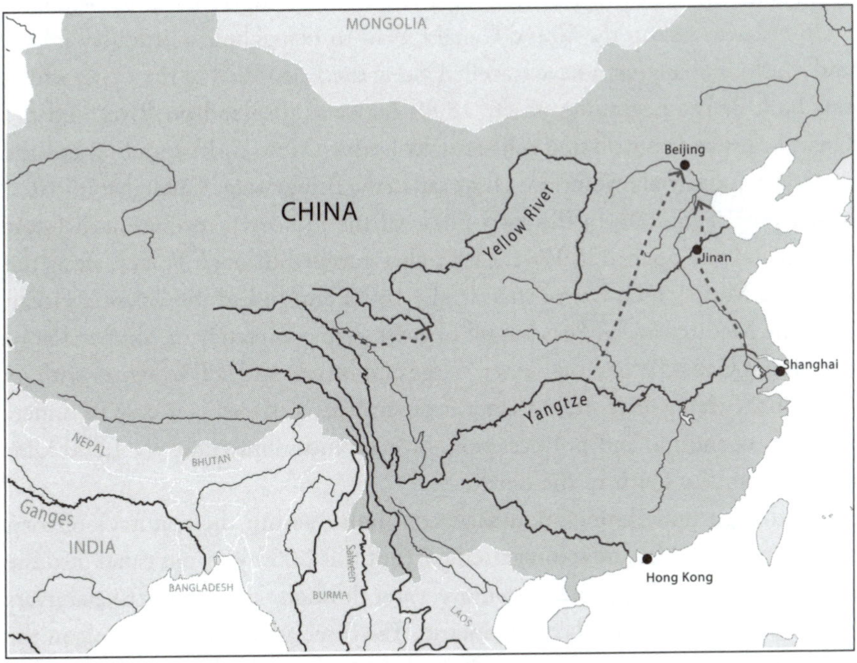

Map 7. Some 5 per cent of the Yangtze's water volume should according to the plan be diverted into three main canals toward dry northern China. The map indicates where they will go and that the project will affect half of China.

'the long river' – or simply Chiang, 'the river'. Referring to the river in this way reflects its position as China's main water highway. The Yangtze has always bound the Chinese to history and has also come to be understood as a messenger regarding the future.

The Chinese leadership has now come up with a vision and a plan involving the Yangtze that overshadows both the Three Gorges Dam and earlier water-moving projects completely; the South-to-North Water Transfer Project. But as always, when it comes to Chinese water history, it has its forerunners.

In China one can talk about a canal epoch that extended for about 1,000 years and started about 300 years before the birth of Christ. It contributed to building the foundations for China's economic development, for a long time being far in advance of what happened in Europe. The most spectacular construction was the Grand Canal or the Emperor's Canal. It had several purposes, both economically, politically and as a weapon of military strategy. It was crucial in all efforts to maintain the unity of the different dynasties and empires. For example; the army and the emperor's administration in Beijing alone required 400,000 tonnes of grain annually, and in the twelfth century around 300,000 soldiers near Beijing and over 750,000 on the northern border were fed by rice that could only be carried by this canal linking the Yangtze Basin to Beijing.

In order to sail on the Grand Canal I went to Hangzhou, a little way inland and south of Shanghai. I have travelled along the Erie Canal in the USA, which was built at the beginning of the 1800s between the Hudson River and the Great Lakes and contributed substantially both to New York's standing and the American industrial revolution; I have sailed the Bridgewater Canal that initiated a transport revolution in the early phase of the industrial revolution in Great Britain and was opened in 1761; I have also travelled through France, along the Canal de Midi, which was opened in the 1600s and linked the Atlantic Ocean with the Mediterranean Sea; but all of these pale completely in comparison to the Grand Canal. When one sees it, large and broad, and still in action with its hectic boat traffic after more than a thousand years of use, it is easy to understand its economic and political role, as it extends approximately 1,800 kilometres from the south to the north.

As though underlining an aquatic continuity within the country's history, the Chinese state has now integrated parts of the 2,000-year-old canal into the new canal project. They intend to move water through three large artificial rivers a total of several thousands of kilometres. The three artificial rivers – one in the east of the country, one in the middle and one right up to the Himalayas in the west – will send 5 per cent of the Yangtze's water north, or about 40 billion cubic metres of water annually, which is equivalent to eight rivers the size of the

River Thames in London. Hundreds of pumping stations, enormous dam sites, tunnels miles long through mountains and under rivers, will take the water from the Yangtze – the world's fifth largest river in terms of water volume, in a list topped by the Amazon and the Congo. It carries almost 1,000 billion cubic metres of water a year, or ten times more than the Nile.

The new canal, which constitutes the most easterly route of the three gigantic canals to be built, looks like many other canals in China – very broad, its bottom composed of white stone, the banks lined by trees as far as the eye can see. But despite the ordinary appearance of the canal, I know that with every step I take along the banks, with every metre I cover by boat on the canal, I am on historic ground. Few places will have greater global significance from a long-term developmental perspective than the site where the first canal's outflow from the Yangtze is excavated.

Right across from this outflow, some hundreds of metres from the Yangtze, there are two gigantic pumping stations filled with technological potency, housed in a cathedral to the possibilities of water management, propelling water up a level and sending it on its way to Beijing, some 1,800 kilometres to the north. The station hall is an architectural masterpiece – and an aesthetic one due to the way the light manages to fall between the large windows, highlighting the row of gigantic pumps – thereby stressing the character of the place, an homage to the ambitions and abilities of the water-moving state.

The project has so many and such grand ambitions that it eclipses everything that has either been built or planned in the West. All the engineers I talk to, and who have established temporary headquarters along the canal, say the same thing as the Vice-Minister I spoke with in Beijing.[67] It is intended both to save agriculture on the North China plains and to expand agricultural lands by millions and millions of acres. It will secure more water for a hundred large cities and stimulate industrial growth. In addition, the project has an even more spectacular task: saving the capital city.

Taking the train across the North China plains is a monotonous experience. There is a steady stream of cities, villages and factories and enormous agricultural areas. From the window, one does not get the impression that this is home to almost half a billion people or that half the grain in China is cultivated here. In the most recent decades the level of the water table here has fallen by as much as 30 metres.

'All you and your glory will perish one day, but the rivers will run forever.' Half aloud, and to myself, I read this ancient verse written by one of the poets of China's T'ang Dynasty, whilst from the window of the train I glimpse the silhouettes of huge factories and note the bone-dry riverbeds. How irrelevant the poet's predictions seem now, for I know that 300 of the rivers on the North China plains have either run dry or become something closer to open sewers than rivers. It has been reported that, due to this water predicament, the CIA watches developments in China's water situation with the same precision that in earlier days it conducted surveillance over troop movements in the Soviet Union. The reason is easy to understand, for if China is forced to import a mere 10 per cent of the grain it needs, it will buy up 20 per cent of what is available on the world market. Increased grain prices globally will threaten political stability in many countries. The Chinese hope that the new rivers will secure productivity and bring about the development of prosperity on these plains.

When I travel along these canals, that are being built at such a rapid pace by the Chinese all the way from the Yangtze to Beijing, I know that I am being borne along by one of the most ambitious and monumental attempts to bend running water to humanity's will.[68] The water taken from the Yangtze is sent from the south toward the north, in a different direction to its natural course (which is from west to east). The waters running along the arrow-straight canals are completely without the powers of the dragon, about which Chinese mythology is replete and which have been feared for thousands of years. The

57. This photo shows a completely new method for saving the Yellow River and, in the future, preventing it from causing still greater flood catastrophes. By thrusting the water at tremendous speed out of the reservoir gates here at the Xiaolangdi Dam, the Chinese intend to force the river to carry more of the silt from the river bed out into the ocean, thus preventing the bottom of the river from continuing to rise.

water of the Yangtze runs across the North China plain like some subdued river god and, fully conscious of the historical and symbolic significance, the Chinese authorities have decided that the canal leading to the centre of power – the capital city – shall terminate at the Imperial Summer Palace. All of those I talk with say the same thing: in the south there is a lot of water, in the north there is little. Therefore the water must simply be moved, cost what it may, for that is the key to China's future and sustainable development.[69]

The project is also intended to save the country's second largest river, the Yellow River, from itself and from over-utilisation. It is, as well, a project of world historic significance since more people live in the Yellow River than reside in the whole of the USA. This river, called 'the mother of Chinese civilisation', and 'China's sorrow' due to the many catastrophic floods it has caused over the course of the past two millennia, more and more infrequently reaches the ocean. Its deterioration is happening quickly and the causes are drought, silting and over-utilisation.

When I had been in China ten years earlier, the Yellow River ran past me here, large and powerful; now, large portions of the riverbed are dry, tinder-dry, almost like a desert. I have seldom experienced a moment that could bear witness, so explicitly and at such magnitude, to the costs of modernisation as I did when squatting down in the bottom of one of the world's greatest rivers and allowing the dry sand from the river bottom to run between my fingers. (And, as it happens, right by a wall bearing the slogan 'Control the Yellow River' – a testimony to a less worrisome period in the relationship between the society and the river.) The mighty Yellow River, which for millennia has emptied its waters into the North China Sea, is in the process of becoming an inland river.

The Chinese have launched a hundred-year plan for the river. New methods have already been put into use to change the water in the river: the sand and the mud will be washed out. When one rides along the river, as it meanders between the terraced hilltops of loess soil, and when one sees the way it runs – not as a clear blue mountain stream, but as a brown current (in some places the river is seven parts sand and only three parts water) – it is not difficult to understand that controlling it requires special measures. I was told that if one were to build a tower two metres in diameter, with walls one metre thick, using the mud brought down by the Yellow River in the course of one year, it would reach the moon. By forcing water out of the reservoirs under high pressure this powerful current will help the river move tonnes of sand further out into the ocean. The aim is to prevent the river bottom from growing ever-higher, in order to defend the country from floods and the catastrophic collapses of dykes and damming. In Xinxiang, Henan province, the river runs between dykes that are 20 metres above the surrounding land. The method makes the control of the river easier, but it is not enough. By feeding in more water artificially, the Yellow River is to be restored to health and once again the mud will be flushed out into the North China Sea, as has been the case for thousands of years previously.

'It is obvious that shooting at the clouds works.' This researcher at one of China's research institutes for weather modification is in no doubt; his colleagues nod energetically in support. They give me DVDs of films that show how it is to be done, as well as references to research reports. Outside Beijing the authorities have set in motion a large programme for shooting the clouds with cannon fire in order to get rain and to be able to control the weather. The Chinese emperors, like overlords in many other locations, had faith in their ability to make rain at their will. Now instead, the Chinese government has set in motion a large programme for modifying the weather, with 37,000 soldiers in the service of the weather war. The weather soldiers pull cannons around and, deployed in small groups, they fire into the clouds in order to increase rainfall. The researchers at the central research institute are in no doubt – indeed, what strikes me is their *certainty* when it comes to the effect of such weather modification projects. But they are all in agreement that this is only one of several initiatives that have to be taken up to solve China's water problem. The capital city must obtain more water than it gets on its own, even in years with good precipitation.

A Beijing resident has only one-eighth of the national average and one-thirtieth of the world average when it comes to access to water, according to the authorities themselves.[70] The water table has fallen well over a metre annually, year after year, ever since the beginning of the 1990s. The water reservoirs have sunk dramatically and the main reservoir has fallen by many metres. According to the political leadership, China's political power centre will threatened without drastic initiatives.[71]

The struggle to solve the water problem of Beijing and North China takes many forms. Those who save water become national heroes. I visit such a family in a down-at-heel suburb of Beijing. I am well-received and they seat me on the sofa under a portrait of Chairman Mao, which hangs in a prominent position in this otherwise bare-walled living room. They are taking part in a water-saving campaign that the state has set in motion and which is led by local committees. The woman at the head of the family tells me proudly that they have won prizes for their water-saving methods. For example, they never let water go down the drain without having first washed their hands or their clothes in it. They have opened the drain so that it runs down into a tub such that it can be used again and again. The narrow bathroom of a couple of square metres is thus crowded

58. The Great Yu, a mythic Chinese emperor, creator of the Middle Kingdom, stands on a plinth and gazes out over the Yellow River. The myths tell that Yu created the country when he tamed the river more than 4,000 years ago. This is the most fundamental trajectory of China's development, or what I call the history of the water-moving state, running from him to today's leaders.

with overflowing buckets and tubs – a primitive system of recycling that could be of real significance if a billion people follow suit. But again China's leaders feel it is not sufficient, and in addition China must chart fresh initiatives.

A water journey in China should naturally be concluded where the great Yu stands majestically on his plinth looking out over the Yellow River: for the myths recount that Yu created the country when he tamed the river about 4,000 years ago. The most fundamental line of development in China runs between him and today's leaders. If the present-day leaders are successful with their gigantic water projects perhaps they too will be remembered and honoured for an equally long time. China will then have laid the structural basis for a lasting national growth and stability. If the project does not succeed, however, not only the regime but the state formation itself will be threatened with collapse. This will be so because of the enormous investment that it demands, the regional co-operation that it presupposes and the state authority it requires. If this gigantic attempt to change China's appearance and its geography fails – either because it proves too complicated to administrate or because future climate change turns the Yangtze and the Yellow into rivers with seriously reduced water flow – this will demonstrate that central aspects of the country's economy were built around an illusion: an illusion of water that is no longer to be found. Given the combination of the legitimacy of the state and its control over society, and the fact that the country's economy continues to grow at around 10 per cent a year, it is not the movement for democracy that is the structural challenge to China's leadership: as I stand at the feet of the statue of Yu it is easy to conclude that in the future, too, China's development will revolve around the question of water. As it has done for thousands of years.

59. Moscow's mayor of about 20 years was behind a whole series of large construction projects there. Here, a 3.5-tonne bridge is being moved 2.5 kilometres along the Moscow River to a new location in the Russian capital. The same mayor put forward the idea of dusting off the old plan to reverse the Siberian rivers, a plan that many consider to be a prime example of Stalinist planning culture and hubris in the face of nature.

CHAPTER 21
TURN THOSE SIBERIAN RIVERS AROUND!

'It is obvious that we have to build this canal.' The then-powerful mayor of Moscow, Yury Luzhkov, is in no doubt. Seated calmly in a beautiful library built in the time of the czars, he looks at me, his hands folded. He says, 'With this we solve problems that are important for all of humanity'.

The *zeitgeist*, the spirit of the times, is a problematic concept, but there can be no doubt that different ideas and visions push their way forward and dominate different time periods and in this way influence what people think as well as what they do. Now and then it happens that a particular year, held up against its epoch and its future, stands out as especially typical of its time, a sort of prism for contemporary visions of the future, precisely because a whole series of epoch-making events reminiscent of one another happen in many places in the world without having any direct causal links. If societies are analysed with regard to how they relate to water, the year 2002 was such a year and. as time goes by, it will go down in history as just such a year. A series of decisions and actions were undertaken in 2002 that will be decisive for the world and the way people talk about it for the coming decades. For the first time, at a summit meeting in Johannesburg, world leaders agreed that water was a principal and extraordinary issue in the fight against poverty. During 2002 the Chinese government started the South-to-North Water Diversion Project that will both change the geography of China and be the largest engineering project ever. In December the same year the Government of India issued a resolution constituting the Task Force on Interlinking of Rivers, the most ambitious water control project ever, and in Russia the influential mayor of Moscow proposed that the country ought to turn the Siberian rivers, which now flow into the Arctic Ocean, around and send their waters through a gigantic canal to water-parched regions in Central Asia.

Mayor Luzhkov, Moscow's leader after 1992 and one of the founders of the ruling United Russia party, insisted that the canal plans are perfectly reasonable.

In the library, he serves tea and, beside it on its own separate dish, very tasty honey from Siberia. Bee-keeping is his passion, he says, while explaining that he is also very interested in the history of water and is in the process of writing a book on the world history of canals. He had won all the elections since 1992 with crushing victories, managed the rapid modernisation of Moscow, and was married to one of Russia's richest entrepreneurs, 30 years his junior, but is criticised for corruption. He gets enthusiastic talking about the canal scheme and takes me down to his office. On the wall there is a map of the old Soviet Union, which also shows the project area, and with his finger he follows the red stripe he has drawn in from where the Irtysh meets the Ob River in Russia and down to Central Asia.

Russia is not only the world's largest country but it is also unusually rich in resources – not least in rivers. The Siberian rivers drain large regions, but these are regions where very few people live, and where most of the water runs completely unutilised out to sea. On the other hand, the new countries in Central Asia are largely water-poor, and they are countries that built their infrastructure when part of the Soviet Union. They have thereby been profoundly affected by the possibility that the Soviet Union could use the river basins without a sideways glance toward the interests of various sovereign states. It is against this background that the plans for turning around the Siberian rivers have surfaced once again – plans that many thought had been shelved permanently with the breakup of the Soviet Union and the state socialist planning philosophy.

The idea itself is more than 100 years old. Already in the 1870s, during the era of the czars, a proposal was put forward by a 16-year-old student, a visionary regarded as divinely inspired, according to Luzhkov.[72] The idea was to take water from the Ob and the Yenisey, two Siberian rivers that flow uncontrolled into the Arctic Ocean, and send it south instead, to where there is a need for it and where large arable regions are simply thirsting for water. Under Joseph Stalin this was developed into a concrete plan. What was known as the Davydov Plan proposed taking water from both rivers and pumping them south toward the Caspian and Aral Seas with the help of a series of dams and reservoirs. A proposal was also made to take water from the Pechora and Vychegda Rivers and send it into the Kama-Volga system and on to the Caspian Sea. Both these plans were put on ice, but interest was renewed in the 1960s under Leonid Brezhnev.[73] Eventually, a more comprehensive project, known by the name Sibaral, evolved and in the 1980s the plans were as follows. A European part, predicated on increasing the water flow in the Volga system and down to the Caspian Sea, was to be ready in the 1990s. There was also to be a Siberian portion, which was both larger and more complicated. The first phase of this was to take 27.2 cubic kilometres of water from the Ob and the tributary Irtysh and lead it into a canal that was to be 2,200 kilometres in length, have a breadth of between 108 and 212 metres and a depth of 12 to 15 metres. This was to start where the Irtysh meets the Ob. Enormous pumps would lift the water over the watershed. For the rest of the distance to the rivers Syr Darya and Amu Darya it would run of its own accord. Stage 2 would increase the amount of water taken to 60 cubic kilometres annually.

Some years later in 1986, the Soviet leader Mikhail Gorbachev called a halt to the whole project, which by then had come to be regarded as an unprofitable environmental catastrophe, and the state no longer had the requisite authority to carry it through. But a couple of decades down the road the plans, or the idea, appeared once again, when the Moscow mayor insisted that it had to be implemented. The idea is still to excavate an approximately 200-metre-wide, 16-metre-deep and 2,500-kilometre-long canal from Siberia's Ob River to Central Asia and the Aral Sea. The mayor of Moscow was conducting a campaign in favour of the plan, as was President Karimov of Uzbekistan. Those who again have supported the plan have called it both an economic bridge and a 'green bridge' between Russia and Central Asia. Opponents think the project is *so* foolish that those who support it ought almost to be met not with rational economic and ecological arguments but with offers of psychiatric assistance.

Map 8. An overview of the Sibaral Project that the mayor of Moscow wants to revive.

The mayor brushes aside the opposing arguments; they are based on emotion and insufficient knowledge, he argues. Technologically speaking, the gigantic canals present manageable challenges, but for Moscow, the Sibaral Project now lacks national economic significance, since it is the dry countries that were formerly part of the Soviet Union which would benefit. Uzbekistan and other countries in that region want to continue to push for this solution, since the water crisis in their region will only worsen.

Central Asia has a warm climate and is rich in mineral resources and labour power, but it does not have enough water. Central Asia's most famous rivers are the Amu Darya (called Oxus in the history books) and the Syr Darya (formerly called the Jaxartes). They originate in the eastern mountains in Asia and run down over the Kara Kum and Kyzyl Deserts, before they end in the Aral Sea, a final station in the desert.[74] The basin is about 1.8 million square kilometres and encompasses parts of Turkmenistan, Kyrgyzstan, Tajikistan, Uzbekistan, Kazakhstan, Iran and Afghanistan. Due to excessive water consumption – and gigantic canals such as the massive Kara Kum Canal, which draws water from the Amu Darya and transports it over 1,400 kilometres to desert land in Turkmenistan – the Aral Sea divided into two at the end of the 1980s. The water level had sunk by 15 metres by the 1990s and the surface area was reduced to half its former size. In the last decade the world's once fourth largest lake fragmented into four bodies of water; the Northern Aral Sea, the eastern and western basins of the Southern Aral Sea and the Tsche-Bas-Gulf, and the large rivers struggle to reach the Sea. The problem is that without using the water of these rivers, large portions of this region will become a dry bush landscape, as almost all the land in the region is artificially irrigated: some 75 per cent in Kyrgyzstan, 84 per cent in Tajikistan, 89 per cent in Uzbekistan and 100 per cent in Turkmenistan.[75]

Development in Afghanistan could also affect the region since about 10 per cent of the Amu Darya's water comes from there, and until now the country has used almost none of it. A further complication is that in earlier times the Aral Sea has grown and diminished, so that what is happening now could be the consequence of climate variation that science does not yet understand. But no matter what the reason for today's situation, what is certain is that the question of water is of extraordinary economic and strategic importance in the area and that the Aral Sea stands as one of the clearest symbols in the world of senseless attempts to gain victory over nature and water.

But there is a 'dark horse' involved in this regional collaboration and in the Sibaral Project, and it is located on the other side of the Himalayas: China. The river that the Russians are considering sending southwards comes from China, or more precisely from the Altay Mountains in Xinjiang Province in the western part of the country. Xinjiang Province is strategically crucial for China because it constitutes one-seventh of the country's landmass, borders the Central Asian states and has potential ethnic problems. Beijing is clear that development in this region, and thereby the pacification of ethnic opposition as well, will require more water, water which they are able to obtain precisely from one of the tributaries of the Ob and Irtysh Rivers, the black Irtysh and Ili Rivers; China has encouraged Han Chinese immigration to the province to balance the Muslim population, which is composed of Uyghurs, closely related to their neighbours in Kazakhstan.

But water management is also a precondition for developing the oil fields of the Tarim Basin.[76] These plans will directly affect downstream developments in Kazakhstan and will also affect the amount of water in the river that the Russians are planning to turn around and run south. China's building of a canal to take water from the Irtysh to the Tarim Basin will reduce the amount of water. The Chinese have plans for at least an increased use of the Irtysh from approximately 15 to 40 per cent.[77] Here, as in other places, cooperation on water will involve many other relationships, not least the energy question. China would like to be involved in oil production in Kazakhstan and can claim that they need more water by way of supporting their building of the oil pipeline to transport oil from Kazakhstan to China.[78] For its part Kazakhstan can, as it has done previously, agree with the oppressed Uyghur nationalists in the country, whom China considers to be a possible threat in terms of social unrest in Xinjiang, unless that is, China promises Kazakhstan more water.

Like almost everywhere else, water management and control has a geopolitical aspect. The Irtysh captures Central Asia's strategic location between two of the world's largest countries: Russia and China. It is a politico-economic weapon that could create a stronger loyalty than state socialist ideology managed to build between the Central Asian states and Moscow. If it is to carry out the project, Russia will put its money on the belief that religious ties between Iran and Turkey will be of secondary significance in relation to Russia's control over the water tap. By means of the Ob, Russia can regain influence and power in Central Asia. Even though many have believed, and continue to believe, that the plan died with Gorbachev's decision in the 1980s, it once more becomes evident that visions promising water-poor countries solutions to their water crises have a tendency to re-surface into the light of day and affect contemporary politics. The Russians have experience in large-scale canal-building: the inland city of Moscow is called the 'ocean port', and thanks to the building of canals, particularly in the last 100 years, one can reach five oceans by boat from Moscow.

On a little island between the Moscow River and the Vodootvodny Canal, Mayor Luzhkov managed to erect a 94-metre-high statue of Czar Peter the Great. The Czar stands energetically on top of a frigate under full sail. Many critics maintain that the figure is much too big and reminds them of an overgrown lead soldier on top of a model ship. This is a monument to the czar who built a new capital city – St Petersburg – on the Baltic Sea, by draining marshes and digging canals and, moreover, planned a canal to run from St Petersburg to Moscow. It was after this visionary tradition that Luzhkov liked to model himself, but whether or not the canal will come into being requires more than ambitious visions.

60. The Guarani Indians have given their name to the greatest underground water reservoir that we know of. The struggle over the proprietary rights to the water has only just begun.

CHAPTER 22
THE LARGEST OCEAN BENEATH THE EARTH – SOUTH AMERICA

The German tourist in the reception at the spa hotel in southern Brazil urges me to sit down. He has to tell me something, he says. He knows I am Scandinavian. He has read Søren Kierkegaard, 'And Søren,' he says with embarrassing intimacy, 'argued that the road to oneself runs through solitude, for in solitude one is brutally thrown back on oneself; it is there you find yourself, when you have lost your way in existence. Kierkegaard,' he says while gripping me by the shoulder, 'looked at the rejection of solitude in modern times as a sign of pathology because solitude was so well-suited for submission to God, intellectual deliberation and soul-searching.' And he goes on: 'As the German philosopher, Otto Marquard, now argues, we have lost our "ability for solitude"; we manage to endure our own company for ever shorter periods of time.'

'But why are you telling me this?' I want to know.

'Because,' he said, 'I saw you at the waterfall today, and what a macabre natural experience that is!'

I reply that I understand what he means but I protest; he has chosen the wrong example. If I were a collector of waterfall experiences, the Iguazu Falls on the border between Argentina and Brazil would definitely be high up on my list. They are three times as broad as Niagara and significantly larger than the Victoria Falls – 275 waterfalls from 60 to 82 metres high are here gathered together in one place in the shape of a horseshoe. Yes we stood there, a whole flock of us crowded in together, but even then the falls made a strong, vivid impression; the deafening sound and the light that made the watery mist to reach up to heaven expressed nature's power – and I thought that precisely by being part of this closely packed crowd of people the feeling of human impotence in the face of this 'big water' became so strong. Iguazu means 'big water' in the language of the Guarani Indians, the dominant people in this area before the coming of the Europeans. And, in reality, it is 'big', for in the rainy season 12,750 cubic metres of water pours over the falls every second, or 240 times more water

61. Iguazu means 'big water' in the language of the Guarani Indians who dominated the area before the coming of Europeans. The falls are three times wider than Niagara and significantly larger than Victoria. Some 275 waterfalls, from 60 to 82 metres in height, are gathered here in one place.

than is carried by the River Thames. Enormous quantities of water plunge, boiling, into a narrow gorge called 'the devil's throat'.

But it is not only to see these falls that I have travelled to South America, nor to study the famous Itaipu Dam, which has changed southern Brazil for good and which produces 90 per cent of the electricity required by Paraguay and 25 per cent of Brazil's electricity needs. No, it is above all to understand something that is visually the least spectacular example one could think of, but which nonetheless will come to have enormous, although yet unknown, significance in the future: there has recently been discovered in the same region a 'lake', one of the very largest, if not *the* largest, groundwater reservoirs in the world.

Map 9. The map indicates the location and size of the Guarani reservoir. Even the portion within Brazil is larger than Great Britain, France and Spain together.

It lies beneath the point where the waters plunge down over Iguazu Falls and under the region where the Iguazu River and a whole series of other rivers wind their way across this great plain. It is called Guarani because it covers approximately the same area that the Guarani people once dominated. Under Brazil alone, the reservoir is the size of Great Britain, France and Spain combined. But it also extends under parts of Argentina, Paraguay and Uruguay as well.[79]

This 'largest ocean beneath the earth' covers an area of 1.9 million square kilometres and contains about 37,000 cubic kilometres of water. The whole

62. I have always been fascinated by Brazil as the world's foremost footballing nation, but it was only very recently that I learned that Brazil is also the world's most water-rich country. Therefore, there can be no doubt that Brazil has a long-term strategic advantage that will strengthen the country's development and international position in the struggle for power and influence.

world could drink from it for 200 years, and the whole Brazilian population of 150 million people could drink it for 2,500 years, before it became empty. Seventy million people are either directly or indirectly influenced by it. It was formed more than 130 million years ago and every year it gives rise to just as much water as the Nile carries in a period of two years, thanks, among other factors, to an annual rainfall of around two metres, for example, in the area around the Falls. Thus, it is actually a gigantic water bank that in part regenerates itself.

The quest for, and the control over, the large and until now hidden water resources of the globe will gain greater significance when more and more countries come to experience water crises due to increased demand and changes in precipitation patterns. The discovery of Guarani, and of other underground water reservoirs that new investigative methods are certain to reveal (large underground water reservoirs have been discovered, for instance, beneath Darfur in Sudan and on the Indian subcontinent as well as in China), will not only open up new arenas for conflict over water but will also cause adjustments to Doomsday scenarios. Of all the water on earth, only 0.0001 per cent of it runs through the rivers that countries are now fighting over and which will be most affected by climate change. Beneath the surface of the earth, in groundwater reservoirs, rather unaffected in the short term by climate change, we find the major portion of fresh water (that which is not ice); a hundred, perhaps even a thousand, times more water than there is in all the rivers and lakes together.[80] Guarani is illustrative of this general scenario and at the same time its discovery has given new possibilities to an already water-rich region.

I drive inland to Araraquara where it is already apparent that there cannot be the least doubt but that the reservoir will become a magnet of national and international industry. The water pumped up out of the ground can be drunk without treatment of any sort. The local water engineer in Araraquara says that he has put a glass into a spring and filled it with groundwater that wells up on the lot belonging to the local waterworks. 'This seldom happens in Brazil, but the water is pure.'

'And it tastes good,' I add.

'Coca-Cola is establishing itself here, and European beer producers and Brazilian juice producers. It has become a magnet for industries that need pure water.'

One of the municipal politicians, Carlos Nascimento, tells me over lunch, which in this part of the world is a sumptuous buffet where various meat carvers stand in a row to give us the portion of beef that we desire, about how this discovery has given a new future to the whole region. But the reservoir is under threat.

He takes us out of the city and after a while we swing off the main road and drive through endless sugarcane plantations.

'Here, you see how the poison mixes with the water and will trickle down into the ground water reservoir, which is only a few tens of metres below us.' He shows me small puddles where the water is bubbling, due to chemical reactions. 'The sugarcane is sprayed from the air with insecticides,' he states. Ethanol production can certainly reduce CO_2 emissions but for the groundwater around here it can be catastrophic. For this reason governments must enact legislation and a use protocol that functions.

One obstacle will be the insecurity as to who owns the water, and how proprietary relations will be regulated. The countries have come together over common institutions, with the support of The World Bank. But the level of mistrust is great. I constantly hear rumours that the USA has plans to seize this resource for itself! Leonardo, our guide, mentions this as well. Will those who own the land above the water also own the water? If so, will the Indians, if they are given rights to the land, also sit on the water resources? And does one establish a just regime for consumption from the reservoir, given that it is difficult to decide what belongs to whom?

I lie down and doze off in one of the many curative baths that have already been established with Guarani water to bring tourists here. This is in Brazil, not far from the Iguazu Falls. The water feels completely untouched and mineral-rich, an impression that is probably affected by the PR of the hotel, which explains that all the water here is changed every four hours, day and night, day after day. The hotel can do this easily, and for little money, because the water is constantly rising from an apparently almost endless source where it is about 37°C at all times. I greet the German I met in the reception but he does not see me, but he also most likely wants to be by himself.

I read more about the aquifer, and it is definitely a blessing to a country that is becoming more and more powerful and is developing rapidly. In an age distinguished by uncertainty over the future of the water landscape, this region has a stable and predictable water bank, a strategic reserve that all other areas can and will envy. The whole area is sitting on what is literally hidden wealth, but which will become increasingly important economically and politically. To apportion the use of a gigantic ocean under the surface of the earth that no one can see and that is difficult to control will also demand forms of cooperation and rules that still have not yet been worked out.

No continent has more water per inhabitant than does South America. They have Guarani, but also large rivers like the Amazon. In 1541, the first European to research the Amazon was the Spanish soldier, Francisco de Orellana, who is said to have given the river its name after having reported hard struggles between tribes with female warriors, whom he compared to the Amazons of Greek mythology. Three centuries later, following his stay in the Amazon realm between 1848 and 1859, the English naturalist H. W. Bates wrote *The Naturalist on the River Amazon*, in two volumes. It is still one of the great classics, but for me, the book about the Amazon, one of the first 'adult books' I read, was *The Lost Steps* by the Cuban writer Alejo Carpentier. This deals with a journey up the river, told as a journey toward the source of life and its origins. The book, or the atmosphere created in the book, makes an indelible impression. A disillusioned musician from New York journeys up the Amazon together with his lover, partly in flight from what he considers an empty existence in New York, and partly to take up once again his project of gathering musical instruments from the far corners of the earth. The book recounts how he is reborn in a village far up the river, a place outside history and without Western civilisation. It is a kind of reverse version of Joseph Conrad's *Heart of Darkness*, where civilisation is in the jungle and where the savages are living in the cities that he has abandoned. What I remember best, for unclear reasons, is the writer's description of how music gradually shifted its sources of inspiration – the music came more and more as if from the world itself; in other words, he came to hear the music that the world is playing – the wind, the trees and, above all, the water.

The Amazon does not resemble most other rivers. By far the world's largest river – it has more water in it than all the next eight largest rivers together – it sends 300,000 cubic metres of water into the ocean every second. When it is at its highest level it accounts for more than 20 per cent of all fresh water emptying into the ocean every year. And at the mouth it looks like a sea. Moreover it illustrates a physical law that will have enormous consequences for large parts of the world: for generations sailors have fooled greenhorn cabin boys by dipping buckets into the ocean, pulling the buckets up over the railing and taking a drink, to the great surprise of the uninitiated cabin boys. But the fact is that, even far out to sea, east of the coast of Brazil and beyond the sight of land, one can drink fresh water!

But the struggle to control water will also take place under the ocean. We already know of 500 fresh-water reservoirs below the ocean floor. Research into what is found in them has only just begun.[81] People have long known that there is drinking water down there and that fresh water rises because it is lighter than saltwater. The Greek geographer Strabo relates how the inhabitants of a city in Syria sailed out to sea, sunk a ceramic pipe under the water surface, and then drew up fresh water.

Some of these reservoirs beneath the bottom of the ocean will surely be gigantic. Nobody knows how big the hidden water riches are. Since we still do not know where they are, we also do not know how they will affect power relations and economic development. The struggle to find them and seize control of them has only just begun.

63. The author at the Nesjavellir factory, one of the world's largest geothermal factories.

CHAPTER 23
THE ISLAND OF THE SAGAS ENTERS THE AGE OF WATER

Some writers have the gift of prophecy and Jules Verne has to be placed among them. In the 1870s he wrote *The Mysterious Island*, about a society and an economy driven by water:

> 'It is to be hoped so' replied Gideon Spilett, 'because without coal, no more machines, and without machines, no more railways, no more steamships, no more factories, nothing of that which is indispensable to modern civilisation!'
>
> 'But what will they find?' asked Pencroft. 'Can you imagine, Captain?'
>
> 'Nearly, my friend.'
>
> 'And what will they burn in the place of coal?'
>
> 'Water,' replied Harding.
>
> 'Water,' cried Pencroft, 'water to heat steamships and locomotives, water to heat water?'
>
> 'Yes, but water decomposed into its basic elements,' replied Harding, decomposed doubtlessly by electricity, which will then become a powerful and manageable force [. . .] Water will be the coal of the future.'
>
> 'I would like to see that,' said the sailor.[82]

Alltinget, the Icelandic National Assembly, was the first and is so far the only parliament in the world that has passed legislation to abandon the age of fossil fuels and enter the 'water age' or the 'hydro-age', publicly stating that their aim was to realise just such a science fiction society described by Smith/Harding in Verne's book.

Compared to most other capitals Reykjavik reminds one most of a fishing village, but as far as trend-setting goes it has long been acknowledged that Icelanders are on the cutting edge of modernity, located as they are on the dividing line between cultural influences from the USA and from Europe (and

64. The world's first bus that runs on water and expels water.

coincidentally on the dividing line between two of the earth's tectonic plates such that the country grows broader by a couple of centimetres each year). To be the first country on the planet to adopt the resolution that the age of fossil fuels must be ended was, from all points of view, an exercise in 'smart state branding'. And in a time when the fear of global warming has become part of the globalised world's collective psychology, the country was simultaneously given an aura of modernity and responsibility. But Iceland has also been in the vanguard when it comes to trying out the technology of the future, because it was here that the first bus to be run on water was being driven around in regular service, among the barren volcanic mountains. To ride on this bus was, above all else, the reason I came here.

From the contemporary point of view, changes of great historical significance often appear to be quite trivial and precisely for this reason they are often difficult to discover or recognise. Such was definitely the case with the 'water bus'. Apart from a large blue 'H2O' sign painted on the outside, it was almost disappointingly normal – the sound, the speed, the suspension brought no surprises. But when the driver took me out of Reykjavik on a special tour, through the black, barren landscape toward Thingvellir, the place where the Vikings gathered in consultation almost one thousand years ago, I felt 'the clamour of history'. I was being driven around in the land of the ancient Vikings in a bus emitting no exhaust, only water. And even more unique, and considerably more revolutionary, a bus that was being driven forward, kilometre after kilometre, fuelled by water. And the mundane appearance of the bus, its very triviality, only added to its power as a symbol of a future that has to come, and as a practical illustration of a technology in its infancy.

We fuelled up from the first station in the world that dispenses hydrogen, which was separated from oxygen with the assistance of water electrolysis and water power. The station produces hydrogen through an electrolysing unit, which for its part – and this the reason why it is possible to say that the bus operates completely pollution-free – is driven by electricity made from water power. While the hydrogen bus glided pollution-free across the volcanic landscape, the driver told me about problems they have had with the project and how expensive the fuel is, but also about encouraging developments internationally. In Japan 50,000 fuel-cell vehicles were to be on the market by 2010 and 5 million by 2020, he told me, and a whole series of countries had established infrastructure for hydrogen vehicles, where cars can be fuelled from their own local stations.

But what is special with Iceland is the way in which they produce the hydrogen. Through the process of electrolysis the water (H_2O) is separated into hydrogen gas (H_2) and oxygen gas (O_2). The environmental properties of the hydrogen that is produced in different countries are no better than the energy source that produces the substance; just as it can be produced using electricity so too can hydrogen be produced using coal, natural gas and bio-energy. At present almost all production of hydrogen in the world is still based on fossil-fuel raw materials, and mostly with natural gas, but in Iceland they also used water – something not considered a possible global solution until now. A study carried out by the World Resource Institute in Washington DC showed that to conduct a hydrogen-driven economy in the USA by means of electrolysis, annually would require an amount of water equivalent to that which pours over Niagara Falls in a three-month period, and it would increase the USA's water demand by 10 per cent. I have not come across any evaluations of this report but it might very well be quite accurate, since today's technology has still not advanced very far. Iceland has considerable water power and considerable geothermal power, such that a carbon-free production cycle, at least in theory, could be achieved before it is possible in other countries. The experiment with buses in Iceland might fail. The technology is still too costly. But supporters of this technology have an unshakeable belief that it is only a matter of time – in the future it will be possible for large ocean-going ships to cross the Atlantic with only a small amount of water as their energy source. In this light, the bus I was driving around in on the island of the Viking sagas has shown its usefulness – a small experiment, but the beginning of a development whose results are as yet complex and difficult to visualise.

'Water will be the coal of the future,' said Harding in Jules Verne's book. Some hundred years after the coal shafts were excavated deeper and deeper under the earth of England and Wales, and which came to change the world forever, the Icelanders are digging their way still much deeper down into the ground – several kilometres deep in fact – for down there is to be found what can replace coal and oil, and thereby change the future world: hot water and terrestrial heat. Few countries have made such advances as Iceland when it comes to utilising the ability of water to retain and transport heat, particularly the heat hidden under the surface of the earth. Science still knows surprisingly little about the world beneath our feet. But one thing is indisputable: there is a gigantic reservoir of heat down there.

To me, the most interesting place in Iceland – even when compared with the regular and spectacular exertions of water at Geysir, or the Blue Lagoon with its air of surrealism, or Þingvellir, near Reykjavik and the Hengill volcanic area where one finds both the crest of the Mid-Atlantic Ridge and the birth place of the Icelandic parliament – is Nesjavellir. Not because it is the world's largest geothermal plant, for the factory building itself is unremarkable and the guest-house smells like it has been impregnated with rotten eggs, and the museum is uninteresting. It is the perfect setting, unrivalled in the way it underlines the particular features of a highly industrialised cultural landscape. The noisy plant manifests a kind of raw primitive power in its solitary setting, surrounded by smoke and the nauseating stench of sulphur – an inferno with volcanic mountains at its back and Iceland's largest lake in front. The whole of this cramped plain is at its most spectacular as the sun begins to set, or early in the morning, when the boiling rivers obliterate themselves in their own steam due to the light and the temperature differences.

It is here that Icelanders tap the rawest of nature's forces. They have bored more than 200 holes 2,000 metres down into the ground. At the surface it would boil off at 100°C at this depth and pressure, the water is a steady 300°C. Ancient rain which has run down through fissures in the rocks becomes heated by the hot mountain, and roars to the surface in the form of steam. This carbon-free energy drives turbines and generates electricity, and at the same time it brings up hot water to warm the houses and the cafes of Reykjavik. Drilling rigs stand here and there around Iceland, accessing this unused, carbon-free and renewable source of energy. Bubbling hot springs, or geothermal areas, are found at 280 locations around the island.

'Yes, yes, that's right. The amount of energy that these fields have is ten billion

65. Transporting hot water to Reykjavik, Iceland.

giga-watt hours, or about three million times Iceland's electricity requirements.' While we drive in his large SUV, the leader of one of the big projects confirms what I have read. We are driving through a landscape where every so often, through the mist and the rain clouds, I can see white steam coming up out of the black earth.

'And what are the plans?' I ask after the engineer has filled me in on all the technical details about the size and capacity of the drilling rigs as we climb a slippery ladder and the wind blows in – wet, cold and horizontal – from the Atlantic Ocean, and makes the job unpleasant for the men who are able to bore down into the boiling hot water, 3,000 metres beneath the crust of the earth, deeper than anyone has bored in other parts of the world.

'We can provide power-demanding industry with carbon-free sustainable energy. We hope that Iceland will become an attractive localisation place. And we want to sell the earth's inner energy,' he says, smiling, while we both settle ourselves, wet and cold, back inside the vehicle.

Iceland is one of just a few countries that have begun to make use of the earth's interior as a source of heat and power on a large scale. For every kilometre that one bores down, the temperature increases by between 20 and 40°C. What is special about Iceland is that the temperature increase is greater: between

47°C and 86°C per kilometre. But everywhere, the earth's interior is an inexhaustible source of heat, a source we have only just begun to utilise.

Once again the properties of water put themselves at the service of humanity, but this time in a completely different way from the forms of control that were fundamental to the rise of civilisation. Water power replaced the muscle power of human beings and animals 2,000 years ago. It played a decisive role in what is commonly called the Industrial Revolution 250 years ago – first by driving water wheels, then in steam engines before oil and other fossil fuels took over. Now water may be able to solve some of the problems it has itself created, by releasing the world from a form of development that is not sustainable; in other words, water can, by being used and exploited in new ways, counteract a development that threatens development itself.

When the aircraft lifts off from the island of the sagas and I see Reykjavik below, and the bay from which smoke also rose when the first Vikings arrived here in their ships more than a thousand years ago, I am in no doubt: qualified technological optimism is the only optimism that endures, but also, by the end of the journey, I am more convinced than ever that it is not sufficient in order to solve the combined challenges of energy production and environmental sustainability.

66. *Mona Lisa*, the most famous painting in the world, was painted by Leonardo da Vinci while he was working on plans to use the Arno River as a weapon against Pisa. One historian has explained the river in the background to the picture as follows: even while he painted the wife of one of Florence's most solid citizens, it seems as though, in the back of his head, Leonardo was preoccupied with the projects on which he co-operated with Machiavelli.

EPILOGUE

The water you touch in a river is the last of that which has passed and the first of that which is coming. Thus it is with the present.
Leonardo da Vinci[83]

The Hindu temple complex at Angkor Wat is a fantastic place to be at any time of the year, but I am here during the New Year celebration in the middle of April. Here, as in many other countries along the Mekong, people throw water at each other. The streets are full of people. Children and youths stand around, half-hidden or out in the open at the roadside, with buckets filled with water. They are waiting for a passing 'sacrificial victim', like three girls on a scooter, a couple on a bicycle, or, what is supremely better – a lorry or an open pickup fully loaded with people dressed in their festive gear. The goal is to get passers-by as wet as possible. As a rule, the families riding in the backs of lorries have equipped themselves with their own water buckets, as weapons of defence and counter-attack.

What is being played out here is a modern variant of an ancient Buddhist tradition, spread from Burma and particularly from Thailand in recent years. According to tradition, Buddha came from heaven on the first day and returned on the third day of the celebration. This was a most auspicious time for washing away all sins. In the palaces they poured water down each other's backs from silver bowls. Outside the palace, the people poured water over one another from buckets. We have to be careful of the camera and microphones; despite everything, we are on the job, but it is difficult not to be infected by the unusually powerful atmosphere of playfulness and carefree merriment, in stark contrast to the historical fate of the region.

Angkor civilisation was made possible through irrigation and trade. The Mekong was the precondition for both. For 600 years, from the tenth to the sixteenth centuries, Angkor was the capital of the Khmer Empire. Angkor was a royal centre that extended from the tip of the Indo-China Peninsula to Yunnan in China, and from Vietnam westward toward the Bay of Bengal. Angkor comes from the Sanskrit word *nagara*, and means 'city'. In a relatively small region, during the 1100s and 1200s, it is estimated that there was a population of almost one million people. The kings built an enormous temple complex in honour of themselves and the gods; a temple complex that is still one of the largest and most beautiful in the world. Many consider the pagoda at Angkor to be the jewel of Indo-China. The roughly 100 temples are generally described as the Khmer people's 'heart of stone'. Around the city was created what was perhaps the most intricate system of artificial watering of that period. The earliest sources describing such large irrigation works date from the late 800s. The Khmers harvested three and sometimes four crops of rice a year in a region that from a natural perspective was not particularly well-suited for more than one harvest in the course of a year.

In 1296, Chou Ta-Kuan, the emissary of the Emperor of China, visited Angkor after having journeyed up the Mekong and over the Great Sea, or Tonlé Sap, a lake extremely rich with fish, where people lived closely together in houses built on poles pounded into the bottom of the lake. In a work entitled *Memorandum on the Customs of Cambodia*, Chou left behind a description regarding the divine position of the king, the heavy chains of gold and pearls he had around his ankles and wrists, about his five wives, the belief that he possessed magical protective powers, and thus for the good of his kingdom he had, every night, to make love to a spirit, a nine-headed dragon dressed as a woman; and about the ritual bathing of the statues of the gods. Angkor was abandoned in the 1500s. The European public first heard about the Angkor civilisation in 1863 in writings by Frenchman, Henri Mouhot, the 'official' discoverer. Later, at a colonial exhibition in Paris in 1931, a reconstructed model of the temple complex became a sensation.

Today, Angkor is accessible on an easy flight from Phnom Penh, and is a tourist attraction. To walk along the moats that encircle and reflect the magnificent temples, to see the Angkor Wat Temple in the sunset (it faces toward the west, the direction of death), or to stroll along the stone-paved road through the main entrance, over the square to the tower that is farthest away – while all the while being aware that historians suppose this construction to symbolise a metaphoric journey back to the Year Zero, or to the time when the universe was created – is a melancholy journey. For me, despite the magnificent elegance of the temples and the hundreds of graceful statues, Angkor radiates melancholy more than anything else. The energy and the organisation of society expressed in these majestic buildings become all the more telling now that we have learned that it was changes to the water landscape brought about by climate change and human intervention that led to this civilisation disappearing from history.

The Bedouins in the desert of Oman have wandered with their camels and their families, from one well to another for generations. In certain places the lack of water is so precarious that they gather up the night's dew by hanging up a sheet and catching the drops. The Bedouins speak about rain as life, and one of the standard questions in their long and involved greeting rituals is thus: 'Do you have life [that is, rain] in your area?'

There has been nothing to indicate that I am in one of the driest places on earth as I arrive in Muscat, the capital of the country. I arrive in a cloud-burst that continues for hours, a cloud-burst in which the rain streams down more violently and in greater quantities than I have ever seen. It is so unusual that a worker watering the grass at the edge of road continues to water even though water stands half a metre deep on the roadbed beside him. The cloud-burst interferes with my plans. I am warned against going to certain places in the desert because I could drown! Indeed, some years earlier eight English tourists had been buried under earth and water, and it happened so quickly that they scarcely had time to be startled. They had gone into one of the *wadi*s or valleys that often have a little surface water at the bottom and are thus popular places for excursions. People go out for picnics, taking along tea, fruit, biscuits and a picnic blanket.

A few days later, Hussein from the Water Department tells me, while we are crossing such a wadi riverbed in a Land Cruiser, that he had taken his family to such a place during one of his free days. The weather was beautiful; it was around that time in the afternoon when the sun's play of colours accentuates the sharp contours of the mountains. Suddenly he heard a violent noise coming from the wadi. He knew immediately a flood was coming, and so he gathered up his children, his wife and some of the picnic things, threw himself into the vehicle, gunned the gas pedal to the floor and hit the horn to warn others. They reached the main road and swung to the left exactly when the flood arrived: a wave of water, stones and mud that would have buried them all in a matter of seconds.

We take the main road out of Muscat, a busy port city on the Indian Ocean that looks like a palm garden, as if it were in the tropics. Here people face the ocean. Oman has had colonies along Africa's east coast and, on the island of Zanzibar, in today's Tanzania, there are groups who would like to withdraw from the union with the old Tanganyika from the 1960s and establish stronger ties with the Sultanate of Oman. And what is perhaps less known is that Oman had trading colonies in today's Pakistan, right up to 1947, when these were disbanded at the same time as the British colonial power withdrew from the Indian subcontinent. We cross the Al-Hajar Mountains, which divide the country in two, and drive on to Nizwa, the former capital and centre of Oman's historical core region. In contrast to the cities east of the mountains, which have been based on shipping and fish, this is an inland city, and like all the other cities it has been dependent on agriculture and trade between the coast and the surrounding districts. It is the beginning of May, right before the summer heat. Oman has a reputation for being one of the hottest places on earth, and before the days of air-conditioning, people would be 'watered' during the night so that they could tolerate the heat. Despite the fact that only about 100 millimetres of rain falls annually, and the heat causes evaporation to be very high, Oman is still the only country on the Arabian side of the Gulf where agriculture has been conducted in great style down through history. This agriculture has always been completely dependent on irrigation.

Since the 1990s Oman has gone in for a moderate policy of modernisation. While earlier sultans refused to allow their subjects to listen to the radio or watch television, and had insisted on personally signing all applications for visas to other countries, Sultan Qaboos, when he assumed power after his father in the 1970s, tried to carry out a step-by-step policy of modernisation. But since development is predicated on increased water consumption, and Oman is a country without surface water and with very little precipitation, it has become more and more clear that the scarcity of water is a central hindrance to development. Around Muscat, on the Al-Batinah Coast, the pumping up of groundwater has led to the growth of agriculture. Seventy-five per cent of the water needs have been met by using groundwater. Drawings and photos of the coastal strip from the beginning of the twentieth century show a desert where now we are driving through an almost endless green oasis. But the groundwater is sinking fast.

A series of towns and settlements is to be found at the foot of the Al-Hajar Mountains in the interior of the country. They have been made possible due to a revolution in the watering system. An underground canal system was dug out thousands of years ago. Irrigation water here does not come from lakes or rivers, as they do not exist. Rather the system is based on the fact that approximately 90 per cent of the rainfall runs down the steep and naked mountainside and on down into the groundwater. Beneath the surface, sheltered from the sun and from evaporation, natural reservoirs have formed.

The *qanats*, long underground tunnels that go from the reservoirs near the mountainside to the fields, perhaps several kilometres away, are very old – so old in fact that no one knows exactly when they were excavated. Legend has it that Solomon, son of David, visited Oman on a magic carpet. His djinns or spirits, built 10,000 such canals in ten days. Those that do not dry out, even in the driest years, are thus still called Daudis, after the son of David. What can be calculated for sure is that the *qanats* were excavated when the Persians controlled this part of the Arabian Peninsula. Some of the long underground canals were therefore ready for use 2,500 years ago. Daris (Darius), which provides water to Nizwa (presumably named after the founder of the Achaemenid Dynasty, the Persian Cyrus who reigned from 550 to 530 BC) is now five kilometres long, of which three kilometres are underground. The *qanat* now waters 16,000 palm trees and provides water to 2,000 licensees.

When I climb down into this underground tunnel, which at its deepest is 34 metres below the surface of the ground, and realise that it has carried water and kept society alive in the same way for thousands of years, almost without any maintenance, it is impossible not to be impressed by the engineering arts of the Persians and their organisational ability. The current is so strong that it is difficult to walk completely upright. The heat and humidity are suffocating, and it must have been this way when Cyrus had it dug out. Here, under the surface of the earth, time has stood still. The *qanat* has not changed. I walk through some that have not changed for 2,500 years but nonetheless are of overriding importance locally. They created the city 2,500 years ago and are life lines today. I feel, as I wade along, sweating and longing for fresh air, that I am walking on what French historian, Fernand Braudel, would have called the 'long dureé' of history, or History's Long Trajectory, in Nizwa. A journey to hunt for the 'hidden' role of fresh water, or the deep structural relationship between society and water, from generation to generation, is a hunt for conditions that change very slowly, almost unnoticeably, but which nonetheless are always creating and recreating the precise conditions needed for social development. Few things could represent the meaning of such hidden 'eternal' structures in the same way as the canals or *qanats* of Oman.

Back from Nizwa, on the emerald green lawn outside the luxury hotel in Muscat where I have been lodged by the Omani Information Ministry, as I allow my glance to drift from the red- and blue-hued mountains across the sandy beaches stretching for kilometres and out over the Indian Ocean, and while the Filipino waiters, discreetly professional, set fruit bowls on the table, my eyes find their way to an article in an Omani newspaper about the lack of water. It starts with a citation from the English poet, Lord Byron: 'Only those who have suffered thirst know the value of water.' I doubt whether he is right, because those who have much water while others suffer from thirst will also know its value.

From Piazzale Michelangelo in Florence, I have a fine view of some of this Italian medieval city's architectural and artistic landmarks: Santa Maria del Fiore, known as Il Duomo, the Church of Santa Croce, where among others, Galileo, Michelangelo and Machiavelli lie buried, and Ponte Vecchio, Europe's oldest arched bridge, which Hitler spared during his retreat during the Second World

War. Not least of my impressions from here is how Florence has been built up around the River Arno, where it comes running down the mountains of Tuscany on its way to Pisa and the Mediterranean.

Around 500 years ago, precisely as the flowering of the Renaissance reached its apex and modern humanism arose, two of the most important people in the European history of ideas – Leonardo da Vinci and Niccoló Machiavelli – got together here to work on their only common project. In relation to the standards of the day it was a gigantic water project. The water project was to transform Florence into a port city by changing the river flow. But they also wanted to use the river as a military weapon against the neighbouring city of Pisa; they would use thirst to bring the enemy to its knees.

Leonardo and Machiavelli were, of course, far from being the first people to think up great plans for the utilisation of water. In Italy the rivers had long been controlled and tamed with dykes and canals.[84] Nor was it a new idea to use artificially controlled rivers in the ongoing rivalry between the city states. Dante, perhaps the foremost writer of the Renaissance, wrote about the peaceful use of the arts of hydraulic engineering in *The Divine Comedy*, but he also fantasised about punishing Pisa by damming up the Arno in order to flood the city. And early in the sixteenth century, the architect Brunelleschi, who built Il Duomo and its famous dome, convinced the government of Florence to try out this weapon in practice. He had the Serchio River dammed up in order to flood the neighbouring city of Lucca. His attempt, however, was unsuccessful.

Leonardo and Machiavelli worked out a much more comprehensive and audacious plan. No other engineering project of that period, in terms of its ambitions, can be compared with their plan to make Florence a port city by directing the Arno by canal through Pistoia (which is located more than 20 kilometres north of the river's normal course), and send it by tunnel under Mount Serravalle, and at the same time deprive Pisa of its share of the river. Leonardo worked out the details of the project in 1503 and 1504: how the river should be moved and the depth that was necessary so that the new canal would be successful in becoming the new course for the river; and he worked out the conditions of the current, how much earth had to be moved and even drew a picture of a sort of model digging machine that would help to remove the earth.

At the same time as he was working on the plans to use the River Arno as a weapon against Pisa, Leonardo was also completing the most famous painting in the world – the *Mona Lisa*. One historian explains the river in the background of the picture as follows: 'Even when painting the wife of one of Florence's solid citizens, Leonardo seems to have had in the back of his mind the projects on which he and Niccoló were collaborating.'[85] Machiavelli, who held a central administrative position, gave the project his full support as well as arranging to have it financed. But the whole project failed. Some historians maintain it was because those who carried out the work ignored Leonardo's technical advice; others emphasised that the plan itself undervalued the Arno and how difficult it was to subdue the river to the will of Renaissance men. Leonardo and Machiavelli experienced – to a profound degree – one of Francis Bacon's aphorisms, formulated only a few decades later: 'Nature, to be commanded, must be obeyed.'[86]

As I stand on the Ponte Vecchio and stare out downriver, as it winds its way toward Pisa, I recite to myself T. S. Eliot's verse from 'The Dry Salvages': 'The river is in us, a strong, brown God – sullen, untamed and intractable.' Machiavelli and Leonardo attempted to control the currents of both the Arno and of history, by combining science, technology and power. The ambition to do so, to use such means to conquer nature and affect history, was a rare occurrence then, but later it was realised many many times, and on a much greater scale. And as we have seen, it is now, and in the coming decades, that the really gigantic plans for the submission of water are being brought to life.

The possibilities of conflict are many, due to the new age of uncertainty, the probable and dramatic changes in the water landscape, and the steady increase in the demand for water. In addition, the water barons of the future will possess a technological and economic power that neither Leonardo nor Machiavelli could possibly have imagined. The temptation to use the power of water in the same direct despotic manner as that of the foremost thinkers of the Renaissance will not disappear, and the only way to counter such possible plans is to establish binding international laws and regulations and international institutions backed with resources and power.

Still, at different places on the globe, every year, thousands of societies both large and small – including the most modern – experience how difficult it is to control the rivers and the local and regional water system. In its time, Pisa was decisively weakened when the mouth of the Arno silted up. So if anything it was nature, as much as hostile city states, that weakened it. Florence has been hit repeatedly by great floods. The great catastrophe came in 1966, when large parts of the city were suddenly underwater and the largest loss of European art treasures in modern time became a reality. No matter how grandiose human attempts to manage water are, water does not allow itself to be completely controlled. Gradually, particularly in periods of climatic uncertainty, it will become ever more obvious that the more dependent society becomes on controlling water, the more it will be society's sovereign, because, always in a fundamental sense, it will be 'sullen, untamed and intractable'.

'Nature, to be commanded, must be obeyed.'

NOTES

Note: since much of the factual information in the text is based on direct observation and discussions, or refers to information such as water quantities and precipitation statistics that are easily available, it has not been thought necessary to refer to the mountain of books, reports and documents pertaining to this subject. In some places where I have referred to assertions considered to be controversial, I have cited the report, the press clipping or the documents from which the information has been taken. Accordingly the notes are limited to information relating to definite important references, to historical analyses I have relied upon and books that I have used.

1 See, for example, Coopey and Tvedt 2006, Tvedt and Jacobson 2006 and Tvedt and Østigård 2006. These three books contain about 70 contributions from researchers from about 50 countries, writing on various aspects of the significance and history of water.

2 To get some idea of the books that give a good picture of the properties of water and its role in nature, and how much there is, see Ball 1999, Botkin & Keller 2005, Berner & Berner 1987, Cosgrove & Petts 1990, Schneider 1996, Šiklomanov & Rodda 2003 and Tollan 2002. The International Bureau of the Permanent Court of Arbitration 2002 provides an overview of some of the difficulties with regard to water and international regulations.

3 For those readers who are interested in London's historic water system and how the rivers have been constructed to flow underground, see for example Trench & Hillman 2000.

4 See, for example, Berner and Berner 1987 on the significance of the hydrological cycle for the climate and the environment and for how climate influences it; Chorley 1969 for an analysis for the links between water, earth and socio-economic relations; Ball 1999 for a fascinating analysis of water's completely unique properties and finally, Cosgrove and Petts 1990 for (certainly a little limited) description of how water forms the landscape.

5 See Cohn 1996 for a short and interesting overview of the flood myths in Western thought. There is an extremely comprehensive literature on the religious significance and meaning of the flood myths and their relationship to factual ecological processes.

6 Also as a commentary to Goudie 1994 who discusses the same theme but from the perspective of dry regions.

7 The articles were Duan and Yao 2002, 2003. It is easy to find interviews with him on the internet.

8 For confirmation of this percentage, see Pradhan & Shrestha 1992, in Eaton 1992.

9 See also Sven Hedin's books on Tibet and Central Asia, Hedin 1898.

10 See Xue-Yong et al. 2002. According to their research, carried out in 1996 there are 336,464.4 hectares of 'severely desertified land', which is termed 'mobile sand land' and 20,047,411.40 hectares of 'desertified land' (p. 189).

11 Citation from *National Geographic News*, January 23, 2007: Alps Glaciers Gone by 2050, Expert Says, by John Roach. Psenner is not a glaciologist but a limnologist.

12 See van de Ven 1994 for a book that documents in technical detail how the Netherlanders have created their country.

13 The Ministry is trying to do something about what it regards as lack of knowledge and lack of understanding. A very illustrative work in this direction is Ministry of Transport & Public Works 2004.

14 Deputy Minister of Transport and Water, Melanie Schultz van Haegen, interview, TV documentary *En Reise i vannets fremtid [A Journey into the Future of Water].*

15 Diamond 2005 has three chapters on this history, see pp 178–277, but he builds much of this on the more fundamental articles by McGovern et al. 1988, and McGovern 1991.

16 *Climate Change: On the Edge*, Jim Hansen, *http://www.ezilon.com/information/article_15998.shtml*, accessed 17.02.2006. Jim Hansen is Director of the NASA Goddard Institute for Space Studies and was the main climate modeller for President George W. Bush.

17 See *National Geographic News*, 20.09.2006: 'Greenland's Ice Melt Grew by 250%, Satellites Show.'

18 Ruskin 1853.

19 See, for example, Ciriacono 2006, one of several books published about Venice's water history in recent years.

20 Keahy 2002: 16.

21 See, for example, Fletcher and Spencer 2003 for a comprehensive description of the situation.

22 & 23 Both these citations are taken from Keahey 2002: 276.

24 Berlusconi to Reuters News, 12 Feb. 2006.

25 See, for example, Dennis Tedlock's *Popol Vuh.*

26 One of the English translations is David Castledine's *An Account of the Things of Yucatán. Written by the Bishop of Yucatán, Based on the Oral Traditions of the Ancient Mayas.* Mexico City: Ediciones Monclem, 2000.

27 A whole series of specialised articles has been published recently about the correlation between precipitation and the fate of the Mayans. Diamond 2005 devotes a chapter to them (Diamond 2005: 157–178). Gill 2000 provides the most thorough account of this issue. This literature has certainly been criticised for being stamped with catastrophe-thinking, but since the findings are still so relatively new, it is possible that with time a more balanced analysis will emerge.

28 Lao Tze's *Tao of War*, Chapter 78. For a comprehensive translation, see Ralph Sawyer, *The Tao of War*, Westview Press, 2002. According to tradition the verses were written around the seventh century by Lao Tze, the 'Old Master' during the Zhou Dynasty. Who really composed the text and when it was actually written down is still disputed.

29 The contents were quoted in the British newspaper *The Observer* on 22 February 2004. The citations taken by *The Observer* come from the report entitled 'An Abrupt Climate Change Scenario and Its Implications for United States National Security', written by Peter Schwartz and Doug Randall. 'Disruption and conflict will be endemic features of life,' they maintain in this report. 'Once again warfare would define human life.' On the other hand, the quality of the report can certainly be discussed for it stands bombastically firm that 'As early as next year widespread flooding due to a rise in sea levels will create major upheaval for millions.' This patently did not happen in 2005. The report can thus be interpreted as an example of how climatic uncertainty is utilised politically, on this occasion during the American election campaign against George W. Bush and in favour of John Kerry.

30 Second UN World Water Report, 2006.
31 See Serageldin 1994 for a representative article from the international aid system, regarding the importance of water.
32 A series of books addressing this problematic has come out in the last few years. Those that have become best known and presumably most used by activists are Barlow and Clarke 2001, and Shiva 2002. A more general but typically journalistic angle on this phenomenon, is Ward 2002. A more academic approach is Finger & Allouche 2002.
33 See Tewari 2006 for analyses of water and justice in South Africa.
34 Roberts 1867 demonstrates how developed Spain already was in the 1860s, in the art of irrigation. Those British functionaries being sent out into colonial service went there to learn. See also Glick 1969.
35 See World Wildlife Fund 2003.
36 Consejeria de Tourismo of the Murcia Region, cited in World Wildlife Fund 2003: 16.
37 For a good overview, see Waterbury 2002. For one of the first detailed and empirical descriptions of the development of the Nile management and utilisation by countries in the region, see Tvedt 2010. Here there are articles by writers from Egypt, Sudan, Ethiopia, Uganda, Kenya, Congo, Tanzania, Rwanda and Burundi.
38 For a broad historical study of the background to the present-day Nile situation see Tvedt 2004/2006.
39 One of many studies of the recent situation on the Nile and with a focus on Ethiopia is Arsano 2006.
40 Personal communication with Torodd Jensen, NVE, 27.06.2007.
41 'Experts Probe Tilting Taj Mahal', BBC News, 20.10.2004.
42 'Concerns over Tilting Taj Mahal Dismissed', BBC News, 04.11.2004.
43 Water in Hindu religion has played a role that confirms social inequality and different forms of impurity, see Joshi and Fawcett 2006.
44 NCIWRD 1999.
45 Verna and Phansalkar 2005: 6. Patkar 2004 consists of a collection of arguments against the plan.
46 Cited in *Dams, Rivers and People*, 1, 2–3, March–April 2003, 6.
47 For a description, see Kamal 2006.
48 Elhance 1999: 168.
49 Two studies that examine this water conflict from a Bangladeshi perspective are Abbas 1984 and Begum 1987.
50 There is of course an extensive literature about this epic. For example, Heidel 1973 undertakes a comparison with the myths of the Flood in the Old Testament.
51 For a description see, for example, Kahlown and Khan 2006.
52 See Oestigaard 2006 for an analysis of the role of the waters of the Bagmati in mortuary rituals in Nepal, related to the Pashupatinah Temple.
53 See Tvedt and Oestigaard 2006. I am currently working on a large volume called 'The Ideas of Water', a history of ideas analysis of conceptions of water in the ideas of the natural sciences, philosophy and religion.
54 See also BBC News, Wednesday, 21.08.2002.
55 The total number of rivers in Nepal has been estimated at 6,000, with a total length of 45,000 kilometres. See Pradhan and Shrestha 1992.

56 Huda 2001.

57 An interesting and popular book on this subject is Halliday 1999, and an interesting article, Hardy 1984. Gandy 2006 gives a more general analysis of the significance of water for reducing mortality in the cities.

58 *The Hindu*, Sunday, 30 July 2006.

59 There is of course an extensive literature on the significance of the Seine for Paris. For me, one of the classics is Demangeon 1920.

60 It is quite obvious that one can draw comparisons between this water bar and the new popularity of water as a health product (this has been lying in a trough since the days of Hippocrates who also offered advice on the efficacious uses of warm and cold water). See Buchman 1994 for a typical volume that argues the importance of water therapy.

61 One of the many books that views California's history in a water perspective is Hundley 1992.

62 See Hisham T. El-Dessouky and H. M. Dettouney 2002 for an overview of the desalination industry, and Latterman and Höpner 2003 for an analysis of the environmental consequences with a focus on the seas surrounding the Arabian Peninsula. Here, as is the case with other industries (such as the geothermal and hydrogen industries) there are innumerable websites of diverse international and national organisations that can be followed up.

63 See Tvedt 2004b for an overview of the literature on the Nile. The bibliography registers almost 4,000 titles and about half of them have been commented upon.

64 Abu Zeid, Egyptian Minister of Water, interview for TV documentary *En Reise i Vannets Fremtid [A Journey in the Future of Water]*.

65 For interesting books and articles about China's relationship to its water, see, for example, Dodgen 2001, Padovani 2006, Rowe 1998 and Spencer 1938.

66 See Derek Bodde, 1981, in Charles Le Blanc and Dorothy Borei, eds. *Essays on Chinese Civilization*, Princeton NJ: Princeton University Press, p. 138, cited by Dodgen 2001: 1.

67 'It will cover half of China. It is very very big.' Jiao Yong, Vice-Minister of Water Resources, China. Interview, for the TV documentary *En Reise i Vannets Fremtid (A Journey in the Future of Water)*.

68 For a description of the project see Liu and Zheng 2002. See as well, Pietz 2006 for a more general analysis of the importance of water management in modern China.

69 After I had left China it became apparent that disagreements about the project were greater than its supporters would have liked. The most westerly canal has been provisionally stopped, obviously because local and regional interests were against sending water out from the Yangtze drainage system and northwards.

70 *China Daily*, 12.06.2009.

71 Ibid.

72 See Luzhkov 2003.

73 See Duke 2006 and Micklin 1987 for an overview of the history of this project.

74 For an analysis of water and high-level politics in the region see Lange 2006.

75 ICG 2005: 28.

76 Pannier and Magauin 1999.

77 Blua 2004.

78 Pannier and Magauin 1999.

79 There are many thick scientific books about groundwater. One that is easily accessible is Chapelle 1997.

80 There are various estimates as to the quantity of water in rivers, lakes, underground, etc. There are reasons to take these numbers with a grain of salt, especially since we still know very little about how much fresh water there is beneath the land surface and under the bottom of the oceans.

81 The new technology is not much reminiscent of the old 'diviner's rod' method, but when it comes to finding underground water there are still some who swear by this method. See Bird 1979.

82 Jules Verne. 1874. *The Mysterious Island/The Abandoned*, Chapter XI. (Sidney Kravitz English translation, 2007). Characters' names vary in different editions. In the French original there is Gédéon Spillet or Spillen for he who is Gideon Spillet in the English and US editions, and 'Neb' in the original is Nab (Nabuchodonosor). Herbert Brown is Harbert Brown. In the Kingston British translation, and in some others, the engineer Cyrus Smith is called Cyrus Harding, and the sailor Bonaventure Pencroff is often called Pencroft.

83 Cited in Masters 1999.

84 See, for example, Squatri 1998, and Masters 1999.

85 Masters 1999: 107.

86 Bacon 1604/2000.

BIBLIOGRAPHY

This list of literature is composed of books cited in the text. It is also meant as a guide to further reading. It is organised in sections related to each part of the book; this has been done in order to increase its utility.

Preface

Ball, Philip, 1999. *H2O – A Biography of Water*. London: Weidenfeld & Nicolson.

Berner, Elizabeth Kay and Robert A. Berner, 1987. *The Global Water Cycle: Geochemistry and Environment*. Upper Saddle River: Prentice-Hall.

Botkin, Daniel B. and Edward A. Keller, 2005. *Environmental Science: Earth as a Living Planet*. New York: Wiley.

Chorley, R. J. 1969. *Water, Earth and Man. A Synthesis of Hydrology, Geomorphology and Socio-economic Geography*. London: Methuen & Co. IBPCA (International Bureau of the Permanent Court of Arbitration), 2002. *Resolution of Water Disputes*. The Hague: Kluwer Law International.

Coopey, Richard and Terje Tvedt, 2006. *A History of Water, Vol. II: The Political Economy of Water*. London/New York: I.B.Tauris.

Cosgrove, D. and G. Petts, 1990. *Water, Engineering and Landscape: Water Control and Landscape Transformation in the Modern Period*. London/New York: Belaven.

Schneider, S. H. 1996. *Encyclopedia of Climate and Weather*. New York: Oxford University Press.

Šiklomanov, I. A. and John C. Rodda, 2003. *World Water Resources at the Beginning of the Twenty-first Century*. Cambridge: Cambridge University Press.

Tollan, Arne, 2002. *Vannressurser*. Oslo: Universitetsforlaget.

Tvedt, Terje and Terje Østigård, 2006. *A History of Water, Vol. III: The World of Water*. New York/London: I.B.Tauris.

Tvedt, Terje and Eva Jakobsson, 2006. *A History of Water, Vol. I: River Biographies*. New York/London: I.B.Tauris.

United Nations Development Programme, 2006. *Human Development Report: Beyond Scarcity: Power, Poverty and the Global Water Crisis*. New York: Palgrave Macmillan.

Villiers, Marq de, 2001. *Water: The Fate of our most Precious Resource*. New York: Mariner Books.

Part 1: The New Uncertainty about Water

Bacon, Francis, 1604/2000. *The New Organon or True Directions Concerning the Interpretation of Nature*, Lisa Jardine and Michael Silverthorne, eds. Cambridge texts in the History of Philosophy. New York: Cambridge University Press.

Buchman, Dian Dincin, 1994. *The Complete Book of Water Therapy*. New Canaan, CT: Keats Publishing.

Burroughs, William J. 2005. *Climate Change in Prehistory. The End of the Reign of Chaos*. Cambridge: Cambridge University Press.

Ciriacono, Salvatore, 2006. *Building on Water: Venice, Holland and the Construction of the European Landscape in Early Modern Times*, Jeremy Scott, trans. Oxford & New York: Berghahn Books.

Cohn, Norman, 1996. *Noah's Flood: The Genesis Story in Western Thought*. New Haven & London: Yale University Press.

Diamond, Jared, 2005. *Collapse: How Societies Choose to Collapse or Succeed*. New York: Viking.

Duan, Keqin and Tandong Yao, 2003. Precipitation Variability in Central Himalayas and Its Relation to Northern Hemisphere Temperature. *Chinese Science Bulletin* 48 (14): 1480–1482.

Duan, Keqin and Tandong Yao, Jianchen Pu and Weiszhen Sun, 2002. Response of Monsoon Variability in Himalayas to Global Warming. *Chinese Science Bulletin* 47 (21): 1842–1845.

Fagan, Brian, 2000. *Floods, Famines and Empires: El Niño and the Fate of Civilizations*. London: Pimlico.

Fletcher, C. A. and T. Spencer, 2003. *Flooding and Environmental Challenges for Venice and Its Lagoon: State of Knowledge*. Cambridge: Cambridge University Press.

Gill, Richardson, B., 2000.*The Great Mayan Drought: Water, Life and Death*. Albuquerque NM: University of New Mexico Press.

Goudie, A. 1994. The Nature of Physical Geography. A View from the Drylands. *Geography* 79 (344): 194–209.

Hedin, Sven, 1898. *En fard genom Asien 1893-97*. Stockholm: A. Bonnier.

Keahy, John, 2002. *Venice against the Sea: A City Besieged*. New York: Thomas Dunne Books.

Landa, Fray Diego de, 2005. *An Account of the Things of Yucatán. Written by the Bishop of Yucatán, Based on the Oral Tradition of the Ancient Mayans*. México: Monclem Ediciones.

Linden, Eugene, 2006. *The Winds of Change: Climate, Weather and the Destruction of Civilizations*. New York: Simon & Schuster.

Matthewman, Steven, 2006. Science in the Social Sphere: Weather Modification and Public Response. In Terje Tvedt and Terje Østigård, eds. *A History of Water, Vol. III: The World of Water*, pp. 409–430, New York/London: I.B.Tauris.

McGovern, Thomas H. 1991. Climate, Correlation and Causation in Norse Greenland. *Arctic Anthropology* 28 (2): 77–100.

Ministry of Transport and Public Works, The Netherlands, 2004. *Water in the Netherlands 2004-2006*. The Hague.

Paterson, W. S. B. 1994. *The Physics of Glaciers*. Oxford: Butterworth/Heinemann.

Ruskin, John, 1853. *The Stones of Venice*. London: Smith, Elder & Co.

Ryan, William B. F. and Walter C. Pitman, 1998. *Noah's Flood: The New Scientific Discoveries about the Event that Changed History*. New York: Simon & Schuster.

Tedlock, Dennis, 1996. *Popol Vu: The Mayan Book of the Dawn of Life*. Dennis Tedlock, trans. and commentary, based on the ancient knowledge of the modern Quiché Maya. New York: Touchstone.

Ven, G. P. van de, 1993. *Man-made Lowlands: History of Water Management and Land Reclamation in the Netherlands*. Utrecht: Uitfeverij Matrijs.

Yang, J. P., Y. J. Ding, R. S. Chen, S. Y. Liu and A. X. Lu, 2003. Causes of Glacier Change in the Source Regions of the Yangtze and Yellow Rivers on the Tibetan Plateau. *Journal of Glaciology* 49 (167): 539–546.

Zou, X. Y., S. Li, C. L. Zhang, G. R. Dong and P. Yan, 2002. Desertification and Control Plan in the Tibet Autonomous Region of China. *Journal of Arid Environments* 51 (): 183–198.

Part 2: The Age of the Water Lords

Abbas, B. M., 1984. *The Ganges Water Dispute.* Dhaka, Bangladesh: The University Press.

Allan, J. A., 2001. *Middle East Water Question: Hydropolitics and the Global Economy*. London: I.B.Tauris.

Arsano, Y., 2006. Nile Basin Co-operation. Prospects for the Twenty-first Century. In Richard Coopey and Terje Tvedt, *A History of Water, Vol. II: The Political Economy of Water*, pp. 324–351. New York/London: I.B.Tauris.

Barlow, Maud and Tony Clarke, 2001. *Blue Gold: The Fight to Stop the Theft of the World's Water.* New York: The New Press.

Begum, Khurshida, 1987. *Tension over the Farakka Barrage: A Technical-Political Tangle in South Africa.* Dhaka, Bangladesh: The University Press.

Bourdieu, Pierre, 1984. *Distinction*. Harvard: Harvard University Press.

Buchman, Dian Dincin, 1994. *The Complete Book of Water Therapy*. New Canaan, CT: Keats Publishing.

Davenport, T. R. H. and Christopher Saunders, 2000. *South Africa: A Modern History*. Basingstoke: Macmillan.

Demangeon, Albert, 1920. The Port of Paris. *Geographical Review* 10 (5): 277–296.

Elhance, A. P. 1999. *Hydropolitics in the Third World: Conflict and Cooperation in International River Basins*, Washington DC: United States Institute of Peace Press.

Finger, Matthias and Jeremy Allouche, 2002. *Water Privatization. Transnational Corporations and the Re-regulation of the Water Industry.* London: Spon Press.

Gandy, M. 2006. Water, Modernity and the Demise of the Bacteriological City. In Terje Tvedt and Eva Jakobsson, eds. *A History of Water, Vol. I: River Biographies*, pp. 347–372. New York/London: I.B.Tauris.

Glick, Thomas F. 1968. Levels and Levelers: Surveying Irrigation Canals in Medieval Valencia. *Technology and Culture* 9 (2): 165–180.

Halliday, Stephen, 1999. *The Great Stink of London: Sir Joseph Bazalgette and the Cleansing of the Victorian Metropolis*. Stroud, Gloucestershire: Sutton Publishing.

Hardy, A. 1984. Water and the Search for Public Health in London in the Eighteenth and Nineteenth Centuries. *Medical History* 28 (3): 250–282.

Heidel, A. 1963. *The Gilgamesh Epic and the Old Testament Parallels*. Chicago: University of Chicago Press.

Joshi, D. and B. Fawcett, 2006. Water, Hindu Mythology and Unequal Social Order in India. In Terje Tvedt and Eva Jakobsson, eds. *A History of Water, Vol. I: River Biographies*, pp. 119-137. New York/London: I.B.Tauris.

Kahlown, M. A., A. D. Khan and M. Azam, 2006. The World's Largest Contiguous Irrigation System: Developments, Successes and Challenges of the Indus Irrigation System in Pakistan. In Terje Tvedt and Eva Jakobsson, eds. *A History of Water, Vol. I: River Biographies*, pp. 35–55. New York/London: I.B.Tauris.

Kamal, A. 2006. Living with Water: Bangladesh Since Ancient Times. In Terje Tvedt and Eva Jakobsson, eds. *A History of Water, Vol. I: River Biographies*, pp. 194–217. New York/London: I.B.Tauris.

N.C.I.W.R.D. 1999. Integrated Water Resource Development: A Plan for Action. Report of the National Commission for Integrated Water Resources Development (NCIWRD), Vol. I, New Delhi: Ministry of Water Resources, Government of India.

Oestigaard, Terje, 2006. River and Rain: Life-giving Waters in Nepalese Death Rituals. In Terje Tvedt and Terje Oestigaard, eds. *A History of Water, Vol. III: A World of Water*, pp. 430–449. New York/London: I.B.Tauris.

Patkar, B. K. and H. M. Shrestha, 1992. *River Linking: A Millennium Folly?* Mumbai: Sanjay, M. G. and Maju Varghese.

Pradhan, B. K. and H. M. Shrestha, 1992. A Nepalese Perspective on Himalayan Water Resources Development: The Ganges-Brahmaputra Basin Water Resource Cooperation between Nepal, India and Bangladesh. In D. J. Eaton, ed. *The Ganges Brahmaputra Basin*, Austin: University of Texas Press.

Ramachandraiah, C. 2006. Inequalities in Urban Water Supply in India: Municipalities in Andhra Pradesh. In Richard Coopey and Terje Tved, eds. *A History of Water, Vol. II: The Political Economy of Water*, pp. 28–41. London/New York: I.B.Tauris.

Regmi, A. 2006. Regimes, Regulations and Rights: Urban Water Use in the Kathmandu Valley. In Richard Coopey and Terje Tvedt, eds. *A History of Water, Vol. II: The Political Economy of Water*, pp.468–500. London/New York: I.B.Tauris.

Roberts, J. P. 1867. Irrigation in Spain. Being a paper compiled from information collected during a residence of several years in that country. London.

Serageldin, I. 1994. Water Supply, Sanitation and Environmental Sustainability: The Financial Challenge. A keynote address to the ministerial conference on drinking water and environmental sanitation: Implementing Agenda 21, Washington DC: International Bank for Reconstruction and Development/The World Bank.

Shiva, Vandana, 2002. *Water Wars: Privatization, Pollution and Profit*. Cambridge: South End Press.

Tewari, D. D. 2006. An Evolutionary History of Water Rights in South Africa. In Terje Tvedt and Terje Oestigaard, eds. *A History of Water, Vol. III: A World of Water*, pp.157–185, New York/London: I.B.Tauris.

Thabane, M. 2006. Developing Lesotho's Water Resources: The Lesotho Highlands Water Scheme. In Richard Coopey and Terje Tvedt, eds. *A History of Water, Vol. III: A World of Water*, pp. 368–390, New York/London: I.B.Tauris.

Trench, Richard and Ellis Hillman, 2000. *London under London: A Subterranean Guide*. London: John Murray.

Tvedt, Terje, 2004a. *The River Nile in the Age of the British. Political Ecology and the Quest for Economic Power.* London/New York: I.B.Tauris.

Tvedt, Terje, ed. 2010. *The River Nile in the Post-colonial Age*. London: I.B.Tauris

Umali-Deininger, Dina, 1993. Irrigation-induced Salinity: A Growing Problem for Development and the Environment. World Bank Technical Paper 215. World Bank Publications.

Verghese, B. G. 1990. *Waters of Hope: Himalaya-Ganga Development and Cooperation for a Billion People.* New Delhi: Oxford & IBH Publishing.

Verma, Shilp and S. Phansalkar, 2005. India Inc. 2050. Potential Deviations from 'Business-as-Usual'. IWMI-TATA Water Policy Research Highlights 6.

Ward, Diane Raines, 2002. *Water Wars: Drought, Flood, Folly and the Politics of Thirst.* New York: Riverhead Books.

Waterbury, John, 2002. *The Nile Basin: National Determinants of Collective Action*. New Haven, CT: Yale University Press.

Part 3: Water Transforming the World

Anton, Danilo J. 1993. *Thirsty Cities: Urban Environments and Water Supply in Latin America*, Ottawa: International Development Research Centre.

Bird, C. 1979. *The Divining Hand: The Art of Searching for Water, Oil, Minerals and Other Natural Resources or Anything Lost, Missing or Badly Needed*. New York: Dutton.

Bodde, D. 1982. *Essays on Chinese Civilization*, edited/introduced by Charles Le Blanc and Dorothy Borei, Princeton, NJ: Princeton University Press.

Chapelle, Francis H. 1997. *The Hidden Sea: Ground Water, Science and Environmental Realism*. Tucson, AZ: Geoscience Press.

Dodgen, Randall, 2001. *Controlling the Dragon: Confucian Engineers and the Yellow River in Late Imperial China*. Honolulu: University of Hawaii Press.

Duke, F. K. 2006. Seizing Favours from Nature: The Rise and Fall of Siberian River Diversion. In Terje Tvedt and Eva Jakobsson, eds. *A History of Water, Vol. I: River Biographies*, pp. 3–35, London/New York: I.B.Tauris.

El-Dessouky, Hisham T. and Hisam M. Ettouney, 2002. *Fundamentals of Salt Water Desalination*. Amsterdam: Elsevier.

Gleick, P. H. 1993. *Water in Crisis: A Guide to the World's Fresh Water Resources*. Oxford: Oxford University Press.

Gleick, P. H. 1996. Water Resources. *Encyclopedia of Climate and Weather, Vol. 2*. S. H. Schneider, ed. New York: Oxford University Press.

Hundley, Norris Jr. 1992. *The Great Thirst: Californians and Water, 1770–1990s*. Berkeley: University of California Press.

Lange, K. 2006. Energy and Environmental Security: The Syr Darya Crisis of Central Asia. In Richard Coopey and Terje Tvedt, eds. *A History of Water, Vol. III: A World of Water*, pp. 404–430. New York/London: I.B.Tauris.

Lattemann, Sabine and Thomas Höpner, 2003. Seawater Desalination. Impacts of Brine and Chemical Discharge on the Marine Environment. L'Aquila: Balaban Desalination.

Liu, C. M. and H. X. Zheng, 2002. South to North Water Transfer Schemes for China. *International Journal of Water Resources Development* 18 (3): 453–471.

Luzhkov, Yuri, 2003. *The Renewal of History: Mankind in the 21st Century and the Future of Russia*. London: Stacey International.

Masters, Roger D. 1999. *Fortune Is a River: Leonardo da Vinci and Niccoló Machiavelli's Magnificent Dream to Change the Course of Florentine History,* Middlesex UK: Plume.

Micklin, Philip P. 1987. The Fate of 'Sibaral': Soviet Water Politics in the Gorbachov Era. *Central Asian Survey* 2: 67–88.

Mount, Jeffrey F. 1995. *California Rivers and Streams: The Conflict between Fluvial Process and Land Use*. Berkeley: University of California Press.

Mumford, Lewis, 1961. *The City in History: Its Origins, Its Transformations and Its Prospects*. London: Penguin.

Naeser, R. B. and M. Griffin Smith, 2006. Water as Property in the American West. In Richard Coopey and Terje Tvedt, eds. *A History of Water, Vol. III: A World of Water*, pp. 500–507. New York/London: I.B.Tauris.

Padovani, F. 2006. The Chinese Way of Harvesting Rivers: The Yangtze River. In Terje Tvedt and Eva Jakobsson, eds. *A History of Water, Vol. I: River Biographies*, pp. 120–144, London/New York: I.B.Tauris.

Petts, Geoffrey E. and I. D. L. Foster, 1985. *Rivers and Landscape*. London: Edward Arnold.

Pietz, D. A. 2006. Controlling the Waters in Twentieth-Century China: The Nationalist State and the Huai River. In Terje Tvedt and Eva Jakobsson, eds. *A History of Water, Vol. I: River Biographies*, pp. 92–120. London/New York: I.B.Tauris.

Postel, Sandra, 1999. *Pillar of Sand: Can the Irrigation Miracle Last?* New York: W. W. Norton.

Reisner, Mark, 1986. *Cadillac Desert.* New York: Viking.

Rowe, W. T. 1998. Water Control and the Qing Political Process: The Fankou Dam Controversy, 1876–1883. *Modern China* 14 (4): 353–387.

Spencer, Joseph Earl, 1938. Trade and Transshipment in the Yangtze Valley. *Geographical Review* 28 (1): 112–123.

Squatriti, P. 1998. *Water and Society in Early Medieval Italy, AD 400-1000.* New York: Cambridge University Press.

Steinberg, Theodore, 1991. *Nature Incorporated: Industrialization and the Waters of New England.* Cambridge: Cambridge University Press.

Symon, Carolyn, Lelani Arris and Bill Heal, 2005. *Arctic Climate Impact Assessment* Cambridge: Cambridge University Press.

Tvedt, Terje, 2004b. *The Nile, An Annotated Bibliography*. New York/London: I.B.Tauris.

Wilf, Mark, Leon Awerbuch, Craig Bartels, Mike Mickley, Graeme Pearce and Nicolay Voutchkov, 2007. *The Guidebook to Membrane Desalination Technology: Reverse Osmosis, Nanofiltration and Hybrid Systems Process, Design, Applications and Economics.* Rehovot, Israel: Balaban Publishers.

Worster, Donald, 1985. *Rivers of Empire: Water, Aridity and the Growth of the American West.* New York: Pantheon Books.

PICTURE CREDITS

1. *(page 2)*: Alf Terje Fotland, IWA
2. *(page 4)*: Erik Hanemann/Panopticom
3. *(page 7)*: O. Louis Mazzatenta, National Geographic Image Collection
4. *(page 14)*: Water festival, Phnom Penh, Cambodia. Courtesy of John Vink/Magnum Photos/All Over Press
5. *(page 16)*: Laurent Monlau/Rapho/All Over Press
6. *(page 17)*: Terje Tvedt
7. *(page 18)*: Mathias Hiekel/EPA/SCANPIX
8. *(page 19)*: Reinhard Krause/Reuters/SCANPIX
9. *(page 20)*: Terje Tvedt
10. *(page 23)*: Terje Tvedt
11. *(page 28)*: Terje Tvedt
12. *(page 30)*: Dura Vermeer, Business Development, BV, Nederland
13. *(page 33)*: Terje Tvedt
14. *(page 38)*: Terje Tvedt
15. *(page 41)*: Terje Tvedt
16. *(page 43)*: Erik Hanemann/Panopticom
17. *(page 46)*: Anders Leines
18. *(page 51)*: De Soye/Rapho/All Over Press
19. *(page 54)*: Terje Tvedt
20. *(page 58)*: Terje Tvedt
21. *(page 65)*: Terje Tvedt
22. *(page 70)*: Amit Dave/Reuters/SCANPIX
23. *(page 74)*: Kim Ludbrook/EPA/SCANPIX
24. *(page 78)*: Gianluigi Guercia/AFP/SCANPIX
25. *(page 79)*: Terje Tvedt
26. *(page 82)*: Erik Hanemann/Panopticom
27. *(page 84)*: Terje Tvedt
28. *(page 89)*: Tony Garriga/EPA/SCANPIX

29. *(page 91)*: Anders Leines
30. *(page 93)*: Terje Tvedt
31. *(page 96)*: Erik Hanemann/Panopticom
32. *(page 99)*: Terje Tvedt
33. *(page 104)*: Terje Tvedt
34. *(page 112)*: Terje Tvedt
35. *(page 114)*: Terje Tvedt
36. *(page 116)*: Terje Tvedt
37. *(page 118)*: Asgeir Helgestad/Samfoto
38. *(page 122)*: Terje Tvedt
39. *(page 126)*: Steve McCurry/Magnum/All Over Press
40. *(page 131)*: Steve McCurry/Magnum/All Over Press
41. *(page 136)*: Christopher Pillitz/Getty Images
42. *(page 142)*: Steve McCurry/Magnum/All Over Press
43. *(page 150)*: Terje Tvedt
44. *(page 156)*: Photo:Terje Oestigaard
45. *(page 162)*: Justin Guariglia/Getty Images
46. *(page 165)*: Terje Tvedt
47. *(page 168)*: Wikimedia by Emmanuel Brunner
48. *(page 171)*: Vestgaard Frandsen/AP/SCANPIX
49. *(page 178)*: Terje Tvedt
50. *(page 182)*: Adrienne Helitzer/ZUMA/SCANPIX
51. *(page 184)*: Ethan Miller/AFP/SCANPIX
52. *(page 191)*: Rick Tomlinson
53. *(page 192)*: Terje Tvedt
54. *(page 196)*: Terje Tvedt
55. *(page 198)*: UPPA/Photoshot/SCANPIX
56. *(page 204)*: Terje Tvedt
57. *(page 208)*: AFP/SCANPIX
58. *(page 211)*: Terje Tvedt
59. *(page 214)*: Sergie Karpukhin/Reuters/SCANPIX
60. *(page 222)*: Reuters/SCANPIX
61. *(page 224)*: Terje Tvedt
62. *(page 226)*: James Nachtwey/VII
63. *(page 230)*: Erik Hanemann/Panopticom
64. *(page 232)*: Terje Tvedt
65. *(page 235)*: Terje Tvedt
66. *(page 238)*: Erich Lessing/All Over Press

INDEX

Page numbers in italics denote illustrations.